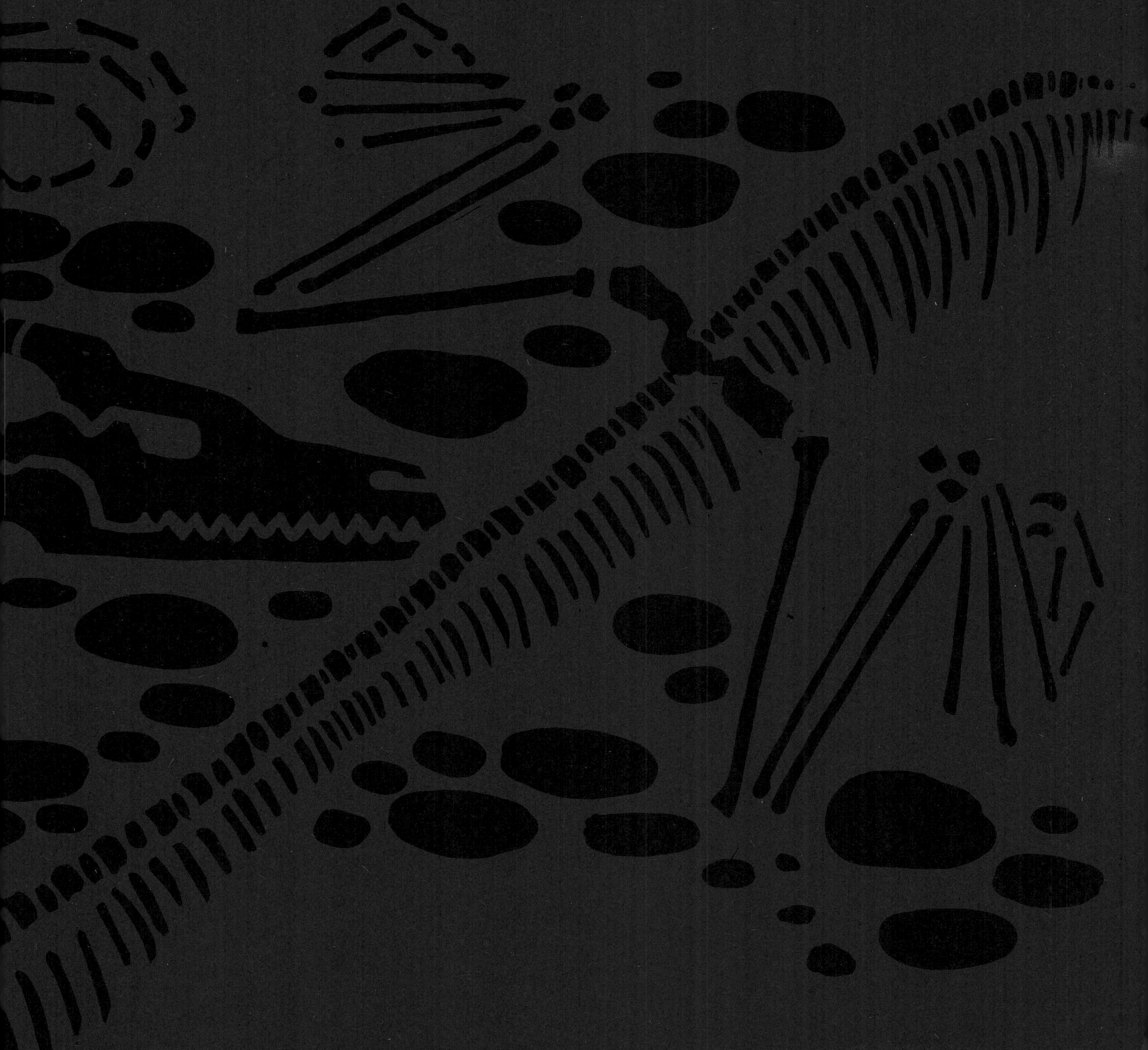

ROSE B. SIMPSON

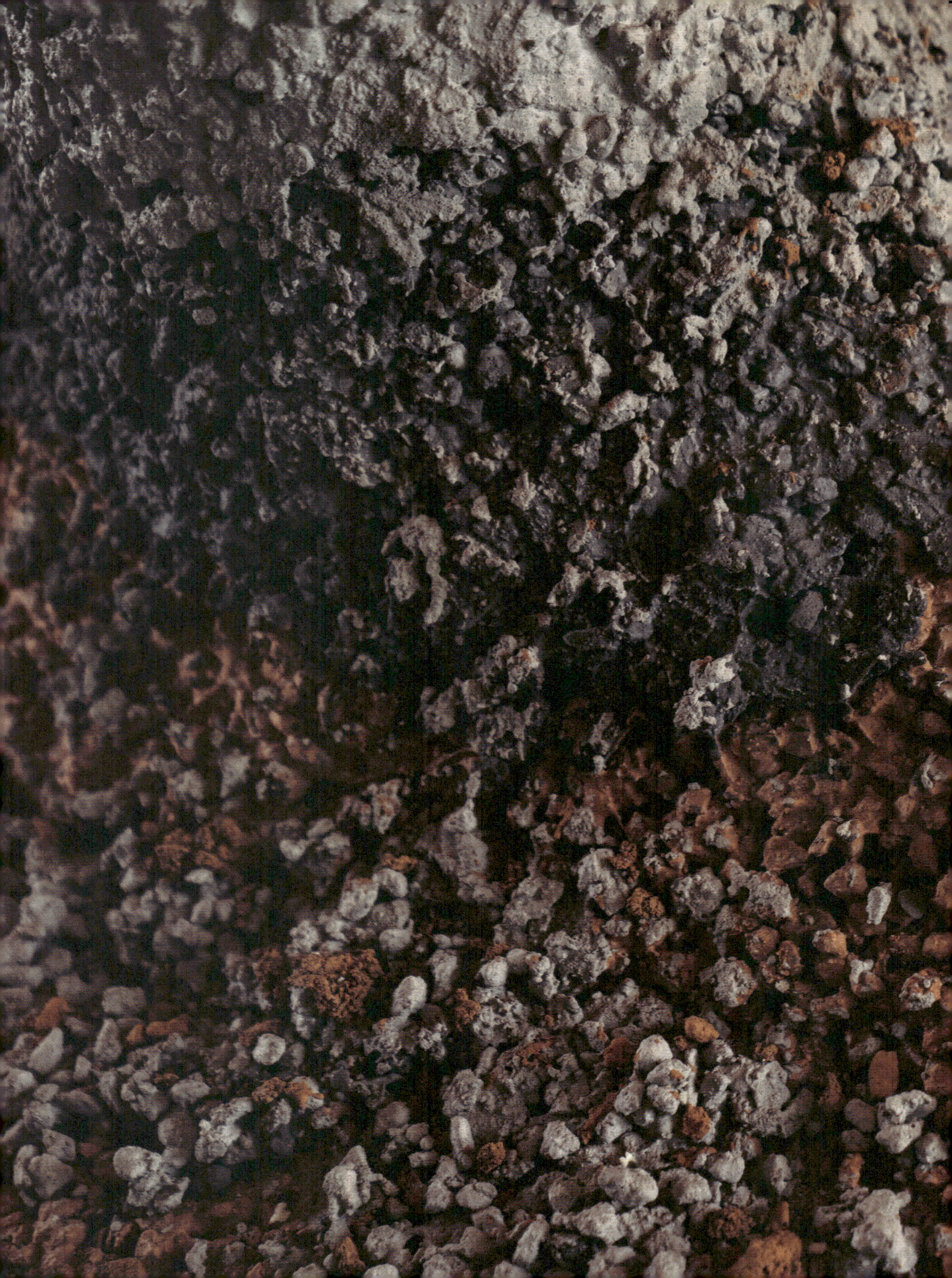

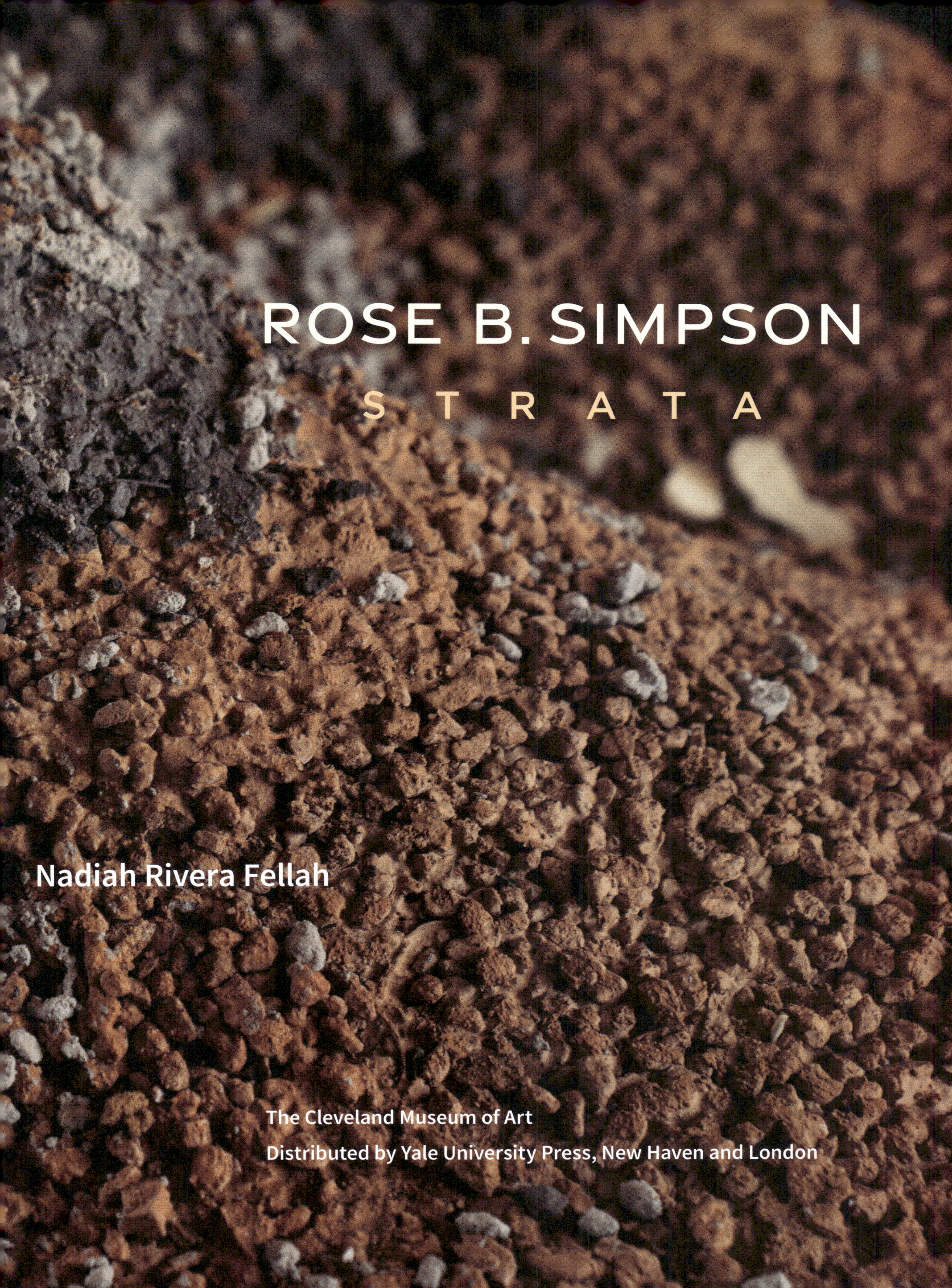

ROSE B. SIMPSON
STRATA
Nadiah Rivera Fellah
The Cleveland Museum of Art
Distributed by Yale University Press, New Haven and London

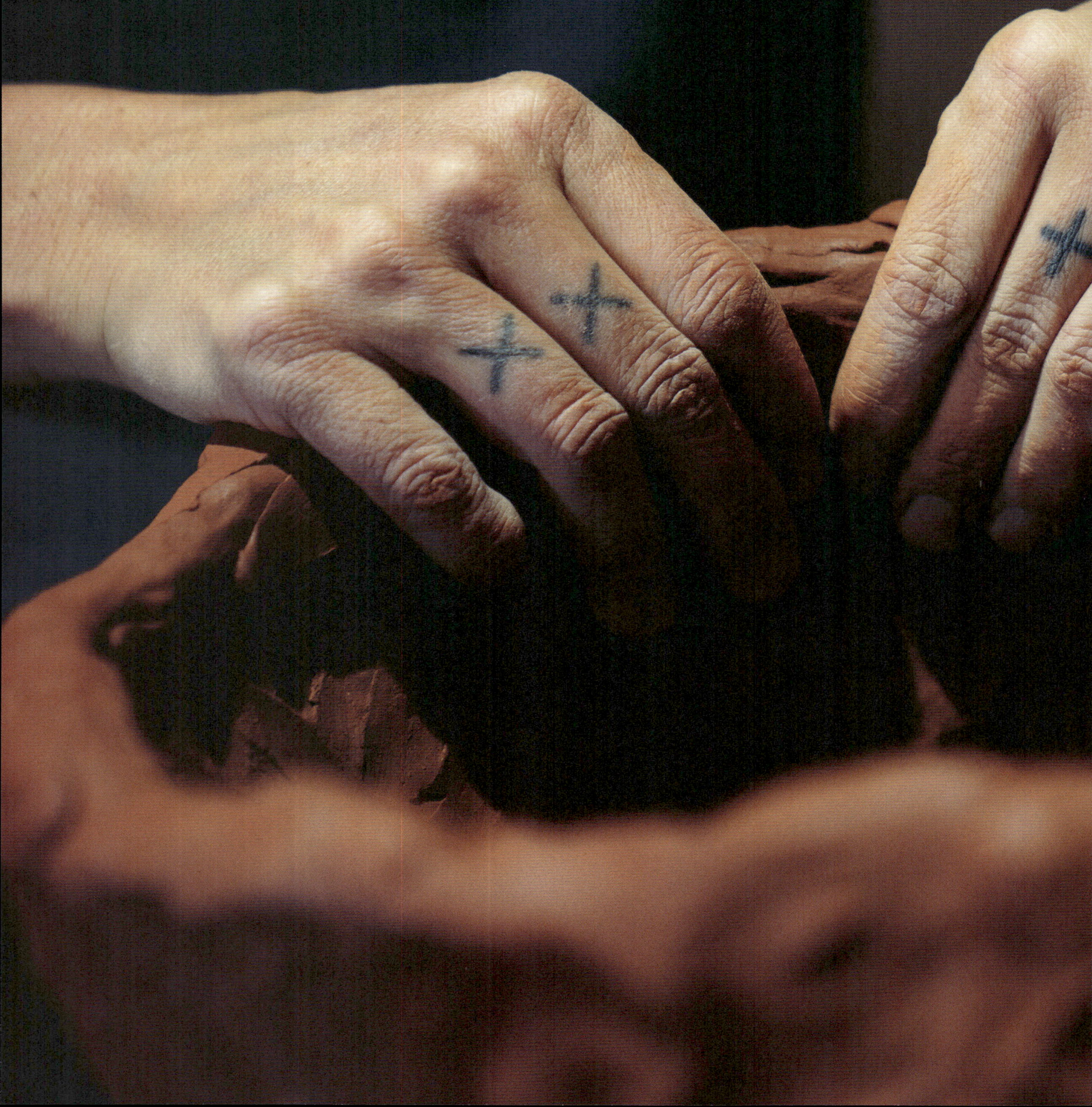

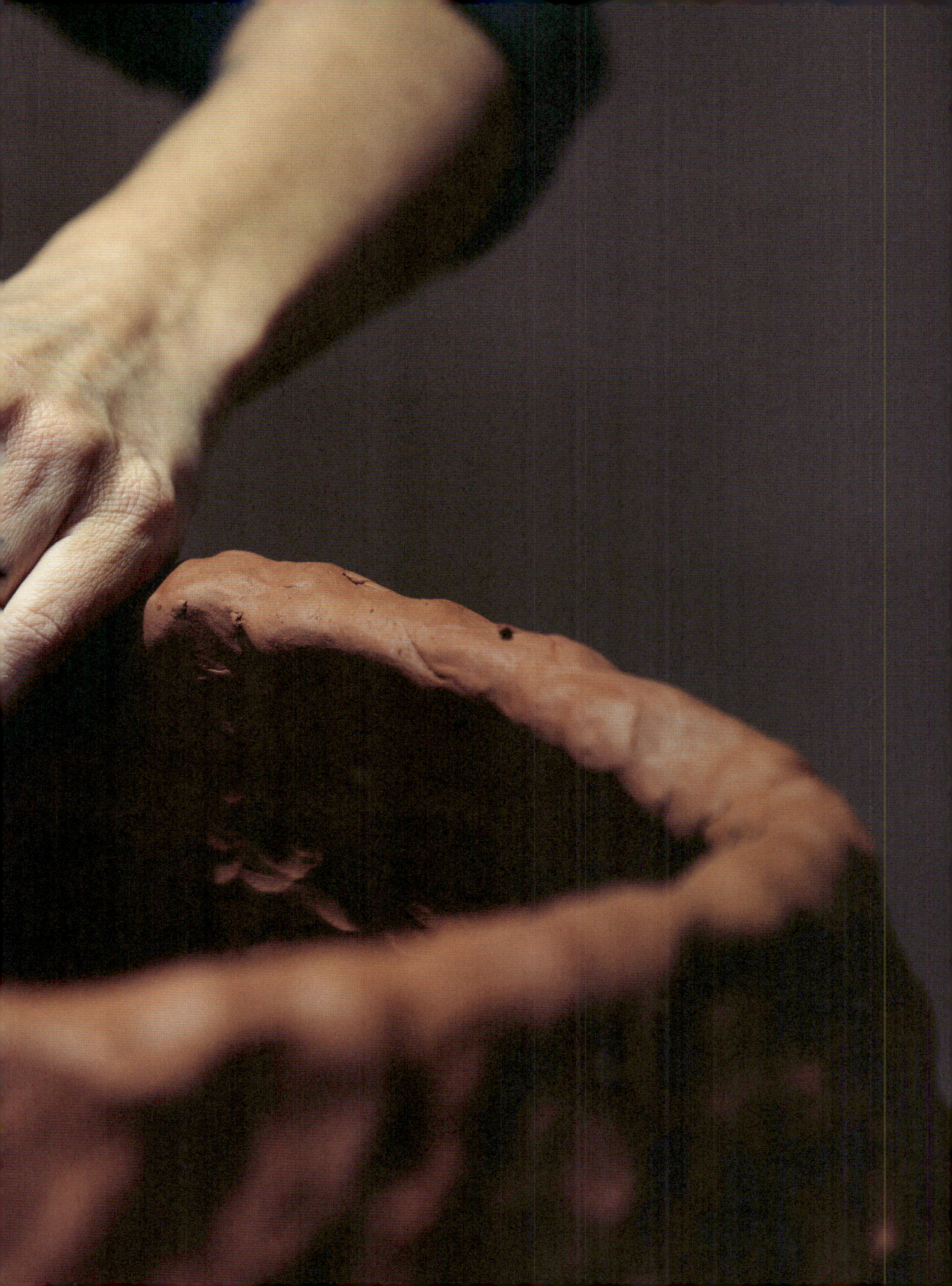

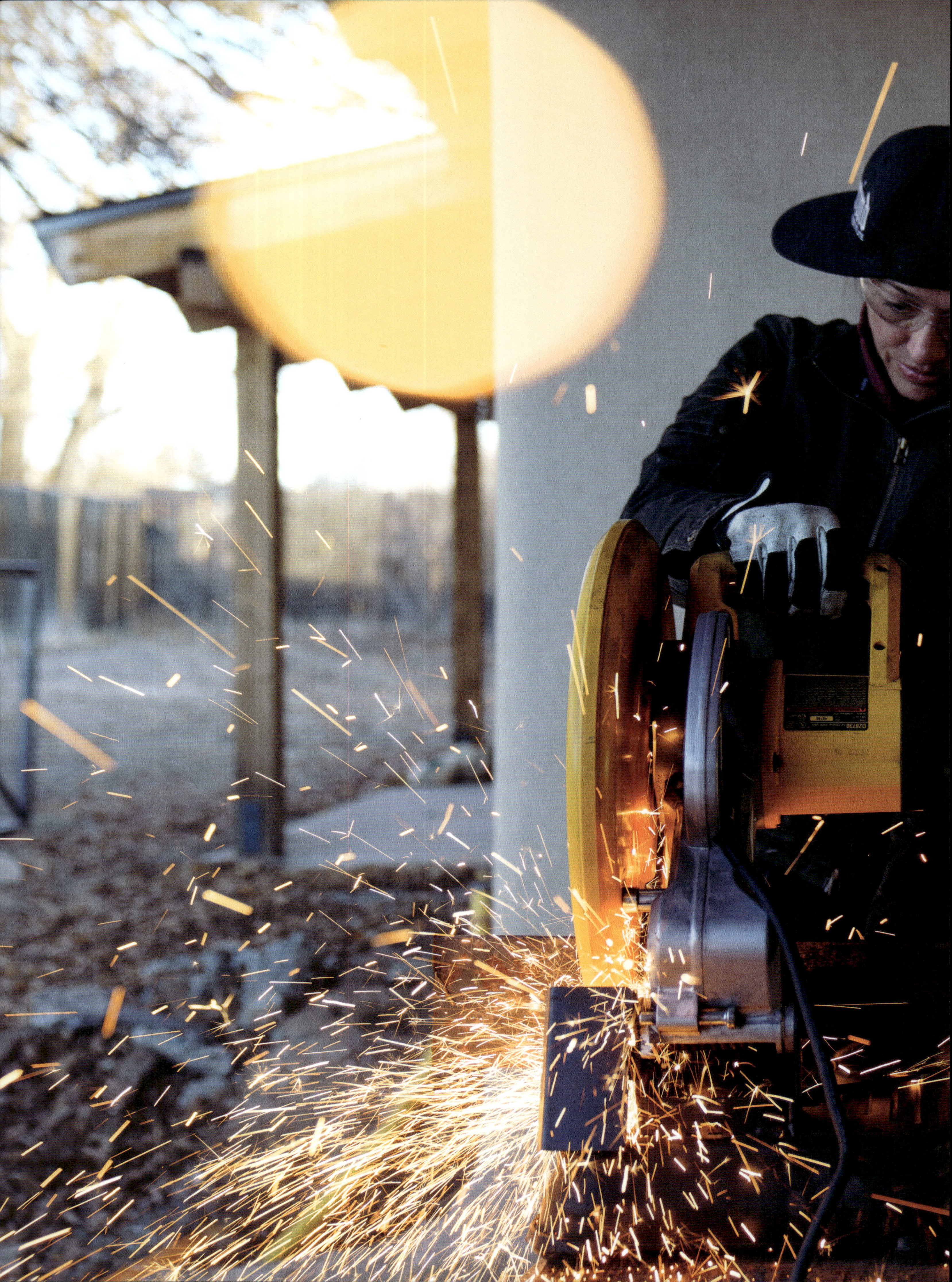

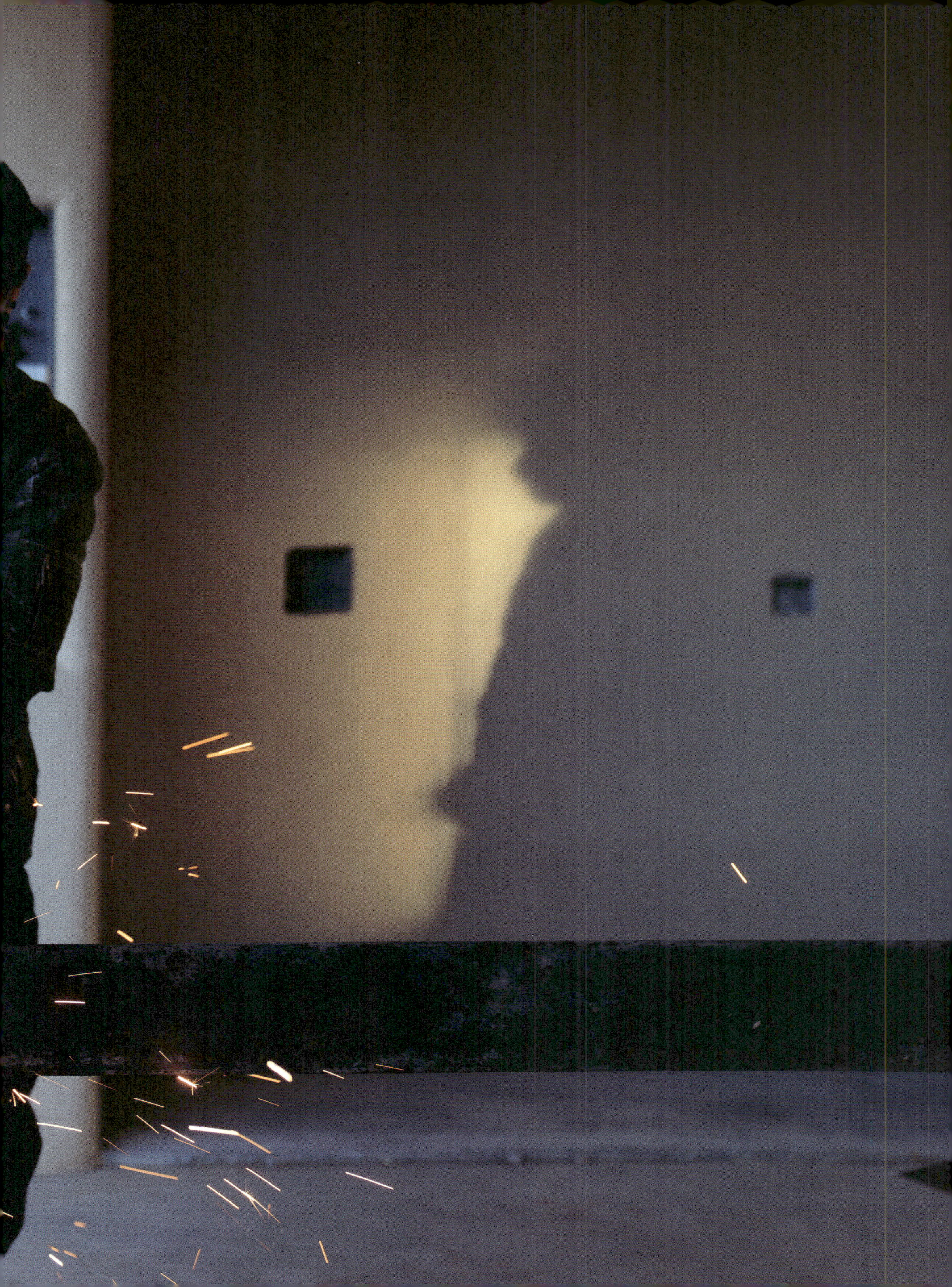

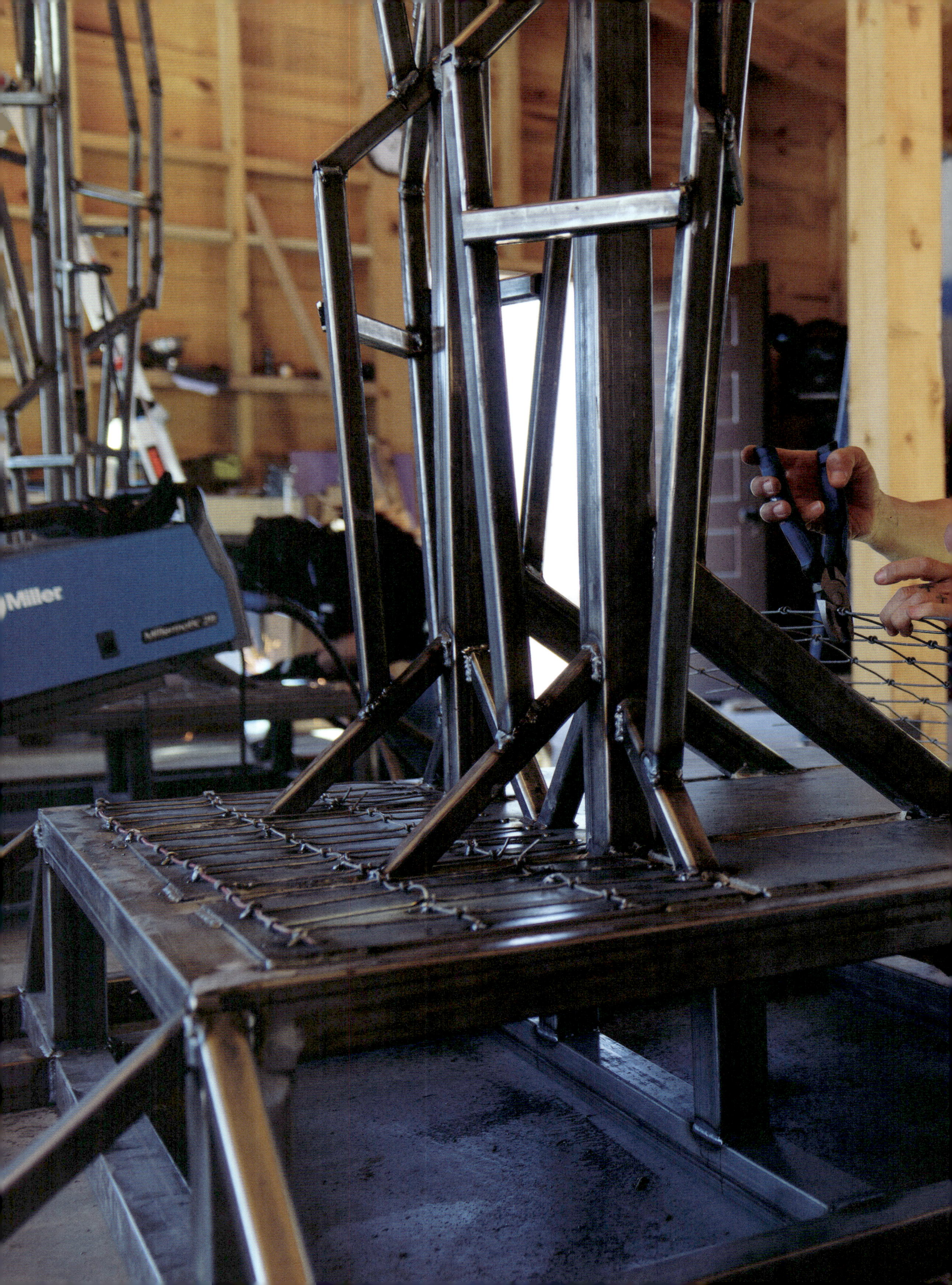

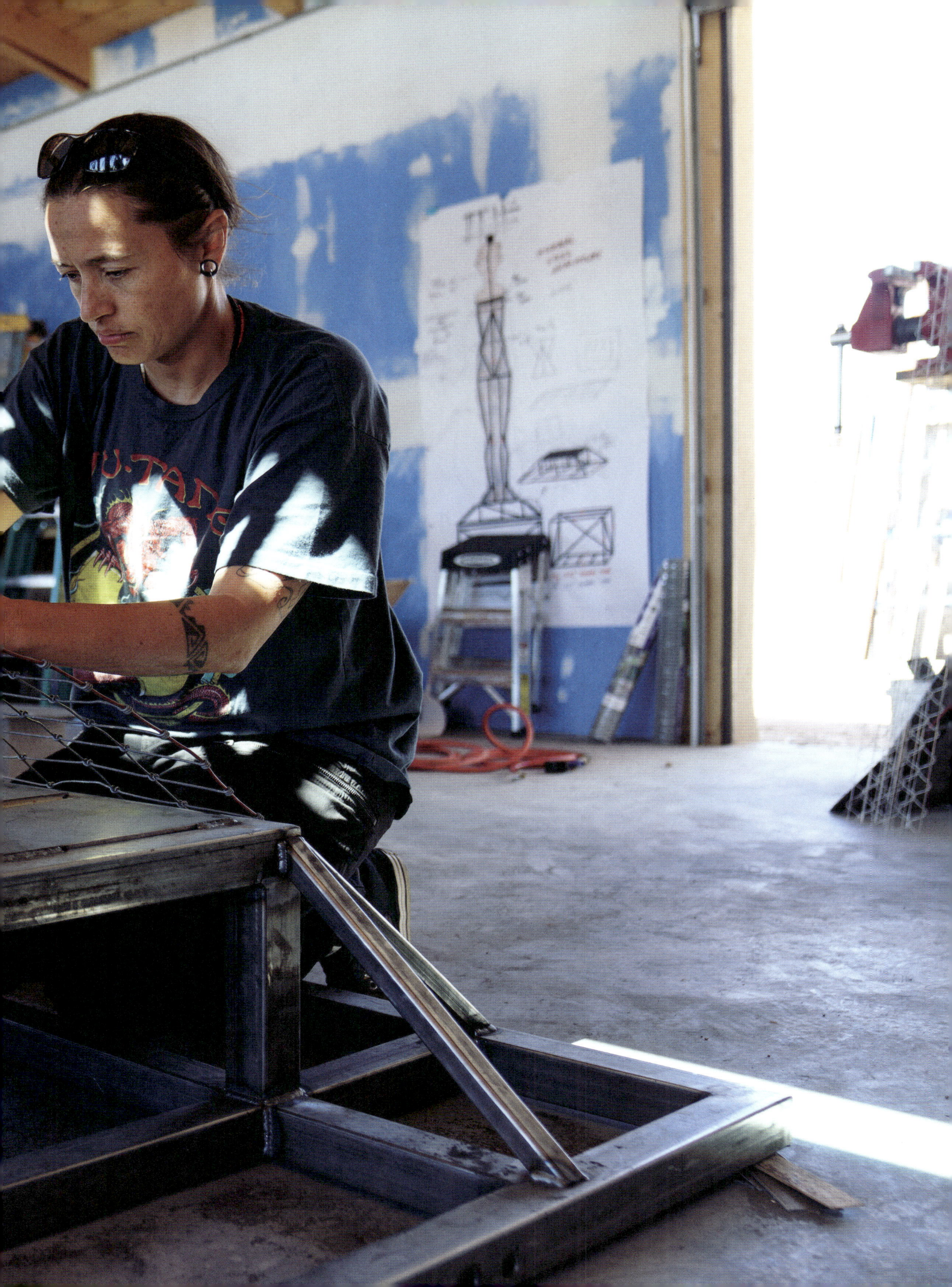

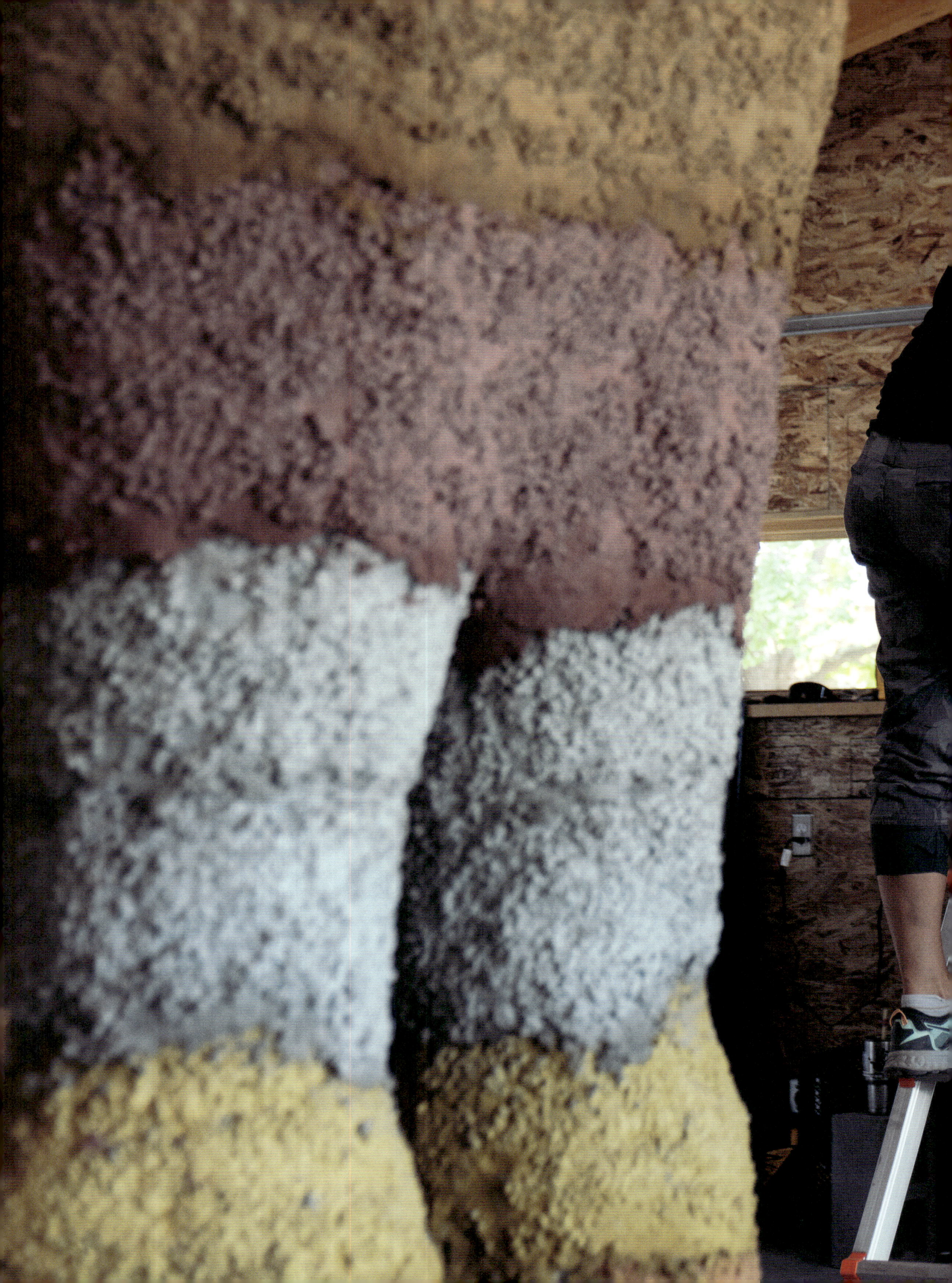

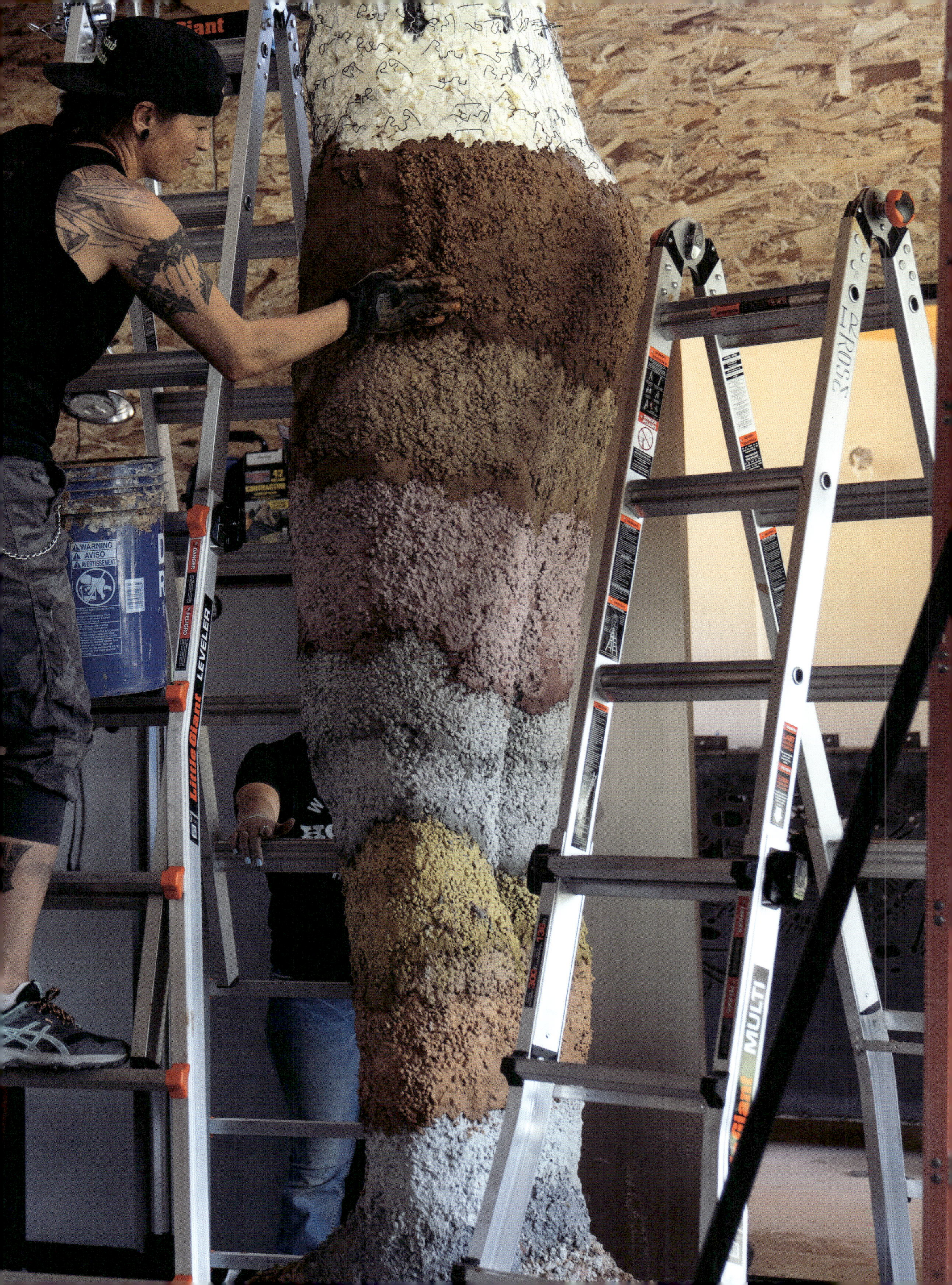

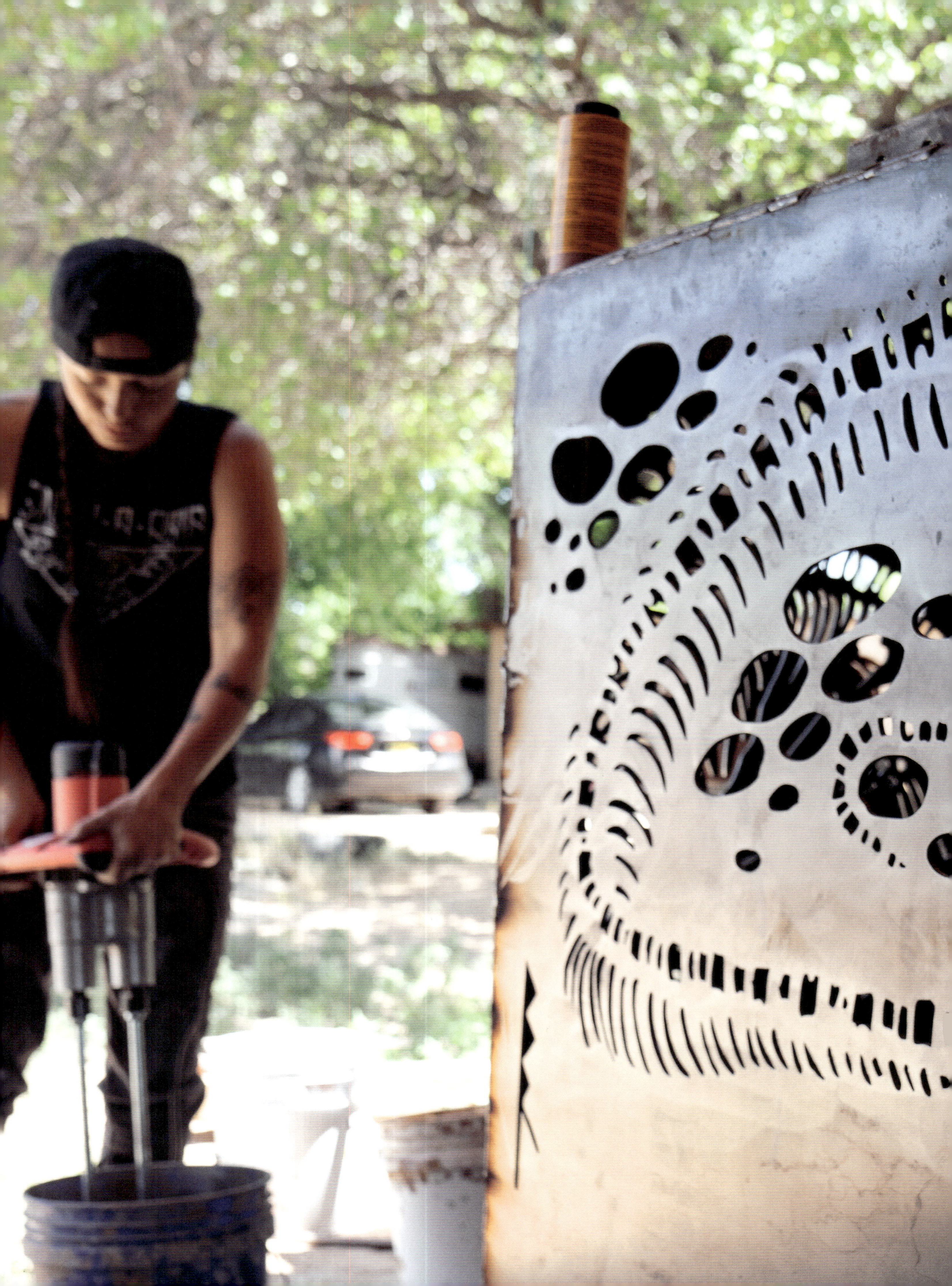

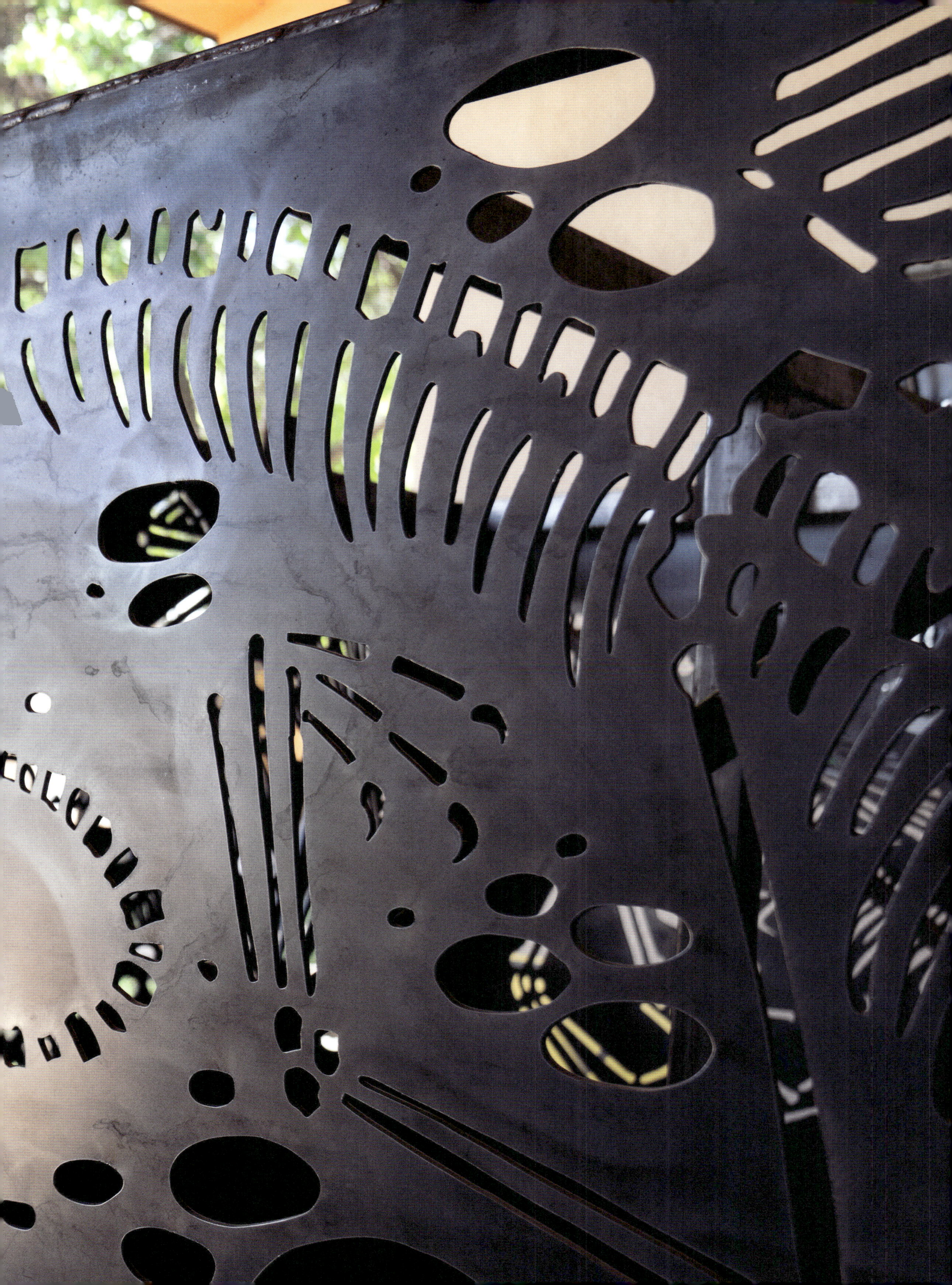

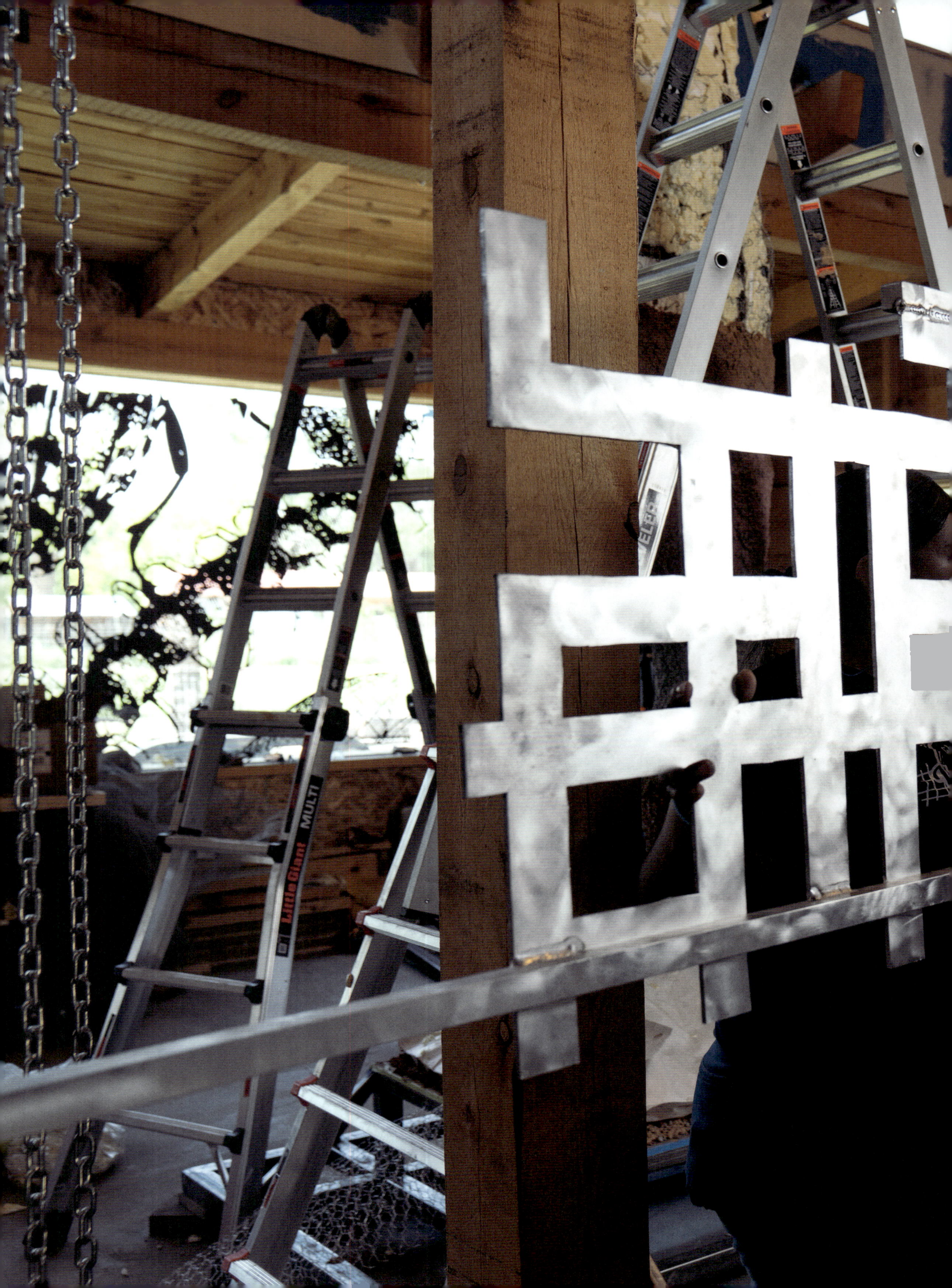

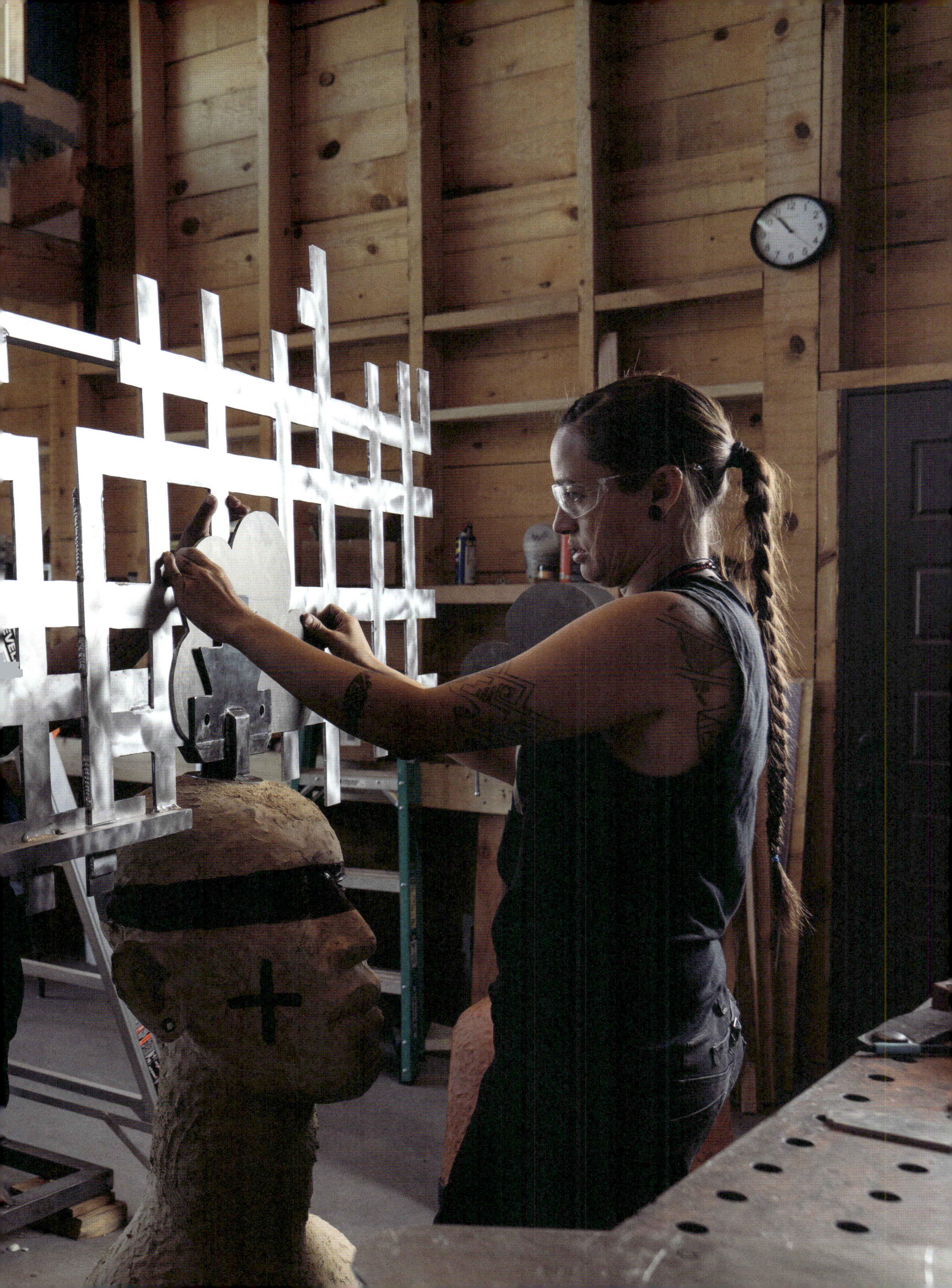

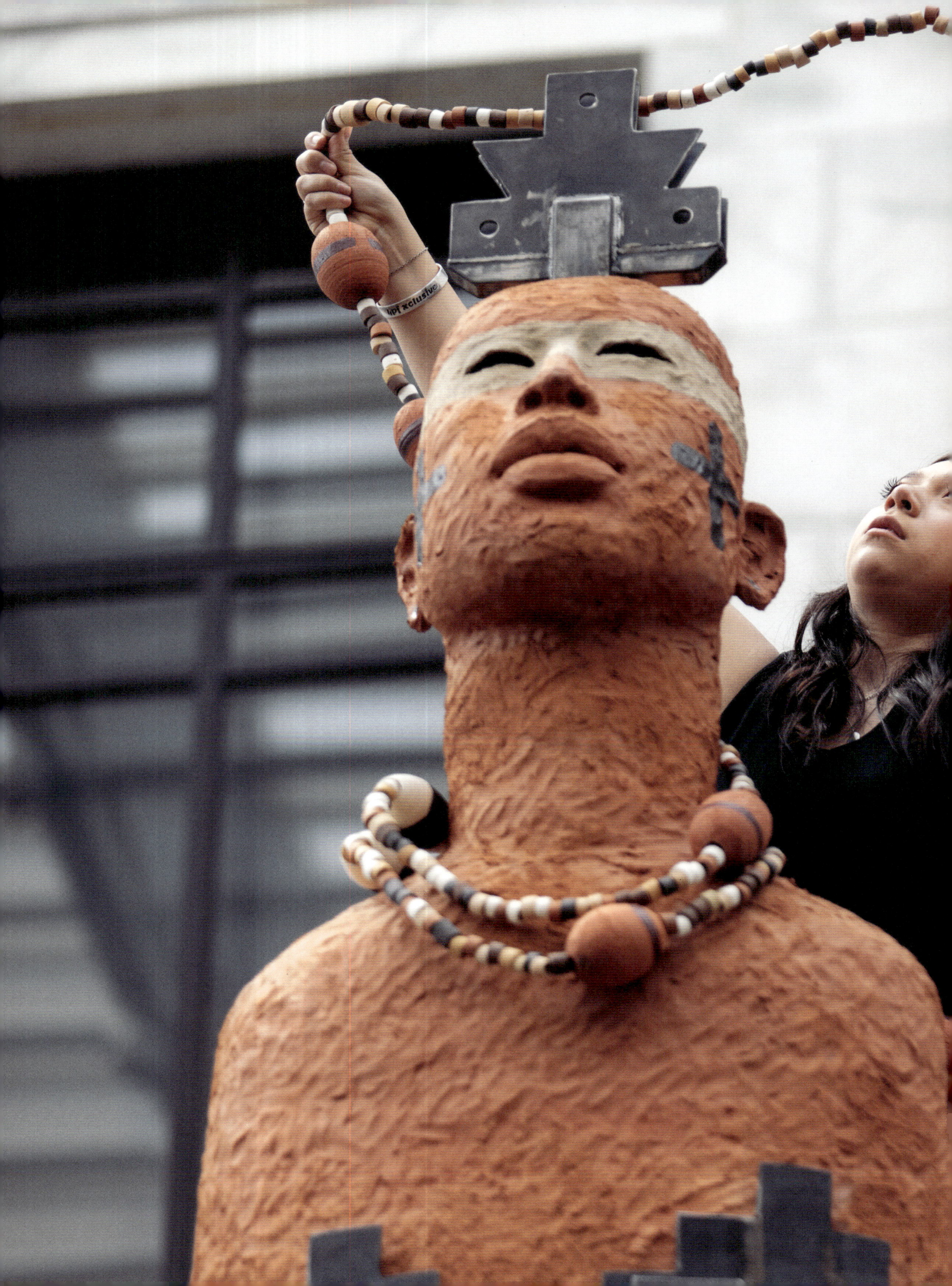

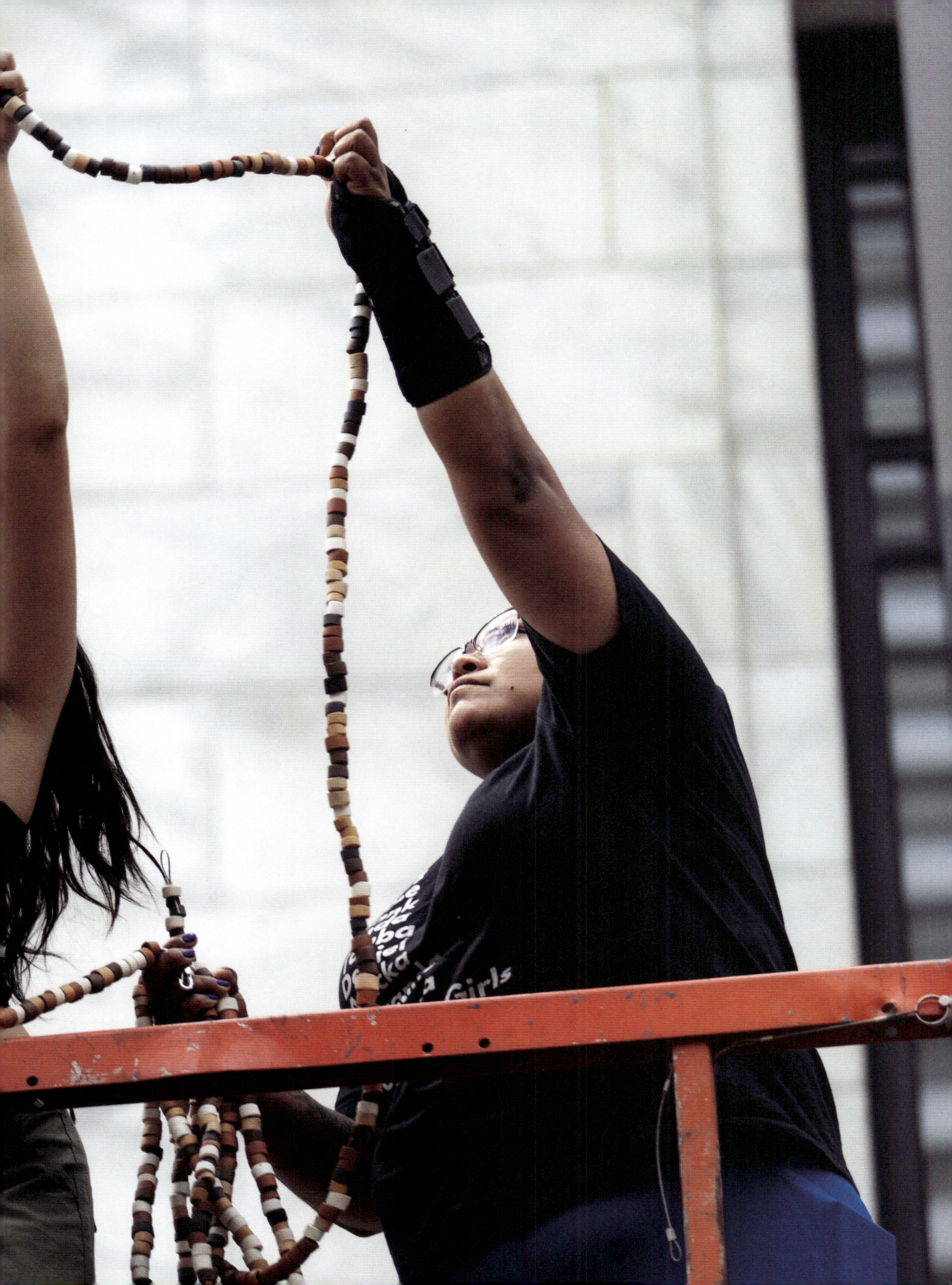

THIS PUBLICATION IS MADE POSSIBLE IN PART BY THE ANDREW W. MELLON FOUNDATION

Published on the occasion of the exhibition *Rose B. Simpson: Strata*, on view at the Cleveland Museum of Art from July 14, 2024, to April 13, 2025.

Major support is provided by the National Endowment for the Arts and the Womens Council of the Cleveland Museum of Art.

NATIONAL ENDOWMENT for the ARTS
arts.gov

All exhibitions at the Cleveland Museum of Art are underwritten by the CMA Fund for Exhibitions. Principal annual support is provided by Michael Frank and the late Pat Snyder, the Kelvin and Eleanor Smith Foundation, the John and Jeanette Walton Exhibition Fund, and Margaret and Loyal Wilson. Major annual support is provided by the late Dick Blum and Harriet Warm and the Frankino-Dodero Family Fund for Exhibitions Endowment. Generous annual support is provided by two anonymous supporters, Gini and Randy Barbato, Gary and Katy Brahler, Cynthia and Dale Brogan, Dr. Ben and Julia Brouhard, Brenda and Marshall Brown, Gail and Bill Calfee, Joseph and Susan Corsaro, Richard and Dian Disantis, the Jeffery Wallace Ellis Trust in memory of Lloyd H. Ellis Jr., Leigh and Andy Fabens, Florence Kahane Goodman, Janice Hammond and Edward Hemmelgarn, Robin Heiser, the late Marta and the late Donald M. Jack Jr., Eva and Rudolf Linnebach, the William S. Lipscomb Fund, Bill and Joyce Litzler, the Roy Minoff Family Fund, Lu Anne and the late Carl Morrison, Jeffrey Mostade and Eric Nilson and Varun Shetty, Tim O'Brien and Breck Platner, William J. and Katherine T. O'Neill, Henry Ott-Hansen, Michael and Cindy Resch, William Roj and Mary Lynn Durham, Betty T. and David M. Schneider, Saundra K. Stemen, Paula and Eugene Stevens, the Womens Council of the Cleveland Museum of Art, and Claudia Woods and David Osage.

Library of Congress Control Number: 2024941874
ISBN: 978-0-300-27879-8

NOTES TO THE READER
All measurements are in centimeters; height precedes width precedes depth.

All works by Rose B. Simpson are © Rose B. Simpson, courtesy of the artist, Jessica Silverman, San Francisco, and Jack Shainman Gallery, New York.

Photos © Kate Russell, pp. 2–17, 20, 23, 26 (top), 28–32, 42–43, 48–49, 56–57, 60–61, 66–67, 69–71, 73–74, 79–84, 86–87, 89–90, 94, 96–97, 108–9, 111, 116, 118–19

Photos © Rose B. Simpson, pp. 26 (bottom), 76–77, 92–93

Views of *Strata* photographed by museum photographer David Brichford, pp. 110, 112–13, 115. Objects in the collection of the Cleveland Museum of Art were photographed by museum photographers Howard Agriesti, David Brichford, and Gary Kirchenbauer. James Kohler prepared the digital files. The museum holds copyright to its images. When known, other copyright holders and photographers are acknowledged in the credits.

Produced by the Cleveland Museum of Art
Designed by Tom Barnard, Director of Publications
Emily Mears, Director of Exhibitions
Rachel Beamer, Senior Publications Project Manager
Edited by Jane Friedman
Proofread by Nick Geller
Color management by Maurizio Brivio
Printed and bound by SYL The Art of Books, S.L. in Barcelona, Spain

The Cleveland Museum of Art
11150 East Boulevard
Cleveland, OH 44106-1797
www.clevelandart.org

Distributed by
Yale University Press
302 Temple Street
P.O. Box 209040
New Haven, CT 06520-9040
www.yalebooks.com/art

Cover: *Strata*, 2024. Rose B. Simpson (Santa Clara Pueblo, born 1983). Ceramic, foam, riveted aluminum, hardware, steel armature, pumice, concrete, and bronze; 792.5 x 152.4 cm

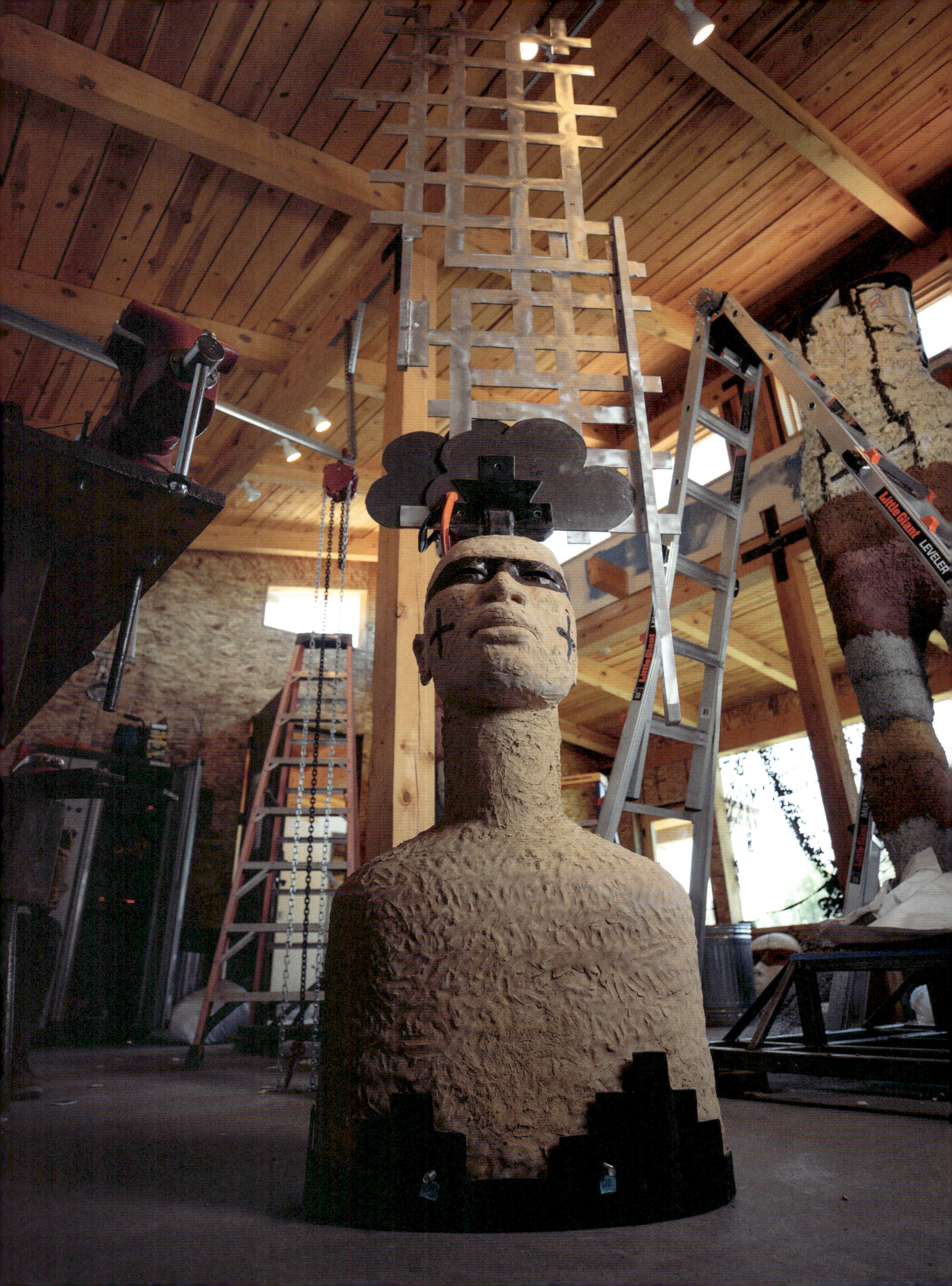

Director's Foreword

The Cleveland Museum of Art's first solo exhibition of a contemporary Native American artist, *Strata* represents an important partnership with Rose B. Simpson, not only in fostering new work but also in signaling our deep commitment to honoring the work of Native artists, both living and past. This publication, on the occasion of the presentation of *Strata*, is an important undertaking for an institution that occupies Native land and is the custodian of many works by Indigenous artists throughout the Americas.

The Ames Family Atrium is one of Cleveland's largest freely accessible indoor civic spaces. Throughout the day, visitors traverse its spaces as they navigate the CMA's galleries or gather to eat, drink, work, or relax. Simpson's sculptures beautifully enhance and enrich this environment.

The two large figures are fashioned from clay—the artist's signature medium—in addition to pumice, or volcanic rock and ash, blended with concrete, metalwork, and local stones. The figures' layers mimic the strata of the Earth's inner layers, drawing connections between the museum's architecture in relationship to nature. Intricate welded metal bases feature stylized depictions of fossils. Simpson hopes the experience of walking between the pair of sculptures in this transitional space will spark awareness in visitors: awareness of their surroundings, of one another, and of the diverse objects they will encounter at the CMA. We are proud that *Strata* is accompanied by an important publication on Simpson's work to date, featuring a range of voices in the fields of Native American art, contemporary art, and literature.

Strata, a brilliant extension of the CMA's ongoing initiative to enhance representation of Indigenous Americans in the museum's galleries, accompanies the museum's broader efforts to collect and exhibit current work. These include several recent acquisitions—works by Jaune Quick-To-See Smith and Edgar Heap of Birds in addition to two by Simpson herself—updated interpretive texts in the Native North American galleries; a formal Land Acknowledgment, drafted in partnership with our community Native American Advisory Committee; and ongoing programming.

A project of this magnitude would not have been possible without the involvement of many individuals. I would like to thank Nadiah Rivera Fellah, curator of contemporary art, whose collaboration with the artist was critical to the realization of *Strata*.

My greatest thanks go to Rose B. Simpson. It has been a privilege to work with the artist, whose extraordinary talent and creative vision have brought an exceptional project into being. We are extremely grateful to her for undertaking this ambitious installation with the Cleveland Museum of Art.

William M. Griswold
Director
Sarah S. and Alexander M. Cutler Chair
The Cleveland Museum of Art

Land Acknowledgment

The Cleveland Museum of Art acknowledges
the many Indigenous peoples who have been
dispossessed from this region. For millennia they
occupied, traversed, lived from, and cared for
land and waterways in Ohio—indeed, the state's
name derives from *Ohi:yó*, an Onöndowa'ga:'
(Seneca) term meaning "beautiful river." Today
Native Americans of diverse ancestries and tribal
affiliations continue to reside in Northeast Ohio,
sustaining their heritages, beliefs, and practices and
making contributions to the region's life and vitality.
With this statement, we affirm our commitment
to creating respectful, enduring, collaborative
relationships with them and with the Native
artists and communities represented by works
in our collection, which embody knowledge and
traditions passed down through generations. We
make this pledge with the aim of including Natives'
perspectives and enhancing Natives' experiences in
our galleries, exhibition halls, program spaces, and
offices.

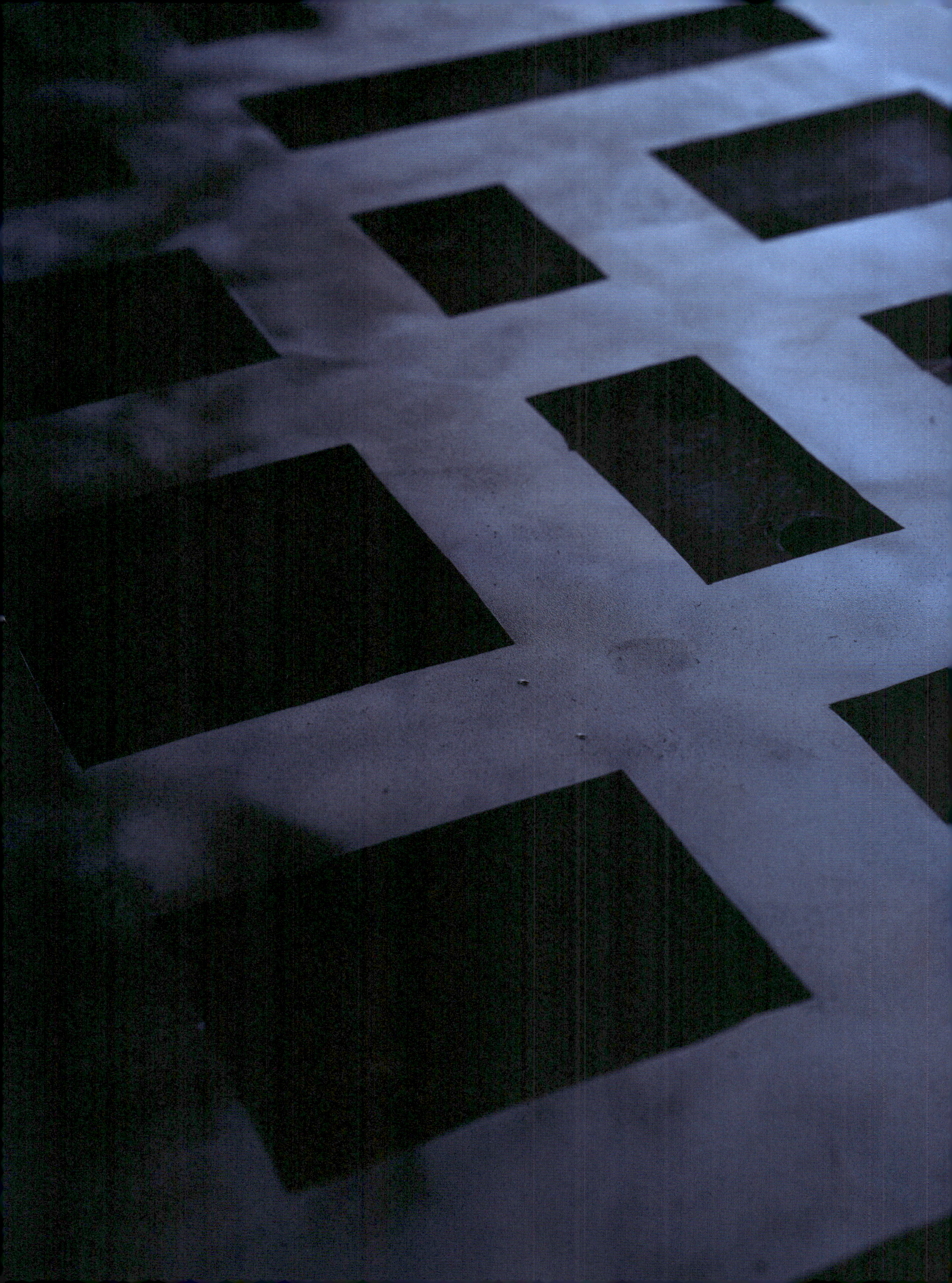

Curator's Acknowledgments

Bringing monumental site-specific artwork to fruition within a museum is a massive undertaking, and we are thankful to the numerous individuals who made *Rose B. Simpson: Strata* possible. First and foremost, it has been a genuine pleasure to work with Rose B. Simpson throughout the inception and development of this project, and I am most grateful for the engineering knowledge, intellectual rigor, and humor she has brought to conversations over the course of many months. Rose has devoted countless hours of labor for the design, realization, and physical installation of *Strata*, a pair of sculptures created specially for the Cleveland Museum of Art's Ames Family Atrium.

The artist's studio assistants—Wanda Abeyta and Celestial Sena—were instrumental in bringing the work into existence. We are appreciative of photographer Kate Russell, who made several visits to Simpson's New Mexico studio to document the process and whose images appear throughout this volume. For their early and enduring support for this project, we are indebted to Simpson's gallerists, Jessica Silverman and Jack Shainman. Kathryn Wade and Marion Cox at Jessica Silverman deserve special acknowledgment, as does Jaci Auletto at Jack Shainman Gallery.

The contributors to this catalogue have revealed various aspects of Simpson's rich oeuvre. My sincere gratitude to Natalie Diaz, Anya Montiel, Karen Patterson, and Dyani White Hawk, along with Rose herself, for their illuminating insights. The time they have spent with the artist's work, in her studio, and in her ancestral homelands contributes to a broader understanding of the sculptures we are privileged to share with the public.

Rose B. Simpson: Strata reflects the dedication and expertise of my exceptional colleagues at the CMA. I am fortunate to work with so many generous and talented individuals in the curatorial division with whom I have been able to discuss this project as it evolved. I especially want to thank Director William M. Griswold for encouraging this project from its inception. Many thanks to Heather Lemonedes Brown, Mark Cole, and Emily Liebert for serving as interlocutors throughout the development of *Strata* and Deirdre Vodanoff for assisting with the many details of the show. My thanks to the Division of Exhibitions, Design, and Publications, led by Heidi Strean. In particular, the exhibition benefited from Emily Mears's skillful management and coordination, with invaluable support from Emma Peters. For their roles in bringing this book to life, I thank Tom Barnard, Rachel Beamer, Jane Friedman, and Nick Geller. I also thank designer Jim Engleman, who situated Simpson's sculptures in real space. Mary Thomas translated the ideas at the core of the exhibition into a graphic identity, and Amy Sparks edited the exhibition materials. In the Department of Collections Management, Elizabeth Saluk ensured that the works comprising *Strata* traveled safely to and from the museum. Our Department of Conservation, led by Sarah Scaturro, helped safeguard the sculptures with precision and expertise; in this department, I thank Beth Edelstein and Laura Gaylord Resch. Above all, our skilled installation crew, including Marty Ackley, Barry Austin, Arthur Beukemann, Joe Blaser, Philip Brutz, Tony Cisneros, Andrew Robison, Dante Rodriguez, and Jason Willis, were instrumental in safely and smoothly positioning the artworks in place.

Translating the exhibition's main ideas into meaningful programming was a key goal from the outset. For their help in realizing this goal, I thank my colleagues in Public and Academic Engagement: Rachel Arzuaga, Ryanaustin Dennis, Erin Fletcher, Stephanie Foster, and Cameron McConnell. I am also grateful to Director of Performing Arts Gabe Pollack for collaborating on associated programming.

I thank the Department of Communications and External Relations, including Todd Mesek and Jacqueline Bon, for helping spread the word about the exhibition, as well as David Brichford in Photographic and Digital Imaging Services for the wonderful images of the show to share with our audiences.

Chief Philanthropy Officer Bruce Loessin and his team, especially Jamie Hardis and Linas Vysnionis, helped make *Strata* possible by securing financial backing. All exhibitions at the Cleveland Museum of Art are underwritten by the CMA Fund for Exhibitions. Principal annual support is provided by Michael Frank and the late Pat Snyder, the Kelvin and Eleanor Smith Foundation, the John and Jeanette Walton Exhibition Fund, and Margaret and Loyal Wilson. This exhibition was supported in part by the Ohio Arts Council. I am deeply grateful for funding from the National Endowment for the Arts, which provided major support for this exhibition.

I would like to recognize the members of the Native American Advisory Committee, not only for their role in drafting the Land Acknowledgment on page 22 but also for their support and encouragement as this project developed over the last two years. Current members include Joseph Connolly, Valerie Evans, Bruce Kafer, Jackie Mendoza, Tory Necklace, Alyssa Rambeau, Marlys Rambeau, Yvonne Shendo, Robbi Swift, Marie Toledo, and Gabe Toledo. We are grateful for your ongoing partnership.

Nadiah Rivera Fellah
Curator of Contemporary Art
The Cleveland Museum of Art

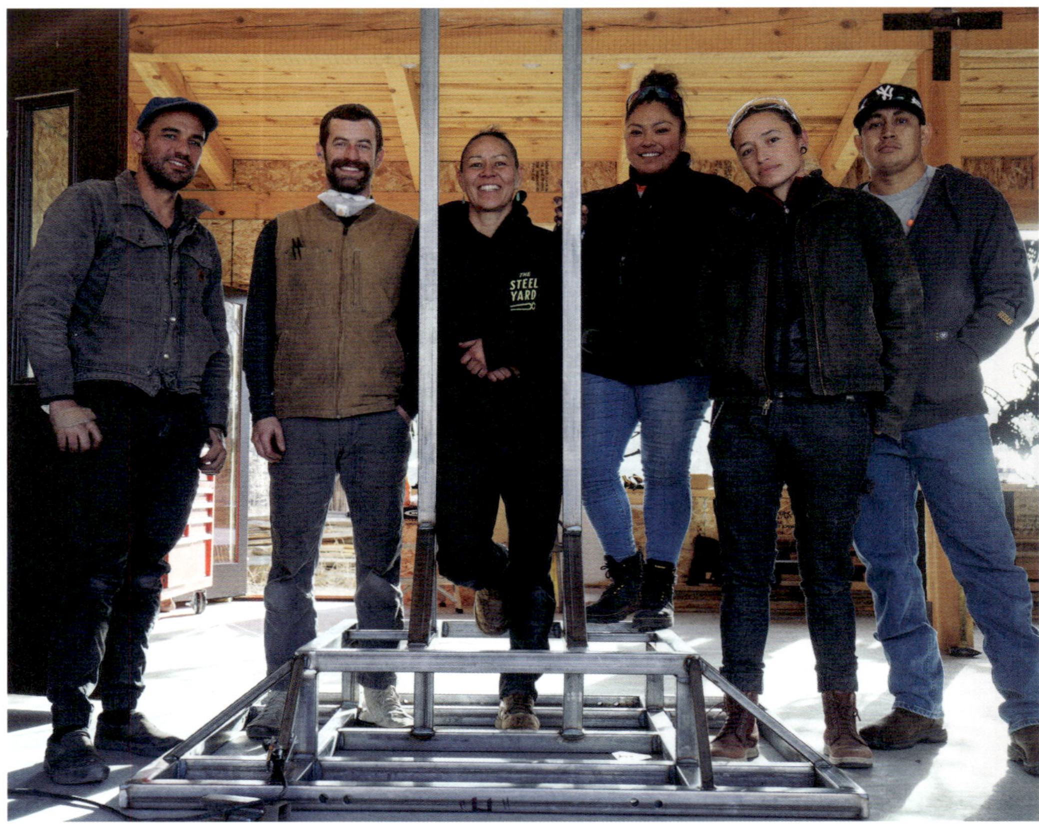

Welding crew (left to right): Steven Thompson, Fulton Forde, Stacy Brossy, Wanda Abeyta, Rose B. Simpson, and AJ Oyenque

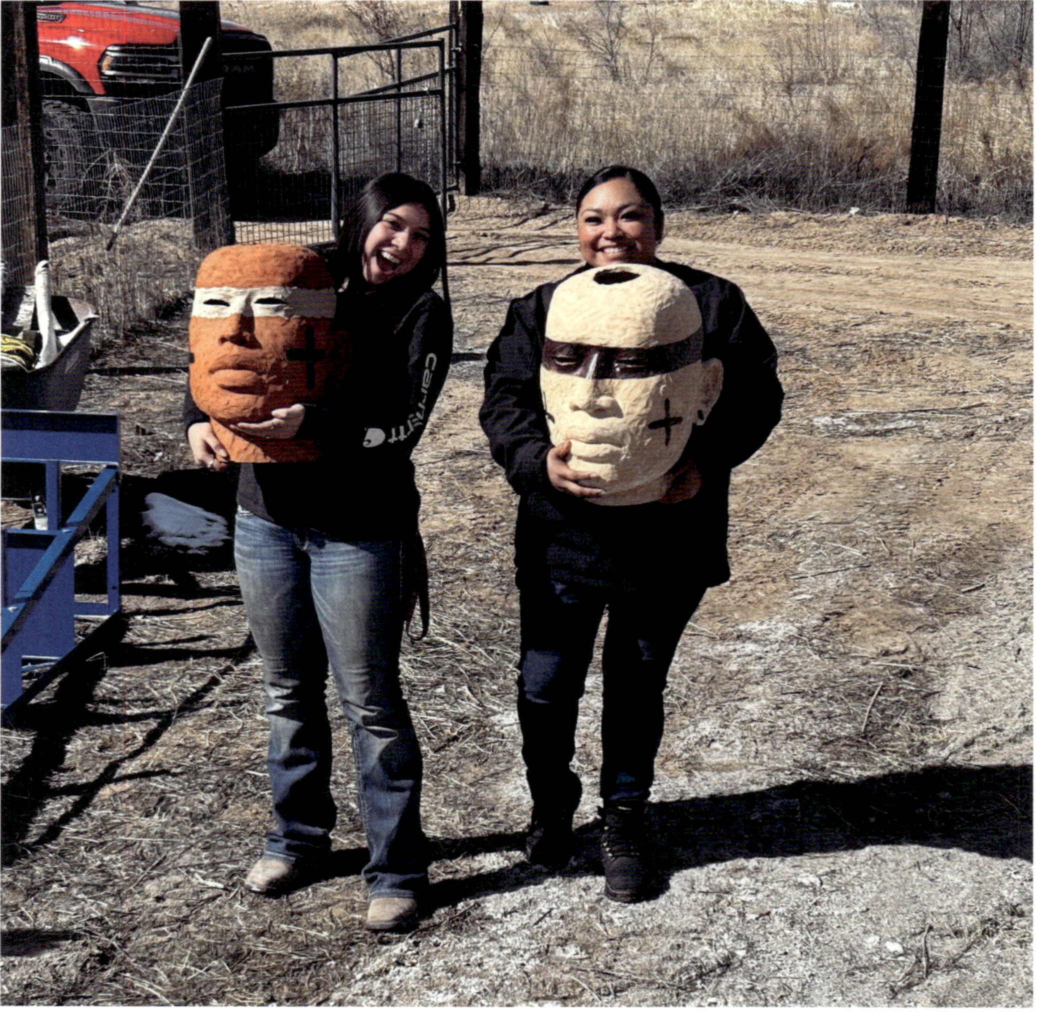

Celestial Sena and Wanda Abeyta

Artist's Acknowledgments

First and foremost, I want to thank Baby Nugget, my Cedar Rain. You are my reason why, and yet my career has made me an absent and stressed mom. I pray that all this that I have been giving away to the outside world somehow comes back as love to you. I pray that I learn fast before too much damage has been done. I love you.

Secondly, thank you to Celestial Sena and Wanda Abeyta. You are not just my studio buddies, my co-manifestors, you are my dear, dear friends. Thank you for going on this adventure with me and for bringing the most beautiful energy to the creative stew. I love you both with all and more of my heart. Goodness, look what we've made! You are teaching me community, you are teaching me collaboration, you are teaching me how to invest joy into the most frustrating tasks.

To Steven Thompson and Stacy Brossy for showing up gracefully in emergency moments to relieve some of the pressure; your presence is inspiring and beautiful. To Harold and Erma Sena for being our community, for being family. To AJ Oyenque for doing your best to be a part of the girl crew. To Kate Russell for being our beloved paparazzi. To Steven Spargur for stepping up to the shipping task. To Kelly Meyers for figuring out how to do the cutting for me. To Mama for your optimism, inspiration, and childcare. Community!

Thank you dearly to Nadiah Rivera Fellah and the Cleveland Museum of Art crew for believing in me—for dedicating yourselves and your space to my vision. What an incredible honor. Thank you!

Thank you to my support systems at Jessica Silverman in San Francisco and Jack Shainman in New York (Jess, Jack, Kathryn Wade, Jaci Auletto); you bookend me and hold me up; you are the oil for my wheels and the gas in my tank. My deepest gratitude.

Thank you to all the plants and animals who gave their lives to sustain us for this project, thank you to all the natural resources that were extracted to complete this vision—from fossil fuels to mineral deposits, I see your sacrifice. Thank you.

Thank you to our bodies for holding strong all the way through. You went through a lot, and you are strong and good and really, really deserve a break.

Love, Rose

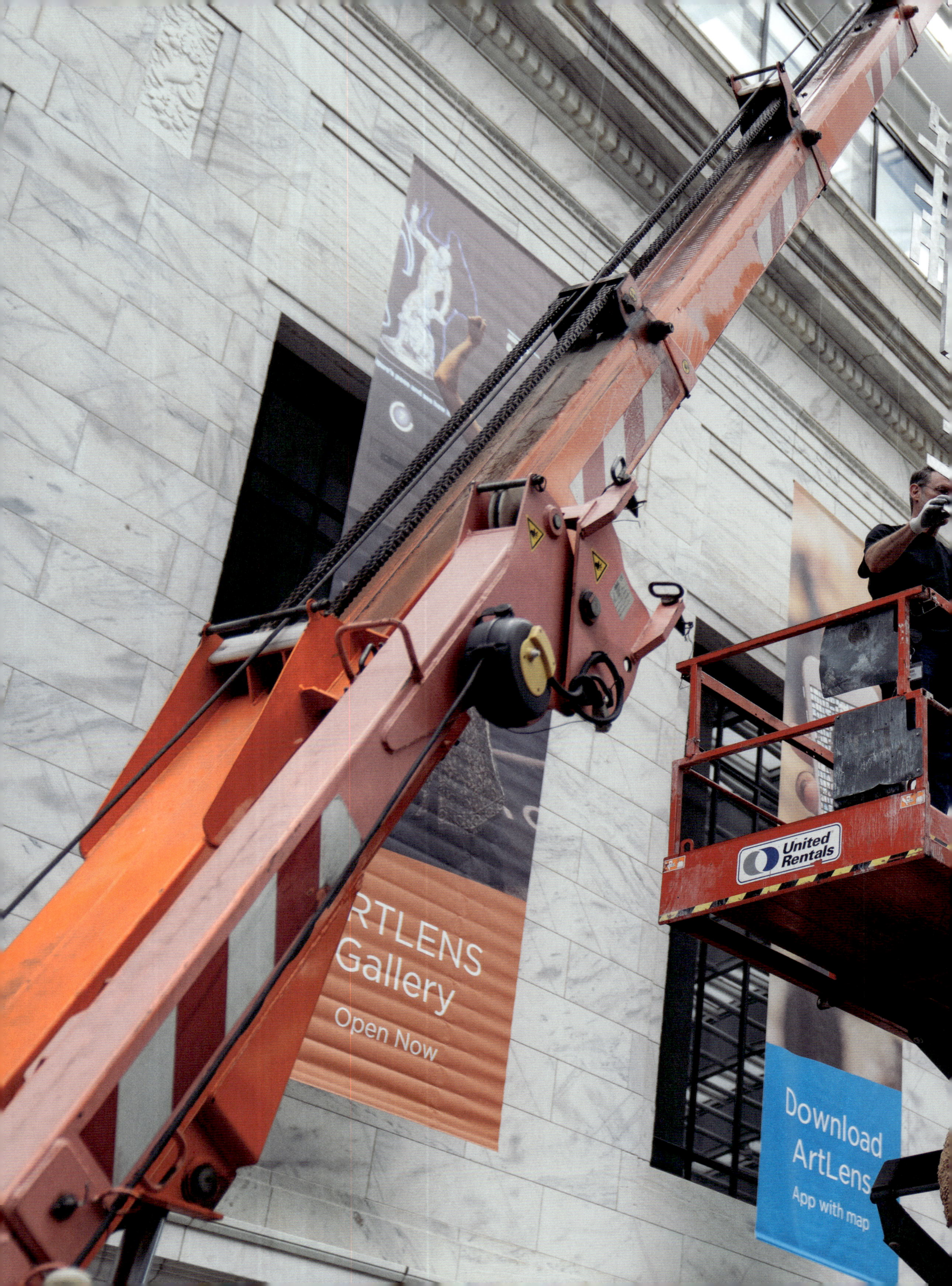

RTLENS
Gallery
Open Now
United Rentals
Download
ArtLens
App with map

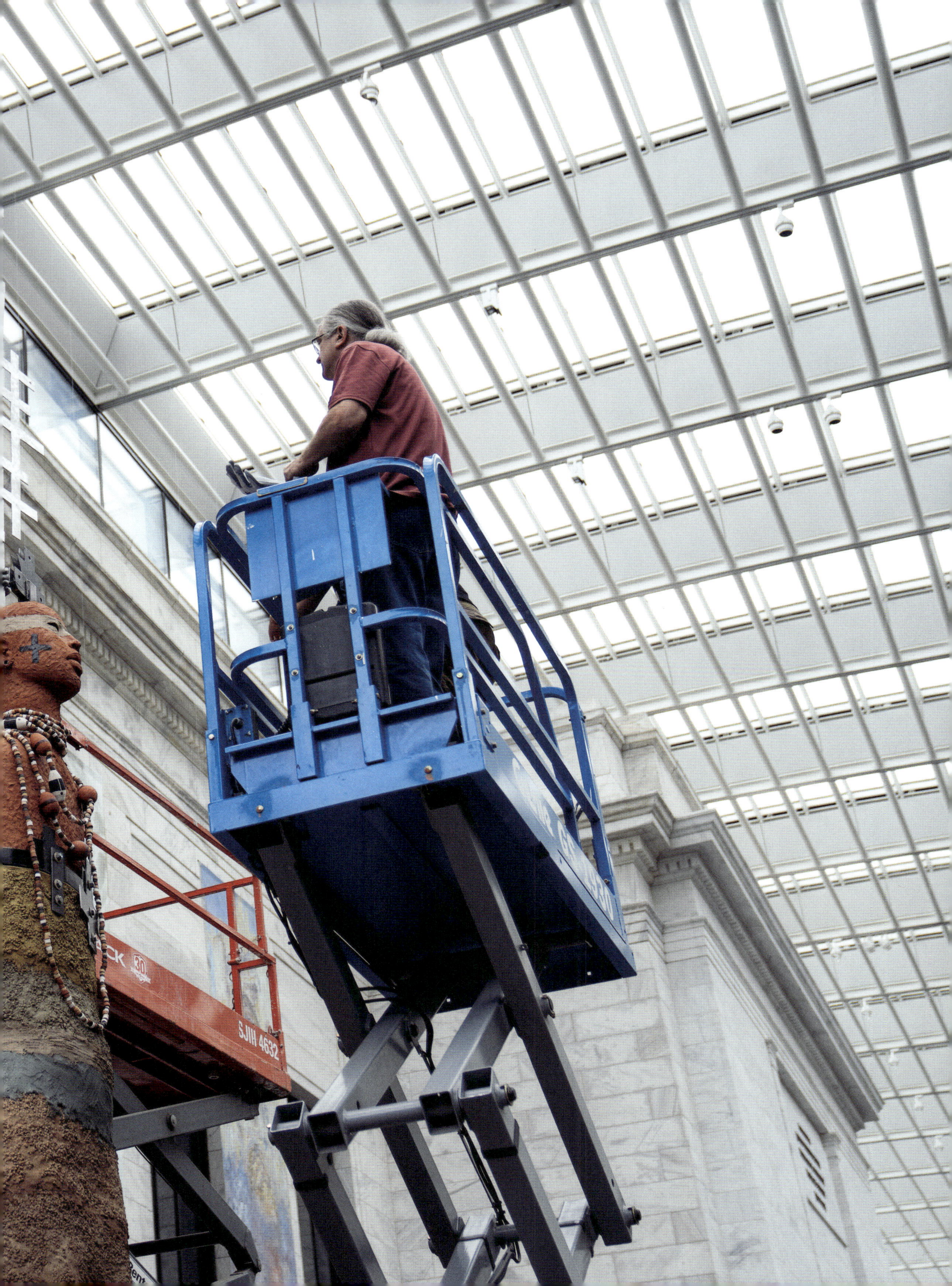

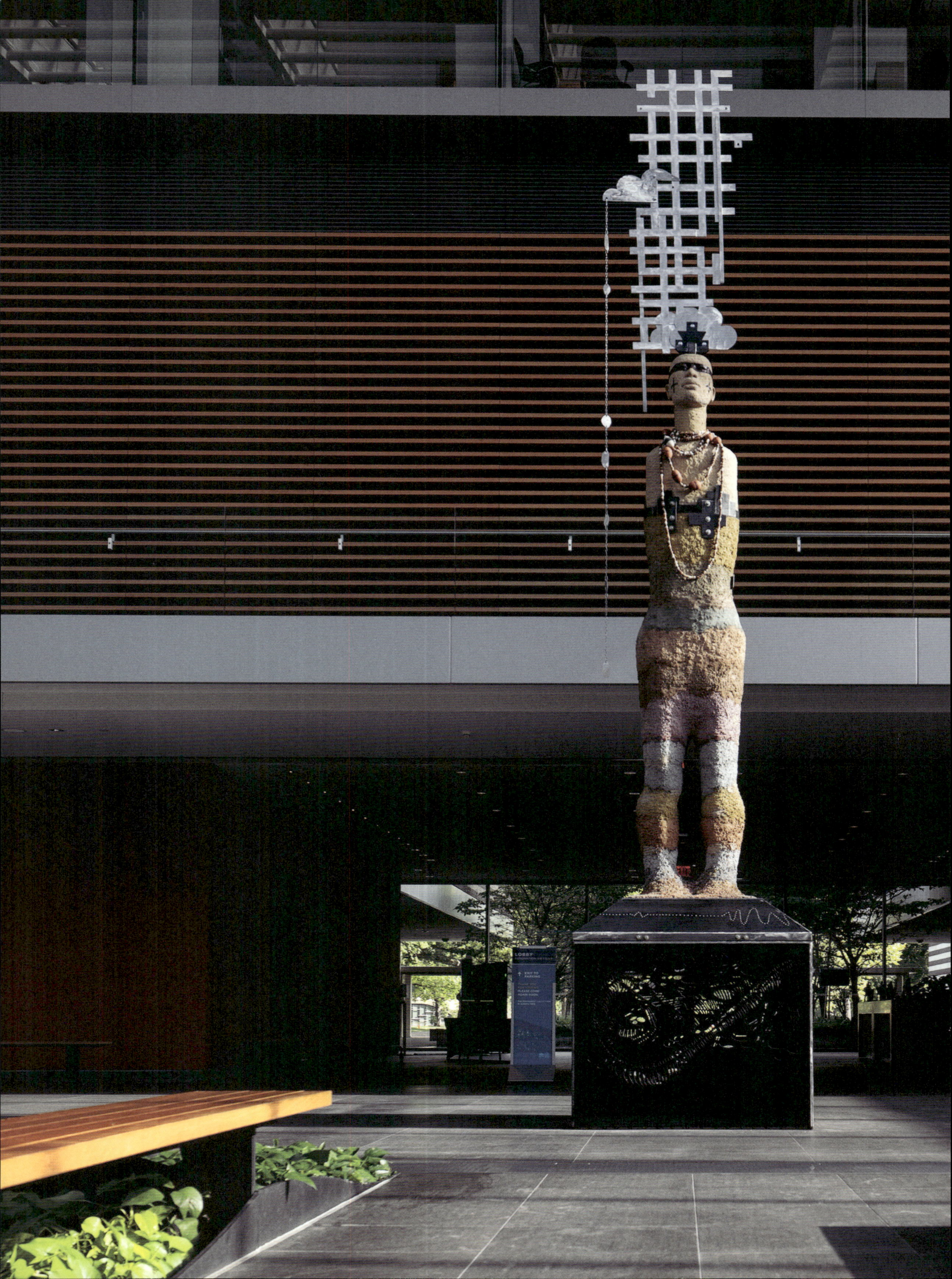

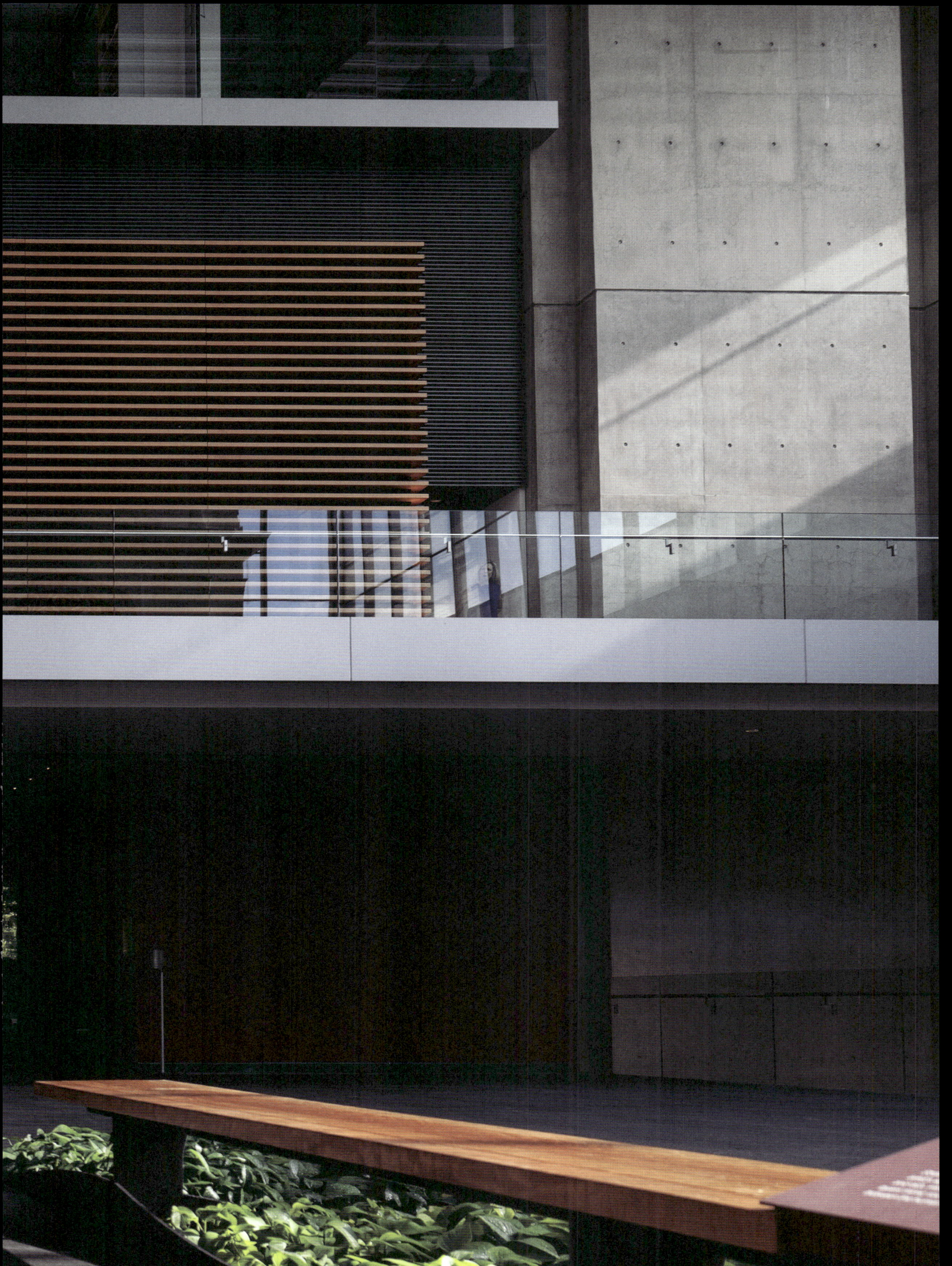

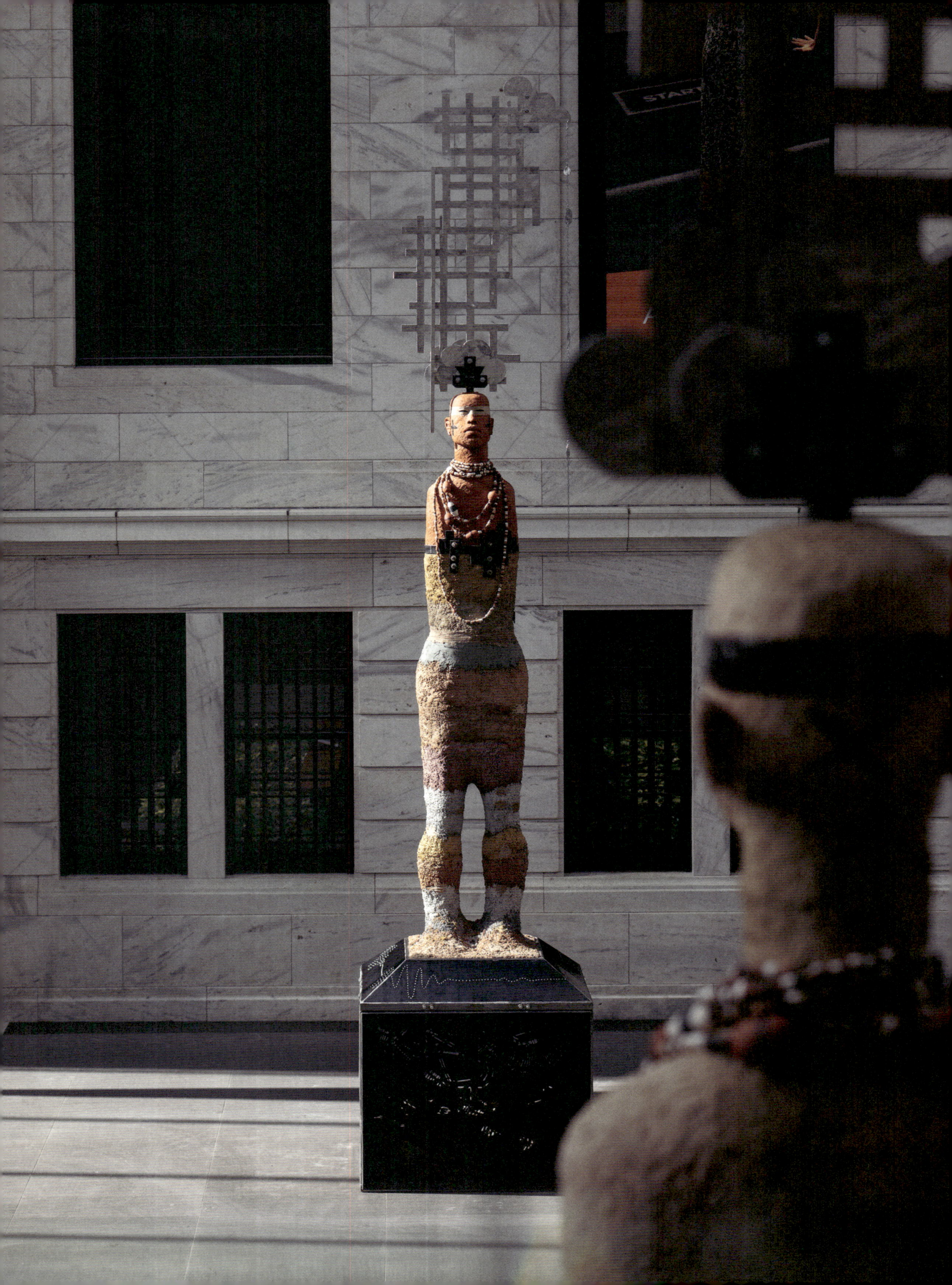

Multiple Layers Emerge

Nadiah Rivera Fellah

Many things are made up of layers. They form the internal structure of the Earth. They indicate the passage of time, show and symbolize growth, and demarcate generational stages of family members. All of these are referenced by Rose B. Simpson's *Strata* (2024), a pair of twenty-five-foot figural sculptures envisioned as a site-specific project for the Cleveland Museum of Art's Ames Family Atrium. In 2022, I invited Simpson (born 1983) to visit Cleveland, Ohio, and consider creating a project for our space. According to the artist, "This piece is inspired by [my] visit to the museum, the architecture of the building, the possibility of the space, tumbled stones from the shores of Lake Erie," as well as her own Indigenous heritage and the landscape of her ancestral homelands of Santa Clara Pueblo, New Mexico, where she lives and works.[1]

Designed as part of the CMA's 2005–2012 renovation and expansion by the architect Rafael Viñoly, the Ames Family Atrium was conceived as an open piazza, with a sixty-foot-tall ceiling; expansive and light-filled, it is one of the largest free indoor spaces in Cleveland. Prior to the renovation, the space served as an open-air courtyard that connected the museum's various galleries. Since opening in 2012, the atrium has been

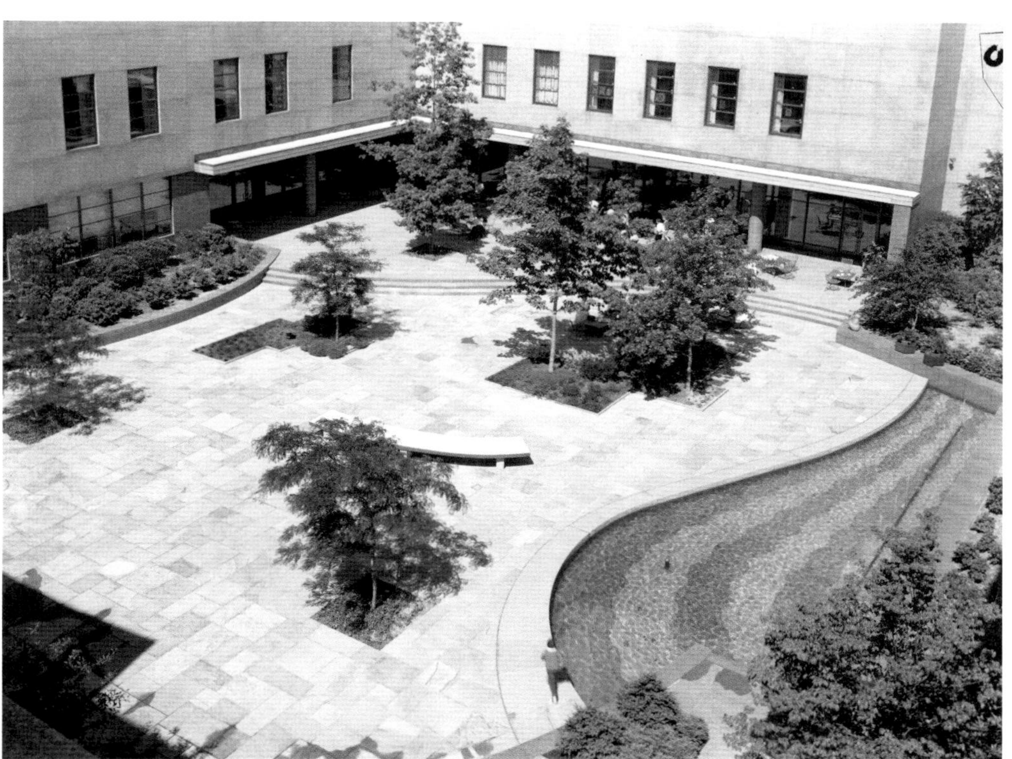

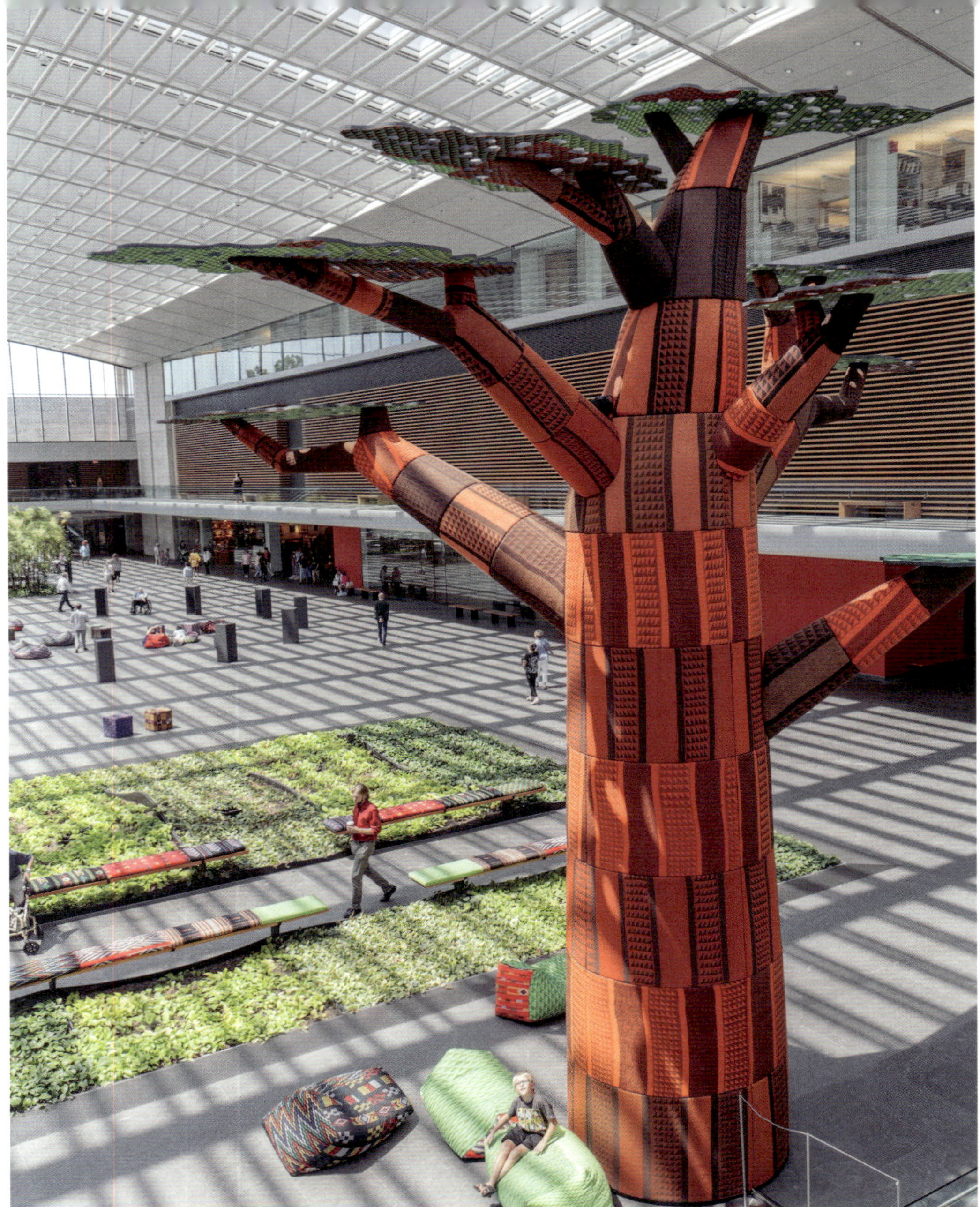

activated with contemporary art on several occasions. *Strata* is the second work commissioned specifically for the site. The first was Emeka Ogboh's 2019 *Ámà: The Gathering Place*, which reimagined the atrium as an Igboh village square similar to those located in the artist's native eastern Nigeria. *Ámà* consisted of a sound installation of choral music, a thirty-foot-tall sculptural rendering of a tree, and traditional Nigerian textiles.[2]

During most days, the gray granite floors of the atrium are bathed in a layer of sunlight. Rectangular patterns created by the glass-paneled ceiling move across the space, depending on the weather. The changing colors of the sunsets can be seen through the windows over the western end of the atrium, and on many evenings the brilliant blue of dusk filters through the windows atop the S. Mueller Family East Wing. During her visit to the CMA, Simpson was struck by the changing light and the way in which it danced and shifted over the granite, steel, wood, and marble of the interior. For this reason, Simpson considers the atrium itself a collaborator in the process of creating *Strata*, stating, the space "spoke to me with its beauty" and inspired the design of her sculptures.

Following Simpson's 2022 visit and our initial conversations, the artist proposed a design for *Strata*. The two figural sculptures gaze at one another; their eye contact creates

Strata proposal drawings, 2024.
Rose B. Simpson

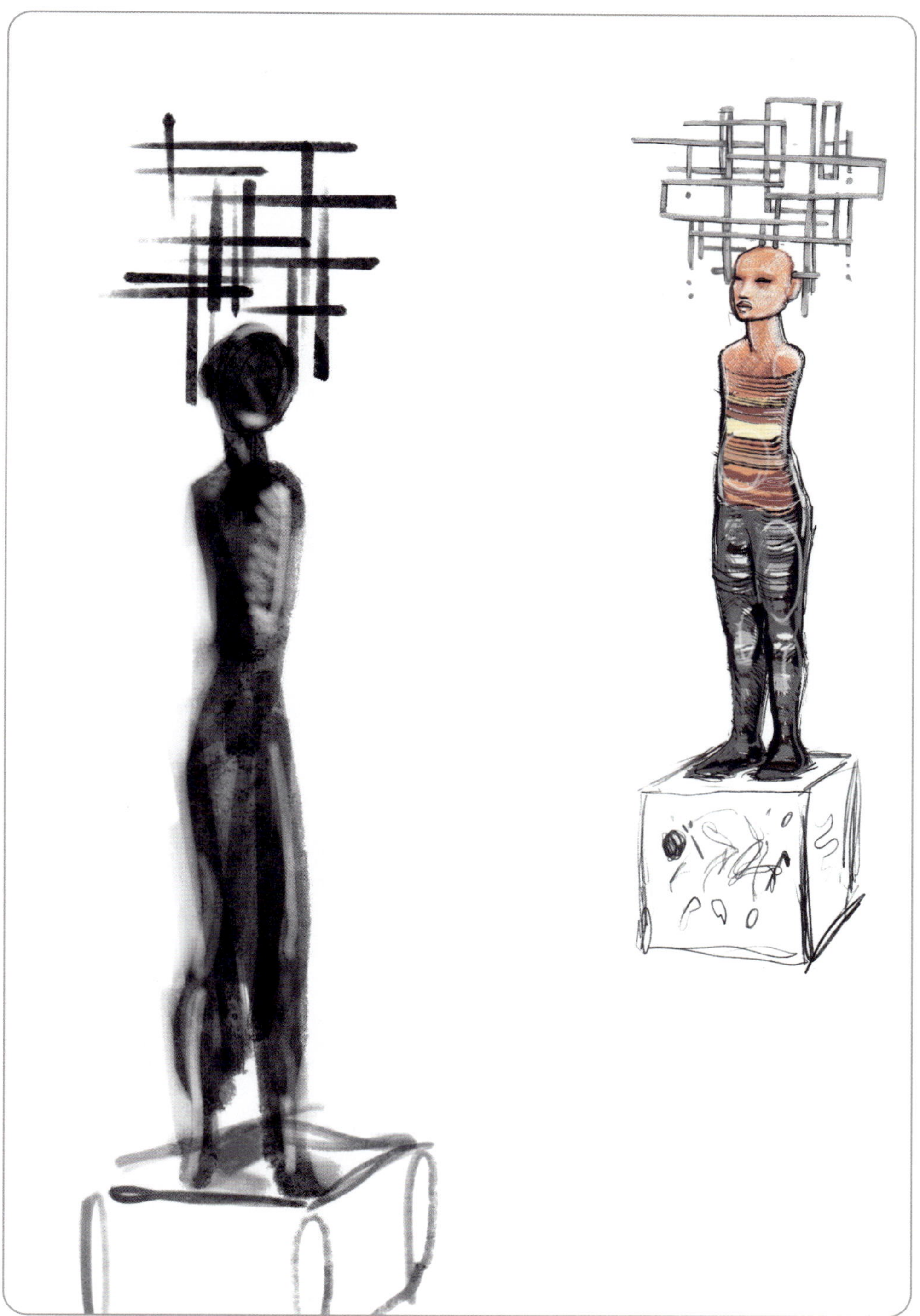

visceral tension between them. The figures are constructed from the artist's signature medium of clay, in addition to pumice, or volcanic rock and ash, mixed with concrete, metalwork, and local stones. The layers, or strata, evoke those naturally occurring layers visible in the mountainous New Mexico landscape, thus drawing connections between the structure and materials of the human-made architecture of the museum in relation to nature. Intricate welded metal bases feature stylized depictions of fossils, inspired by the Tewa water serpent deity, Avanyu, a motif often used in Pueblo art. Structures mounted to the heads of each figure cast shadows, evoking cerebral processes and how their interaction with time and space influences our perceptions of reality. Simpson hopes that the experience of walking between the pair "allows visitors to begin to feel the influence of intention in artistic objects in their bodies. So that they are transformed by that, and they will witness the rest of the museum in a different way—seeing artistic creations as beings other than objects."[3]

Strata's siting in the dynamic, light-filled space of the atrium adds another layer to the visitor's experience, as the sculptures are constantly transforming throughout the day in their interplay with the natural environment. In addition to being striking from a distance, the work also rewards close looking. Seeing Simpson's beautifully handmade and delicate clay sculptures up close, one has a sense of the artist's hands and her finger impressions in the clay, the manner in which she works the surface of the objects. As the poet Natalie Diaz (Mojave / Akimel O'odham) observes of Simpson's clay sculptures, "These objects are never static. They're imbued with, embodied with, embedded with life, with all the marks that have been made on them, with all the marks that they've made on [the artist] . . . these beings are always capable of another layer, another bit of growth."[4] Simpson affirms, "I feel like as much as I'm working with [clay], it's also working me. Our bodies can hold that experience, of how that relationship to materials transforms you."

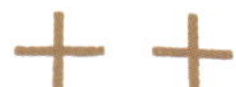

Simpson was born and raised on the Santa Clara Pueblo (Tewa: Kha'po Owingeh) near Santa Fe, New Mexico, and apprenticed with her mother, the well-known Native artist Roxanne Swentzell (born 1962; see pp. 55 and 102). Simpson and Swentzell come from a long line of women working in the Santa Clara Pueblo tribe's ceramic tradition, dating back to the 500s CE. By creating ceramic figures, as opposed to the traditional clay vessels for which ceramic artists in their region are known and which are often sold to tourists and outsiders, Simpson and her mother disrupt colonial legacies of dependency, erasure, and assimilation. Simpson's identity as a Native woman is evident in her work, but she balances her deep-rootedness in her heritage with modern methods, materials, and processes, incorporating elements such as metalwork and concrete along with clay.

Simpson's two works in the CMA's permanent collection, *Heights III* (2022) and *Maria* (2021; see p. 40), speak to two areas of her diverse practice, including the combination of multiple media seen in *Strata*. *Heights III* is a clay self-portrait of the artist holding her daughter. The "bridges" between their heads manifest the artist's concern with passing down Indigenous traditions to her child as she grows up. Simpson recalls, "In the fall of 2022, I homeschooled my [then] six-year-old daughter. The process helped me realize how my beliefs create a foundational belief system for her. When she asks complex questions, it is a moment where I realize it is up to me to help guide her forth. It is a

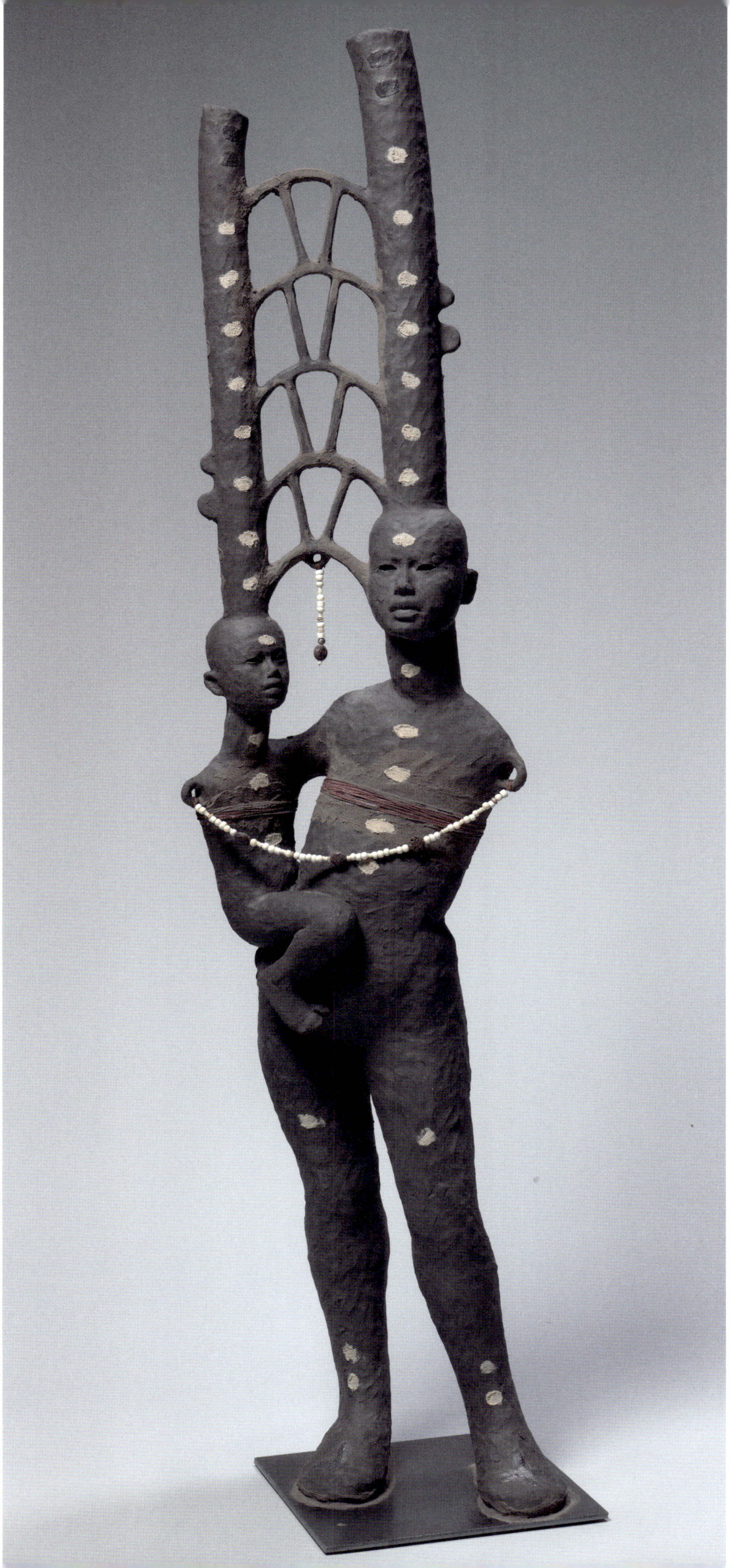

Heights III, 2022. Rose B. Simpson. Clay, steel, twine, grout, and beads from bone, wood, lava, trade, glass, pyrite, and stone; 190.5 x 58.4 x 58.4 cm. The Cleveland Museum of Art, Severance and Greta Millikin Trust, 2023.49

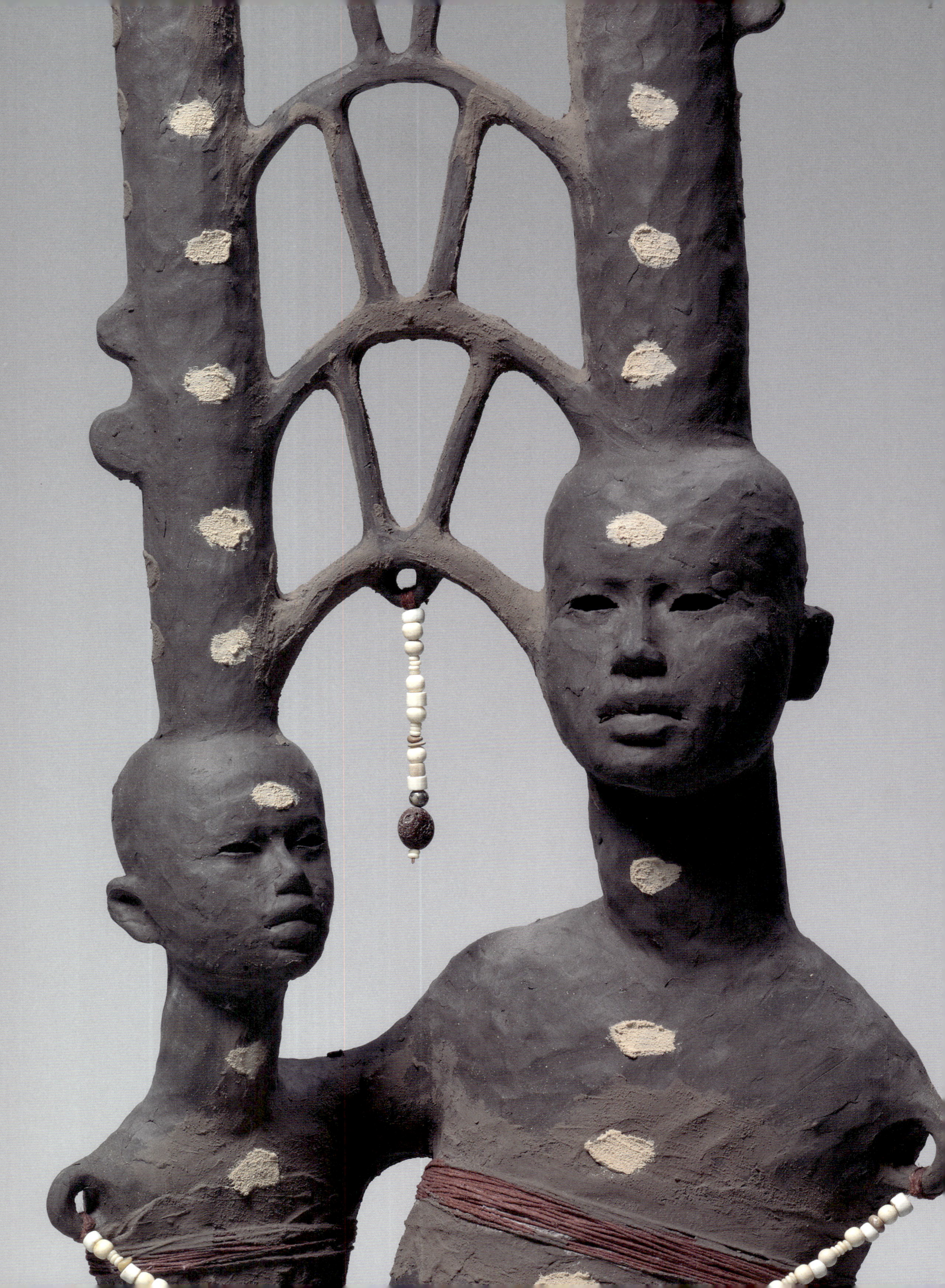

loving job, one that requires a delicate balance."[5] Positioned with her growing daughter on her hip, the mother in *Heights III* is posed in a gentle contrapposto stance to offset the weight of the child, a formal manifestation of the "delicate balance" evoked in the artist's description of the piece. The figures' arms are replaced by handles, underscoring their resemblance to double-handled ceramic vessels. The jewelry hanging between the figures, featuring colored beads also made of fired clay, is one of the artist's trademark elements. Typical of Simpson's oeuvre, the piece is exquisitely sculpted, showing traces of her hand-molding throughout the surface. The black clay used in *Heights III* recalls signature Pueblo blackware pottery but in updated form.

The other work by Simpson in the museum's collection is the diptych *Maria*. This pair of color lithographs reproduce an earlier work by the artist—also titled *Maria* (2014; see pp. 56–57)—a restored and customized 1985 Chevy El Camino whose exterior was painted to look like Tewa blackware pottery. The black-on-black pottery technique was invented by the famed potter Maria Martinez (1887–1980; see pp. 44–45 and 58), after whom the piece is named, and her husband, Julian Martinez (1879–1943), at San Ildefonso Pueblo in 1918–19. In addition to being a ceramic artist, Simpson is also a skilled auto mechanic. *Maria* pays homage to Simpson's own training in Northern New Mexico College's Automotive Science program, as well as the lowrider car culture of Española, New Mexico. Since creating *Maria* in 2014, Simpson has used the car in performances and shown it in exhibitions, in addition to creating the printed diptych (see pp. 60–61).

Bowl, c. 1948–49. Maria Martinez (San Ildefonso Pueblo, 1887–1980). Ceramic, slip; diam. 23.1 cm. The Cleveland Museum of Art, Gift in memory of Dr. Henry L. Tapp by his family, MaryLou, Carl, and Richard Tapp, 1999.191

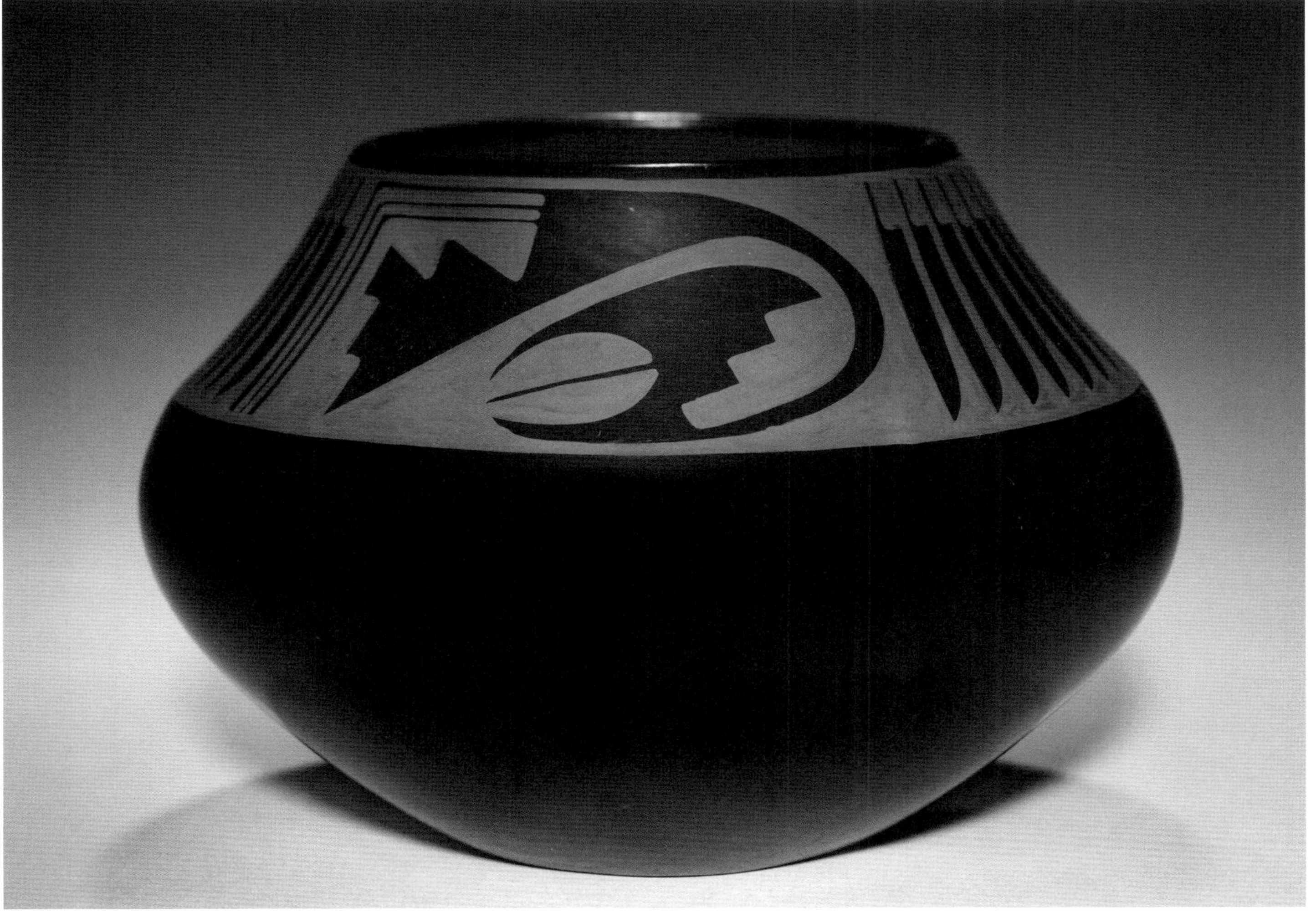

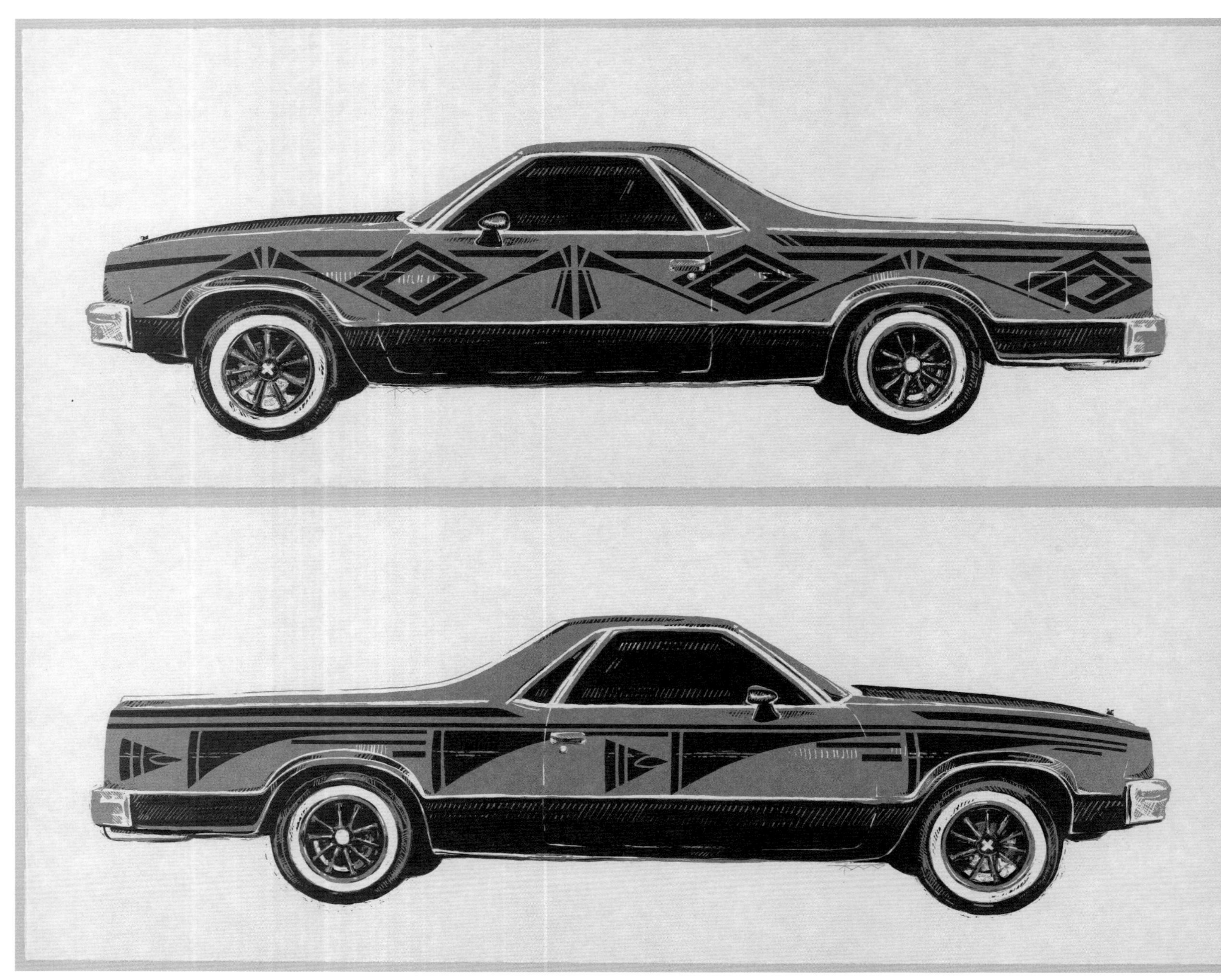

Maria, 2021. Rose B. Simpson. Color
lithograph (diptych); 91.4 x 116.4 cm.
The Cleveland Museum of Art,
Anne Elizabeth Wilson Memorial Fund,
2023.14

Producing site-specific, large-scale work is an integral component of Simpson's artistic practice. In 2022, at Field Farm in Williamstown, Massachusetts, she made *Counterculture*, a series of twelve concrete standing figures placed in the outdoor landscape for ten months. In 2024, she created a temporary installation for Madison Square Park Conservancy in New York City titled *Seed*, composed of towering, welded structures and clay figures emerging from the ground. In both cases, a deep awareness of and appreciation for the surrounding landscape in which the work was sited was a primary concern, factoring into the artist's choice of scale, materials, and design. At Field Farm, for example, the eyes of each figure are carved out, so that "it [is] like the sky is seeing *you*."[6] And in New York, the welded totems of *Seed* interact with the buildings surrounding Madison Square Park in Manhattan's Flatiron District.[7]

Scale is important to how Simpson hopes visitors will engage with *Strata*. She reflects on her experience seeing the fossils on display in the neighboring Cleveland Museum of Natural History. "You realize your own experience of life in a larger context . . . we are so tiny." In this regard, "*Strata* is about history, about something bigger than humanity." Each statue is like the Earth itself, watchful and witnessing the passage of time and the changing effects of light. Simpson hopes that visitors' interaction with the work will foster self-awareness, "so that we can build a more reverent relationship" with the natural world.

Simpson's practice also extends to installation art. This includes *Dream House*, a site-specific project the artist conceived for the Fabric Workshop and Museum in Philadelphia in 2022, which Karen Patterson discusses in her essay in this volume.[8] In *Dream House*, as in *Strata*, Simpson reflects on facets of familiar spaces and how impressions of home can shift and transform when transported to other places. Thus, a project like *Strata* transcends spatial notions of home, combining inspiration from diverse locales into a single work.

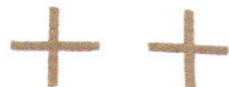

The transformation of the natural world is key to Simpson's conception of her artistic practice. As she puts it, "I often think about how I transform materials. How am I the wind? How am I the water? How am I just part of the natural influence of things that have intention?" She continues, "I don't think my intention in sculpting is any different than the wind. I want to believe the wind has intention as well. It's just that I have an anthropomorphic investment because I see myself in things. And maybe the wind is sculpting to make things look like itself."

While driving with Simpson in New Mexico alongside the Rio Grande, as I had the opportunity to do in December 2023, one can see how the wind and water shape the terrain. The formations they have carved reveal stratified layers of rock faces, ranging in color from deep red to light terracotta. Hues shift with the time of day, revealing new vistas depending on the light. As she drives on roads that weave through deep canyons, Simpson adds layers to the experience with a steady stream of stories—stories about the landscape, the Pueblos we drive through and the people who live there, the UFOs she sees frequenting the evening skies. Her daughter, Cedar, chimes in at various moments from the backseat, joining her mother in song as we pass Black Mesa, an Indigenous stronghold against Spanish colonizers during the seventeenth-century Pueblo Revolt.[9]

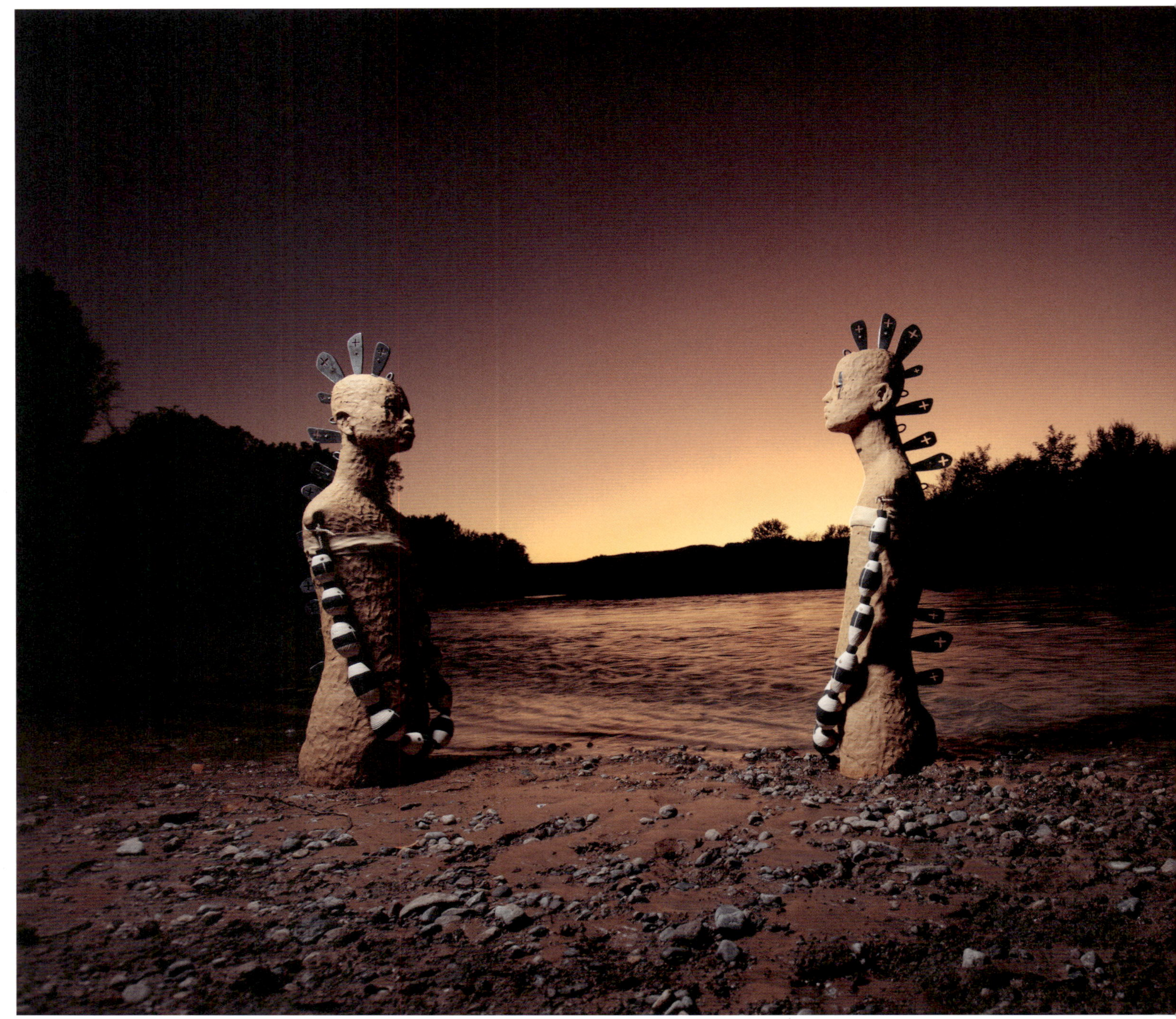

Rose B. Simpson's *River Girls* (2019) in the New Mexico landscape. Consisting of a pair of immortal punk warriors on the water's edge, this work was made in response to the Missing and Murdered Indigenous Women and Girls (MMIWG) crisis in communities across North America and beyond.

The volcanic activity in New Mexico is present as well in the materials of *Strata* via the pumice, or pieces of volcanic ash, that are blended with the concrete to form the lower torso of each sculpture. In conceptualizing the piece, Simpson felt that solid concrete would appear too industrial. But when she mixed the concrete with particles of pumice, roughly one-half to one centimeter in size, they imparted a rough and textured surface—the exact effect she sought to achieve. Furthermore, there are poetic metaphors to be drawn from the additive. Simpson explains that because of its volcanic past, pumice does not expand or contract because it has already been through intense heat and pressure, transforming from a solid to a liquid and then back to a solid. Thus, "it creates stability because of everything it's been through." Natalie Diaz remarks how the analogy could extend to Indigenous survival and resistance. "Beautiful that stability would come from what it has been through. Maybe a better way of saying survivance [of] Indigenous

peoples is to say because of everything [we've] been through . . . it has [created] strength and stability."[10]

Simpson often reflects on history and human relationships with the environment. She states, "What we put out into the world becomes a natural resource that is harvested by the generations to come. Whether it's the work we do, whether it's the mistakes we made . . . what we construct, what we stand for, what we take apart, what we dismantle, is all so that it can eventually transform." Even within her own work, Simpson recognizes the maturation that has come with years of practice and the growth that transpired in her art prior to *Strata*. "Our colonized modern culture is very youth-centric and doesn't value elders. It doesn't value experience. It doesn't value maturity." Patience is part of that growth, as is the slow transformation of oneself into an elder, a valued and revered member of the community. The human forms often present in her work go a long way toward fostering this way of thinking. For Simpson, the anthropomorphic quality of her work elicits empathy from the viewer, as there is an inherent human response to encountering another human-like figure. In this sense, *Strata* opens up yet another layer not only in Simpson's growth as an artist but also in the possibility of others' growing awareness of the natural world, Native histories, and one another.

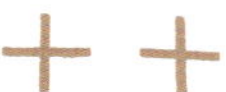

Layers can also provide the opportunity to heal, to suture what was previously torn, without necessarily forgetting or denying the past. "No matter what has happened in the strata, what better way to live than to always be open to the possibility of another layer?" In this regard, Simpson's work asserts a pride of place and belonging on land where Native residents have historically been forcefully dispossessed of their territories and cultures. It also contributes to evolving conversations with historical examples of Pueblo pottery in the museum's collections.

The decision to feature Simpson's work at the Cleveland Museum of Art grew in part out of the extensive discussions leading up to the museum's Indigenous Peoples and Land Acknowledgment, announced on January 31, 2023. In late 2021, the CMA convened an Indigenous advisory committee to address whether an acknowledgment should be made, to seek guidance on how Native Americans and their arts are presented in the galleries, and to explore ways to develop a long-term relationship with the region's Indigenous communities. Committee members represent a range of ancestries and tribal affiliations; some have deep roots in Northeast Ohio, while others arrived more recently and have tribal affiliations from across the country. The resulting acknowledgment is posted as a plaque in the museum's Horace Kelley Art Foundation North Lobby and appears in the opening pages of this publication, with a longer statement on our website explaining its purpose and background. These efforts begin to recognize the Native Americans who were dispossessed from this region in the past and to inaugurate a new era of collaboration with Indigenous peoples living in Northeast Ohio today.

In addition to caring for past examples of Pueblo pottery in our collection of Indigenous art of the Americas, we also have a unique piece of Pueblo history in the holdings of our Education Art Collection (EAC). The EAC was founded in 1914 to spread awareness of visual arts and global cultures in advance of the museum's official opening in 1916. Among the EAC's ten thousand objects is a process kit from Maria and Julian Martinez demonstrating the methods and materials used to create their renowned black-on-black pottery. On June 30, 1930, the CMA's education curator, Charles F. Ramus, wrote to the Archaeological Institute of America in Santa Fe, asking for help in procuring a process kit from Maria Martinez. In July, he received a reply from the institute's curator, Mary R. Van Stone, reporting that the Martinezes "will make the complete set of pots and accompanying implements etc., to demonstrate the pottery making, for thirty dollars."[11] The CMA agreed to the price, and later that year the museum received a set of nearly forty objects, including vessels in varying states of completion, shaping tools, pigments, powders, and brushes, along with fourteen photographs of Maria Martinez at work and basic descriptive labels of each item.

Absent from the labels are aspects of the couple's work that we have only fully come to appreciate decades later: the remarkable engineering, specially designed tools, and time-consuming study of ancient and modern pottery techniques it took the Martinezes years to perfect. The pair's innovative and systematic approach to pottery transformed

Maria Martinez's process kit. The Cleveland Museum of Art, Education Art Collection, 30.620

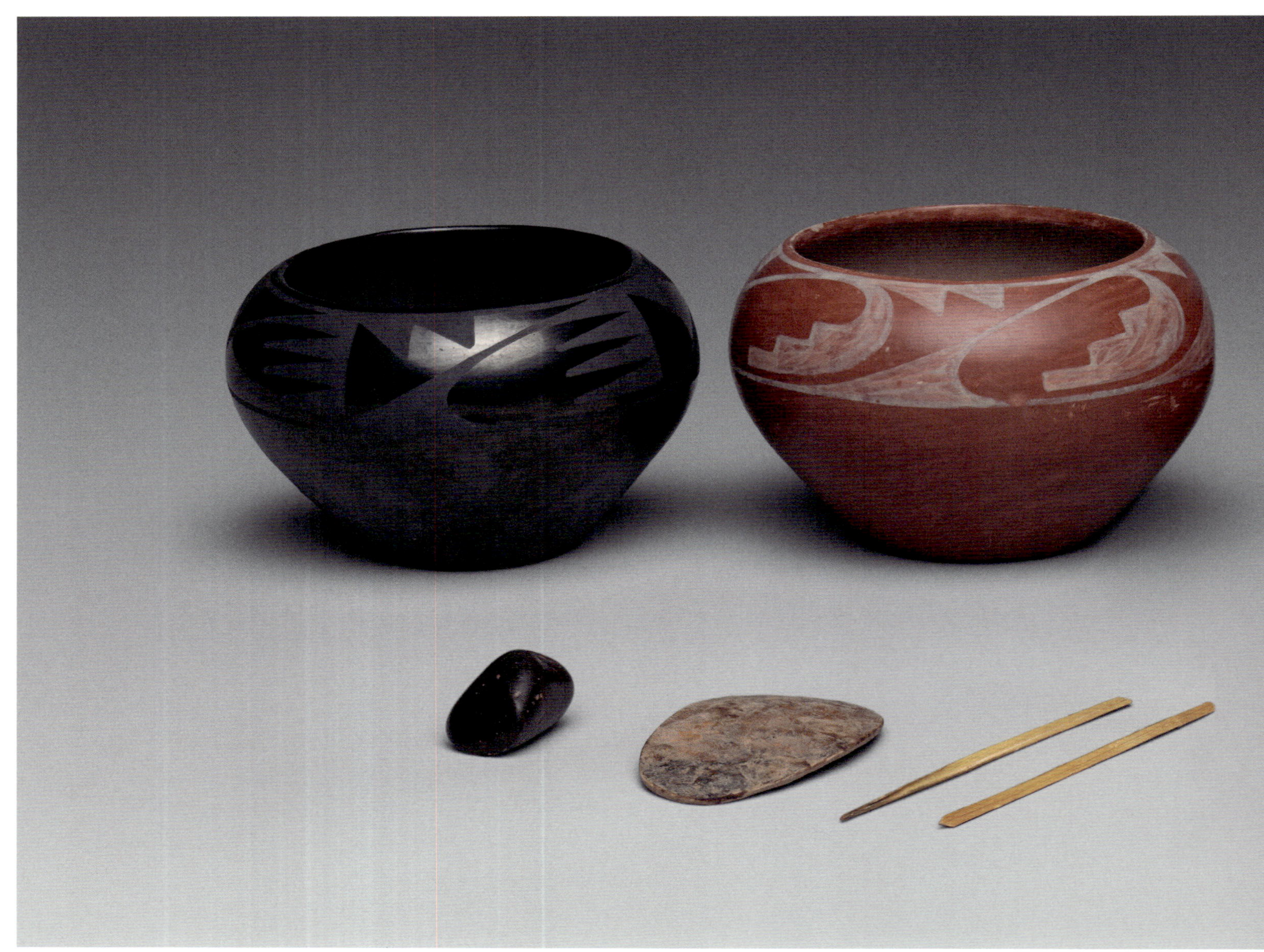

utilitarian Pueblo vessels into works of art in their own right. Although the kit was created almost a century ago, it bears strong contemporary resonance. There is something about seeing each layer of the Martinezes' process iterated and laid out, piece by piece, that is akin to a conceptual exercise, the telling of a story, or even the generous sharing of a tried-and-true recipe. Like the rock faces of a canyon, the kit reveals the layers that underpin the making of a singular vessel but also build a history of the generations-long pottery traditions practiced in the Pueblos of modern-day New Mexico. Reflecting on *Maria* (2014), her 1985 El Camino made to honor Maria Martinez's iconic Tewa pottery, Simpson affirms, "I have the utmost amount of reverence for the Tewa potters who have come before me . . . when I look at the wall of a particularly sharp Maria Martinez vessel, I see myself. I see the simultaneous layers of existence I navigate . . . . We are here together through time."[12]

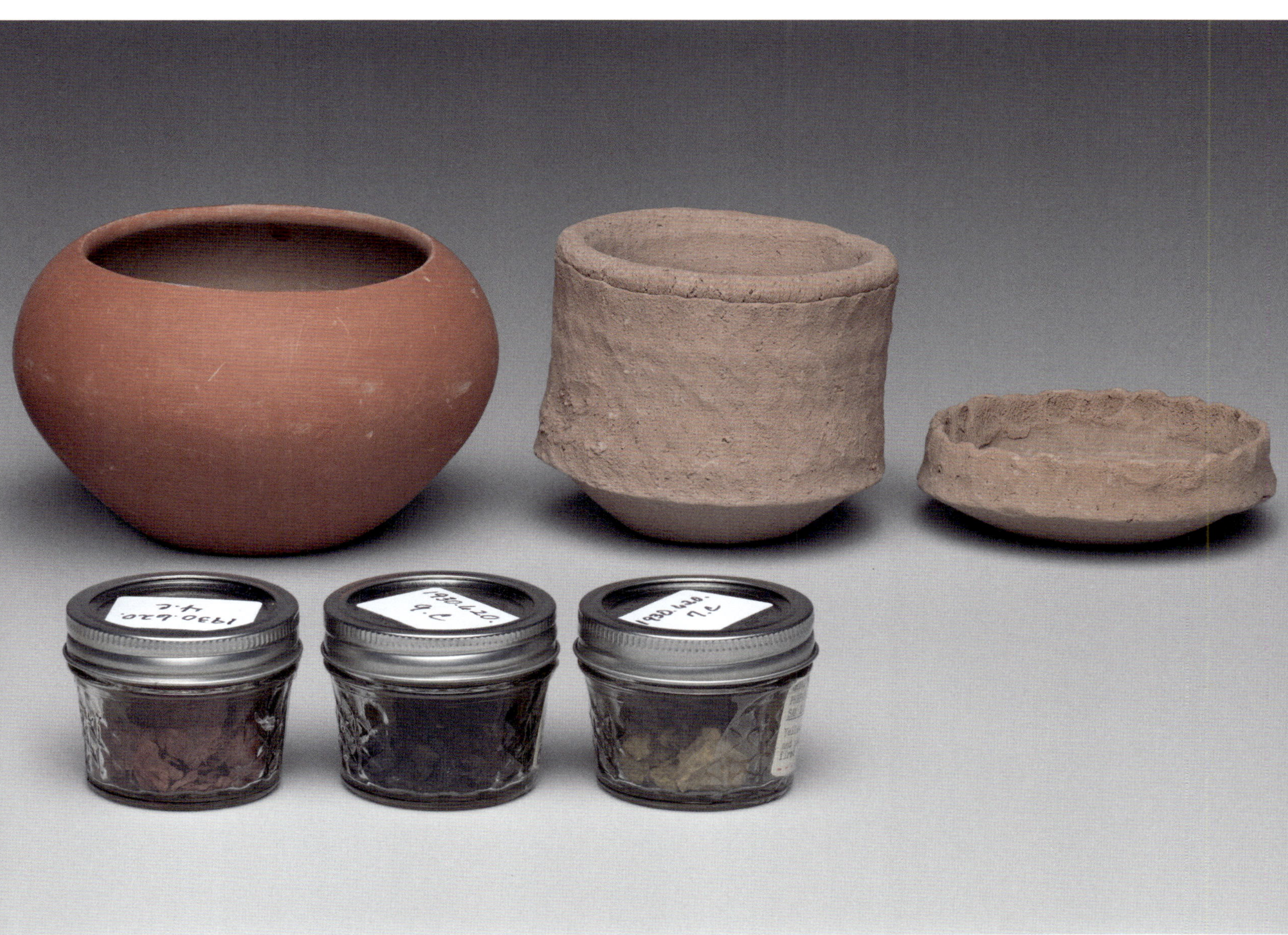

Maria Martinez with fellow potters building and shaping clay pots. These photos accompany Martinez's process kit. The Cleveland Museum of Art, Education Art Collection, 30.620

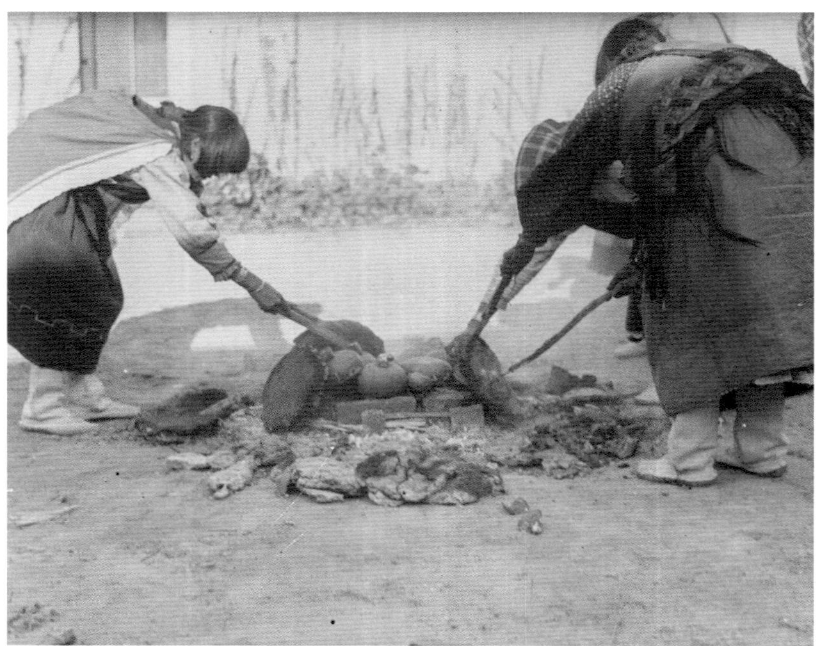
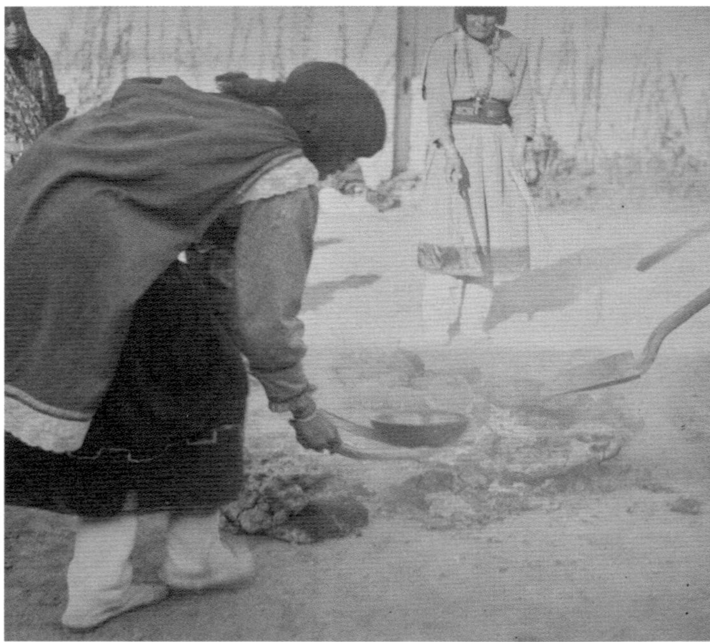
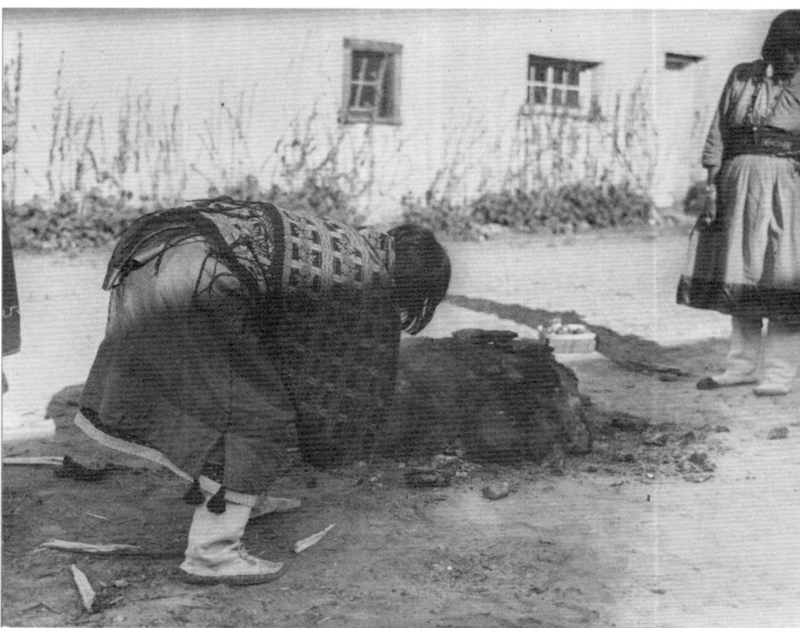
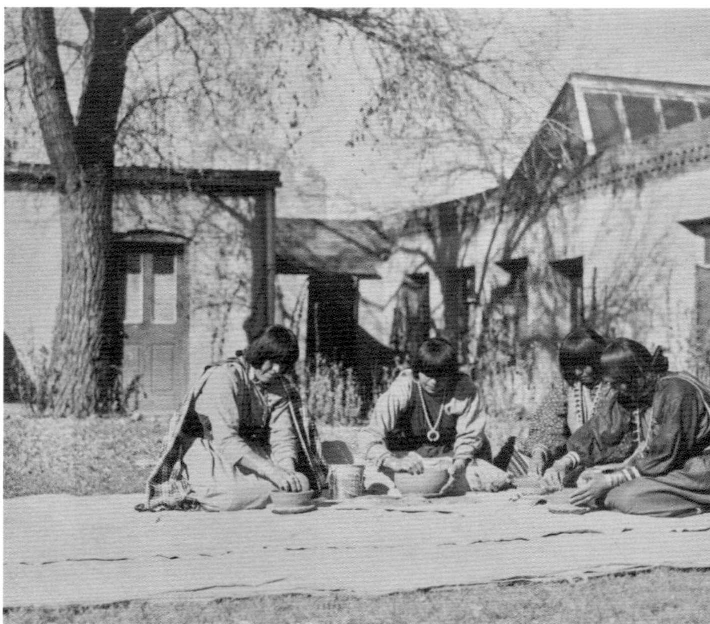

1. Rose B. Simpson, artist proposal for *Strata*, 2022.

2. *Ámà: The Gathering Place* was on view in the Ames Family Atrium at the Cleveland Museum of Art, August 2–December 1, 2019. The multichannel electronic sound installation *The Ties that Bind* (2019.34) remains in the museum's permanent collection.

3. Unless otherwise noted, all quotes by Rose B. Simpson are from the author's interview with the artist, March 1, 2023.

4. "Molded by Life," 103.

5. Rose B. Simpson, email to the author, January 18, 2023.

6. Rose B. Simpson quoted in Jori Finkel, "Rose B. Simpson Thinks in Clay," *New York Times*, June 16, 2022.

7. Part of the installation of *Seed* was sited at Inwood Hill Park, as well as in Madison Square Park, both in New York City.

8. Karen Patterson, "A Dream House," this volume, 80–95.

9. The Pueblo Revolt, also known as Po'pay's Rebellion, occurred in 1680. See Roxanne Dunbar-Ortiz, *An Indigenous People's History of the United States* (Boston: Beacon Press, 2014), 125–26.

10. "Molded by Life," 101.

11. Mary R. Van Stone to Charles F. Ramus, July 17, 1930, The Cleveland Museum of Art, object file for EAC 30.620, Maria and Julian Martinez Process Kit, Maria Martinez (San Ildefonso Pueblo, 1887–1980), Julian Martinez (San Ildefonso Pueblo, 1879–1943).

12. Rose B. Simpson, "*Maria*, '85 El Camino," in *Maria & Modernism*, ed. Diana F. Pardue et al. (Phoenix, AZ: Heard Museum, 2024), 182–87.

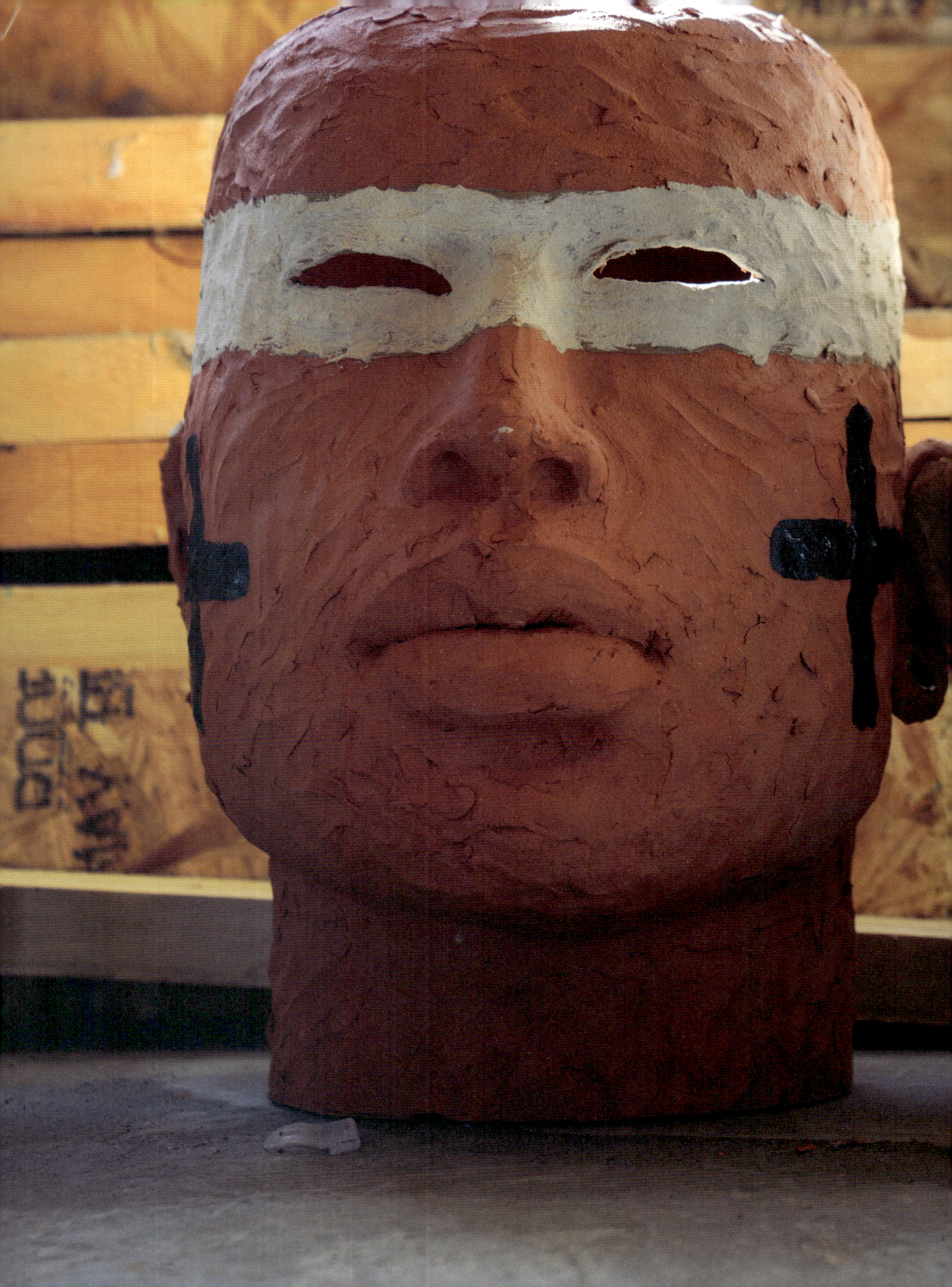

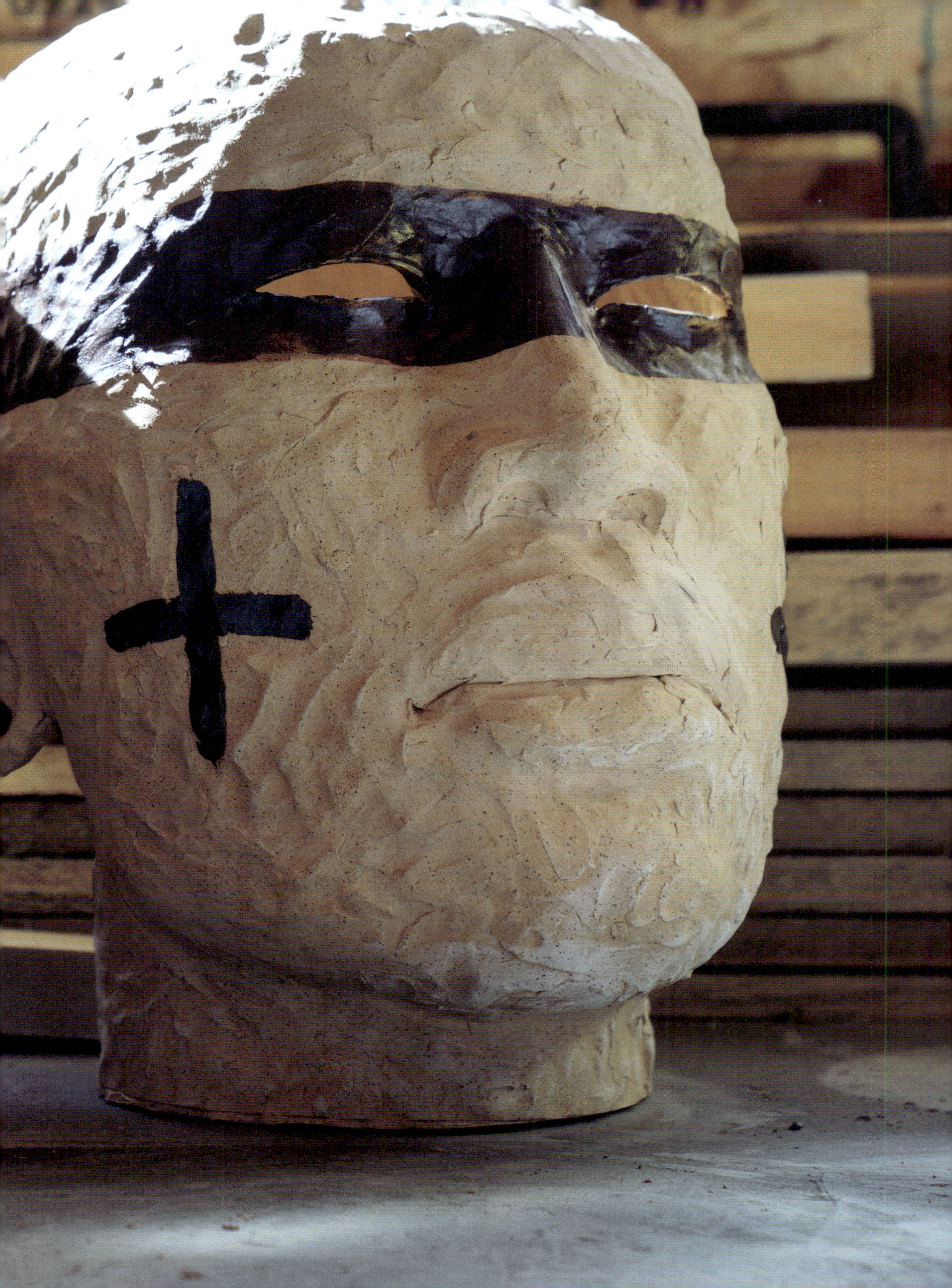

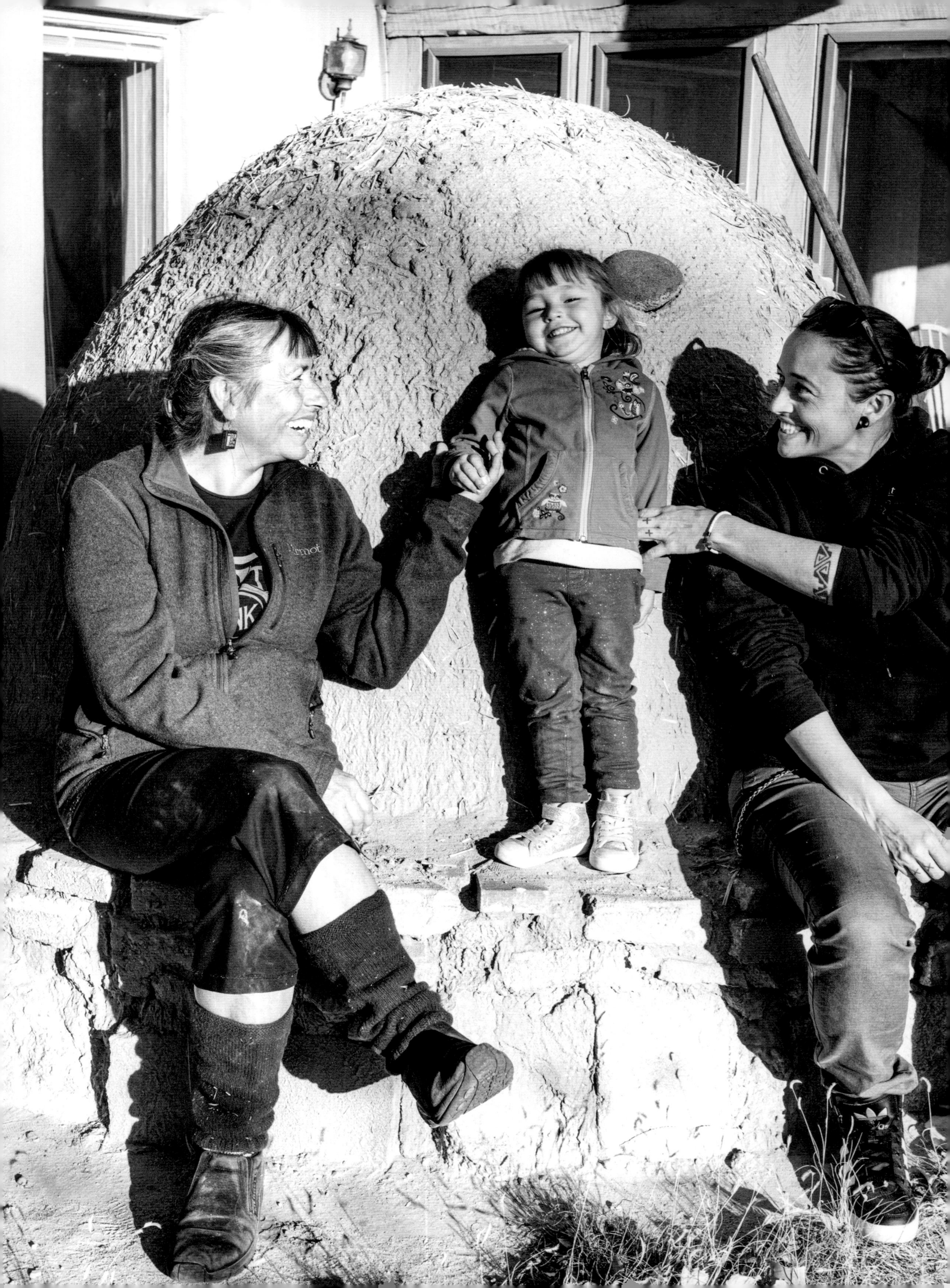

Daughter, Mother, Pueblo Woman, Indigenous Woman: Rose B. Simpson in Four Artworks

Anya Montiel

Because of her, I sculpt clay. Because of her, I don't question whether I am able to build cars. Because of her, I can wield a chain saw and chop an adobe the exact right shape. Because of her, I was raised on our ancestral homelands, participating in our cultural practices. Because of her, I can usually figure out a way to get something done with what I have on hand.[1]

—Rose B. Simpson

Rose B. Simpson (born 1983) is an artist who is the daughter, granddaughter, and great-granddaughter of artists. For most of her life, she has lived on her ancestral homelands at Kha'po Owingeh (Santa Clara Pueblo) in northern New Mexico. The "her" Simpson references and applauds in the epigraph is her mother, Roxanne Swentzell (born 1962), who is a clay and bronze artist, builder, farmer, food activist, and permaculturist (see pp. 55 and 102). As a child, Simpson observed her mother challenge societal, cultural, and gender expectations—which, in turn, enabled and inspired Simpson to do the same.

In her art, Simpson creates and builds using multiple materials and resources; she works in clay and metal figurative sculpture, automotive design, installation, performance art, fashion, and poetry. Her artworks often expose aspects of the human condition, but they emanate from deeply personal experiences and her worldview as an Indigenous woman. When she was only twenty-five, one writer described Simpson's art as "the insides of all of us made visible" but, was also "no longer defensively Indian."[2] With the latter characterization the writer, Richard Nilsen, exposed his bias and his patronizing view of Native American art. For Nilsen, Simpson's art prompted an emotional, personal response from deep within, but he identified with the art, not the artist. Simpson, however, while giving a keynote address before hundreds of fellow ceramic artists, declared, "a lot of my work isn't gendered, but everything is me. It's a piece of me. They're all my own truth. My own experience."[3] Her artworks are manifestations of her life as an Indigenous woman/mother/daughter living on her Pueblo homelands. Examining four of Simpson's artworks reveals that her identity and worldview are inextricably linked.

Roxanne Swentzell and her daughter, Rose B. Simpson, with Simpson's daughter, Cedar, Flowering Tree, San Pedro, 2018. Photo by Ungelbah Dávila

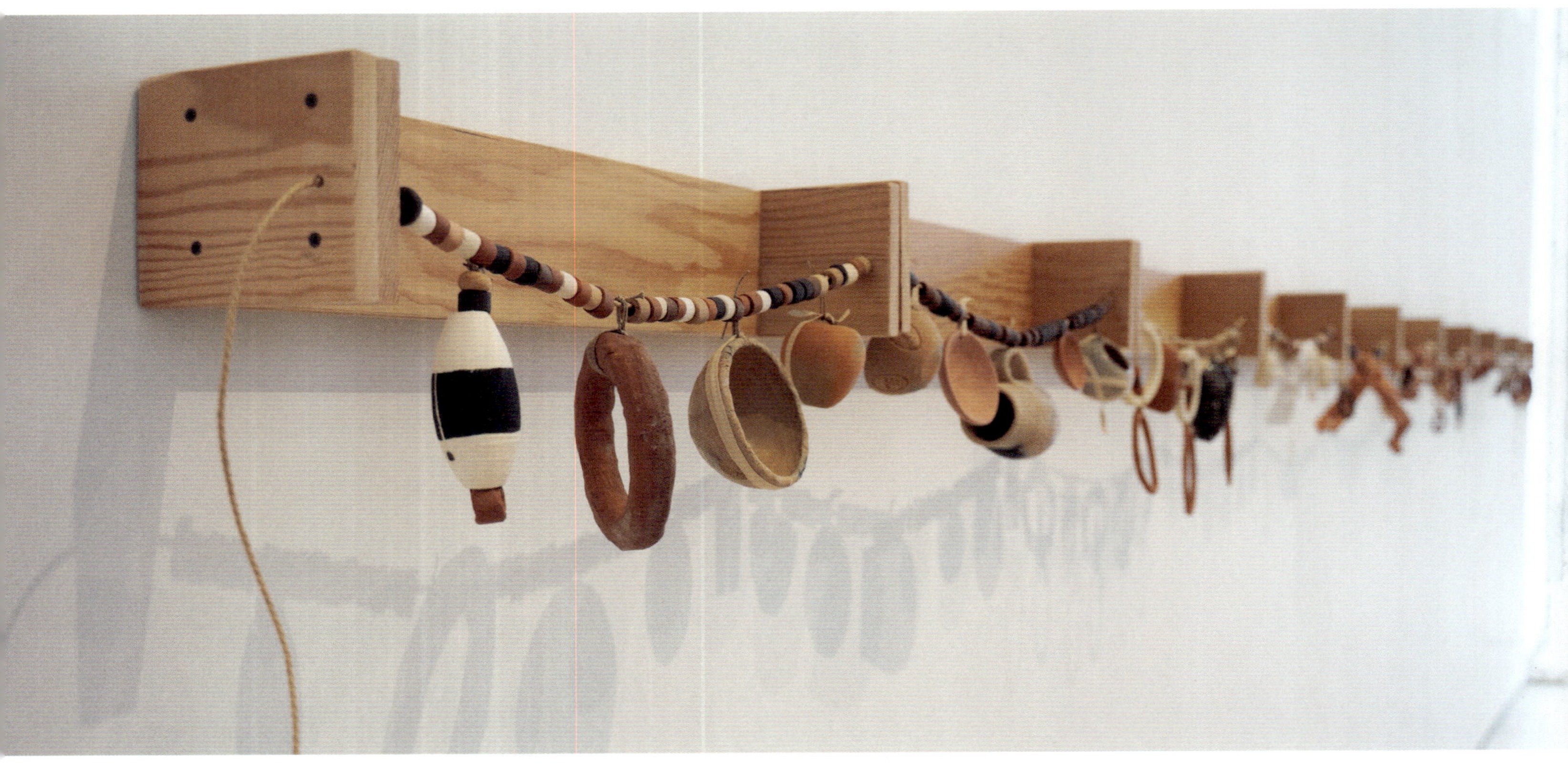

Installation view of *Untitled (Timeline Necklace)*, 2019, from the exhibition *Form & Relation: Contemporary Native Ceramics*, Hood Museum of Art, Dartmouth College, January 6, 2021–July 23, 2022. Rose B. Simpson in collaboration with Roxanne Swentzell. Ceramic, glaze, leather, wood, string, mud beads, and wire; 61 x 640.1 x 22.9 cm. Installed in ten separate wooden bracket sections with cleats. Photo by Brian Wagner

DAUGHTER: *TIMELINE NECKLACE*

In 2019, Simpson and Swentzell collaborated on an artwork for the group exhibition *Form & Relation: Contemporary Native Ceramics*, at the Hood Museum of Art at Dartmouth College. Twenty-one feet long, the work, *Timeline Necklace*, consists of clay beads, hoops, masks, figures, bowls, and vessels strung horizontally with twine, wire, and leather. In its form, materials, and motifs, the necklace speaks to the transfer of inter-generational knowledge between Simpson and Swentzell—the only parent-child pair in the exhibition—as mother and daughter, artists, and Pueblo women. The symbols and figures represent experiences and events from their lives, some comprehensible to outsiders and others more obscure. There are babies, hands with open palms, hands with clenched fists, a couple with their arms intertwined, and, toward the center, a figure cradling its pregnant belly. The various elements that make up the work blend perfectly, and it is difficult to discern which artist made which elements.

Discussing the inspiration behind *Timeline Necklace*, Swentzell reflected, "Instead of sitting there and talking to each other with words, how about we talk to each other with clay?"[4] Swentzell had a speech impediment as a child, and sculpting with clay was her means of communication, noting that "I sometimes consider clay my first language because words were not there. I was able to start making these little figurines that would explain to my mother what I wanted her to know."[5] Just as Swentzell expressed herself through clay, Simpson would learn and adopt the same language.

Simpson has described her mother as "a farmer, builder, professional sculptor, and cultural preservationist, and my closest ally."[6] When Simpson was a child, Swentzell established the Flowering Tree Permaculture Institute, a nonprofit organization, at Kha'po Owingeh. Run by Native women, Flowering Tree draws from Indigenous knowledge systems of the local ecosystem to teach sustainable home building, high-desert farming and irrigation, solar energy, seed saving, beekeeping, and animal husbandry. Also during Simpson's youth, Swentzell built the family home from adobe and became well-known

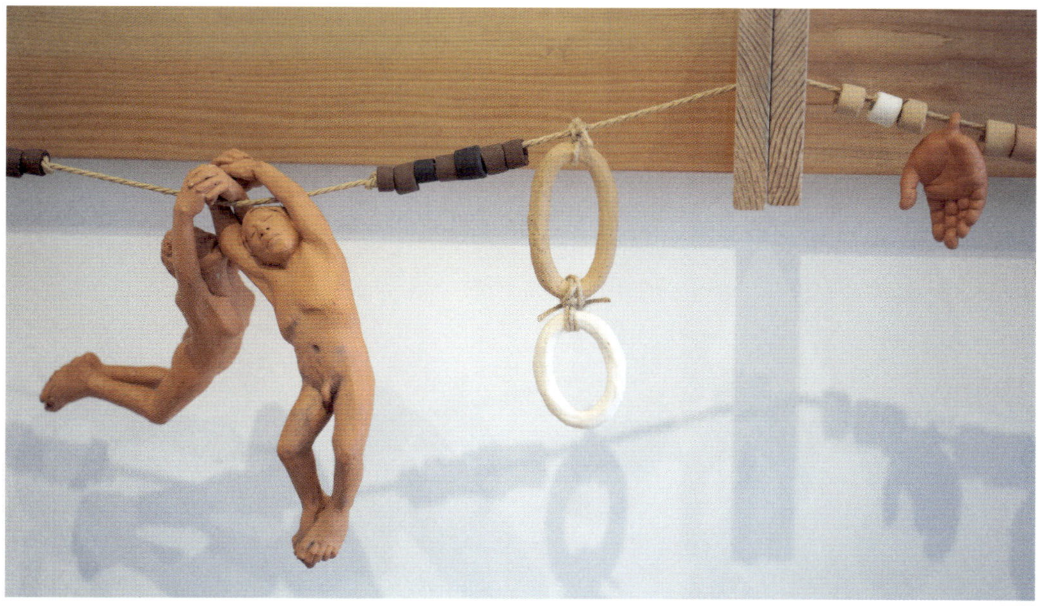

for her clay figural sculptures, often winning awards at Native art fairs and exhibiting in museums. By watching her mother create and provide for those around her, Simpson recognized the limitless possibilities for her own future.

Reflecting on everything her mother has accomplished, Simpson observed, "The challenges and the questions that my mother put out into the world—asked of society, asked of the art world, asked of ceramics, and asked of the Pueblo people—were big when she started asking them. She was pushing the boundaries in so many ways, and I'm not having to do that in my life."[7] When Swentzell launched her art career in the 1980s, the Native art world had not previously seen figural sculptures like hers, sculptures that unsparingly commented on social issues, human frailties, and gender disparities. Swentzell's honesty in her life and art provided Simpson with a crucial model for her own life and art. The two have collaborated on other artworks as well, but *Timeline Necklace* is perhaps the most evocative, rendered in a uniquely shared language and acting as a visual mnemonic for their memories.[8]

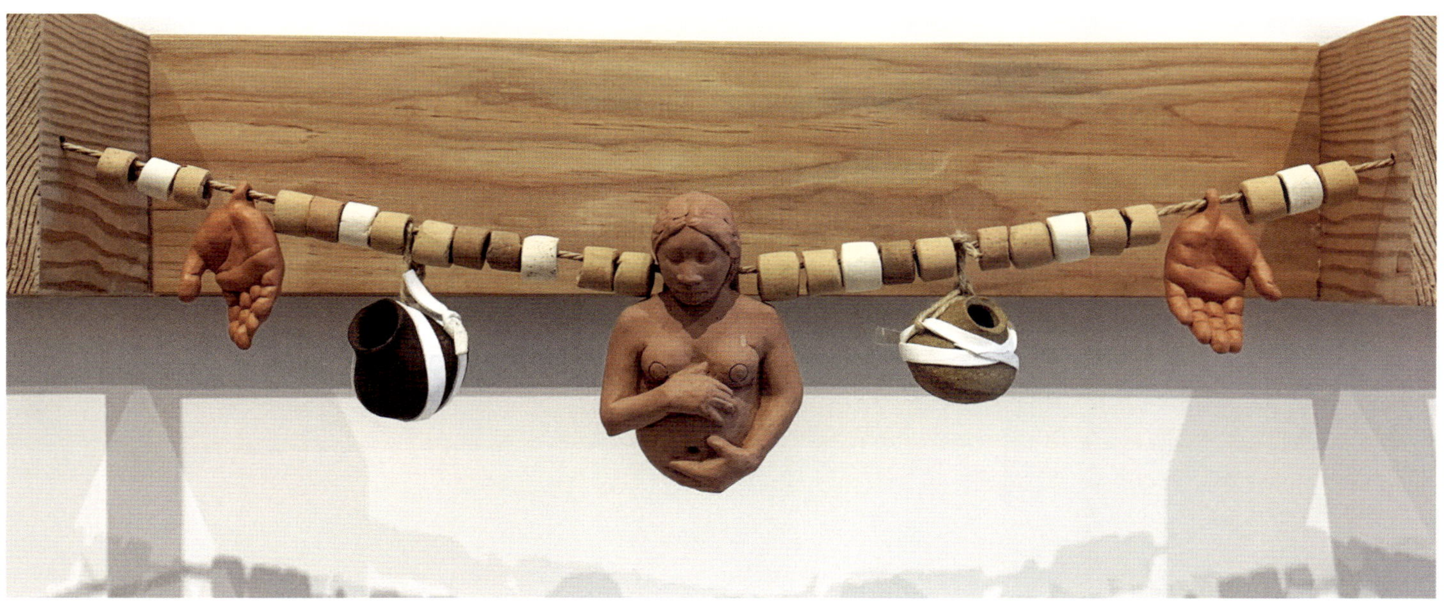

Detail of *Untitled (Timeline Necklace)*, 2019

MOTHER: *GENESIS*

In 2017, after giving birth to her daughter, Cedar, Simpson completed a clay figural sculpture entitled *Genesis*, depicting a mother holding her baby to her chest. Wearing a sash around the hips, the mother figure stands tall, with feet firmly planted on the ground. Atop the head is an oval-shaped metal piece that is an automotive steel clutch plate. The clutch plate suggests a halo, likening the figure to a Madonna image, while also signifying Simpson's newfound understanding of empowerment that came with motherhood. She noted, "One of the biggest things that happened in my life was becoming a mom, a parent, an only parent . . . it changed me and my idea of what power looked like, what strength looked like."[9] Being a parent and loving, nurturing, and protecting are now sources of Simpson's empowerment.

Motherhood also prompted a change in Simpson's outlook on the world and its future. Formerly she had espoused an attitude of "Let's burn it all to the ground" as a means to advance change; this attitude is reflected in some of Simpson's early figural sculptures,

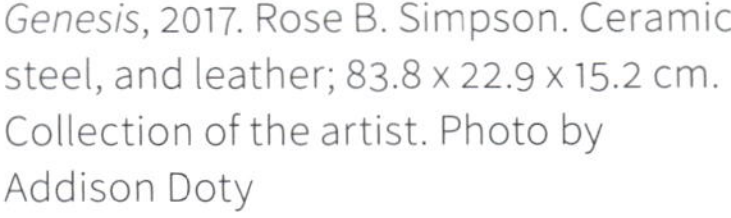

Genesis, 2017. Rose B. Simpson. Ceramic, steel, and leather; 83.8 x 22.9 x 15.2 cm. Collection of the artist. Photo by Addison Doty

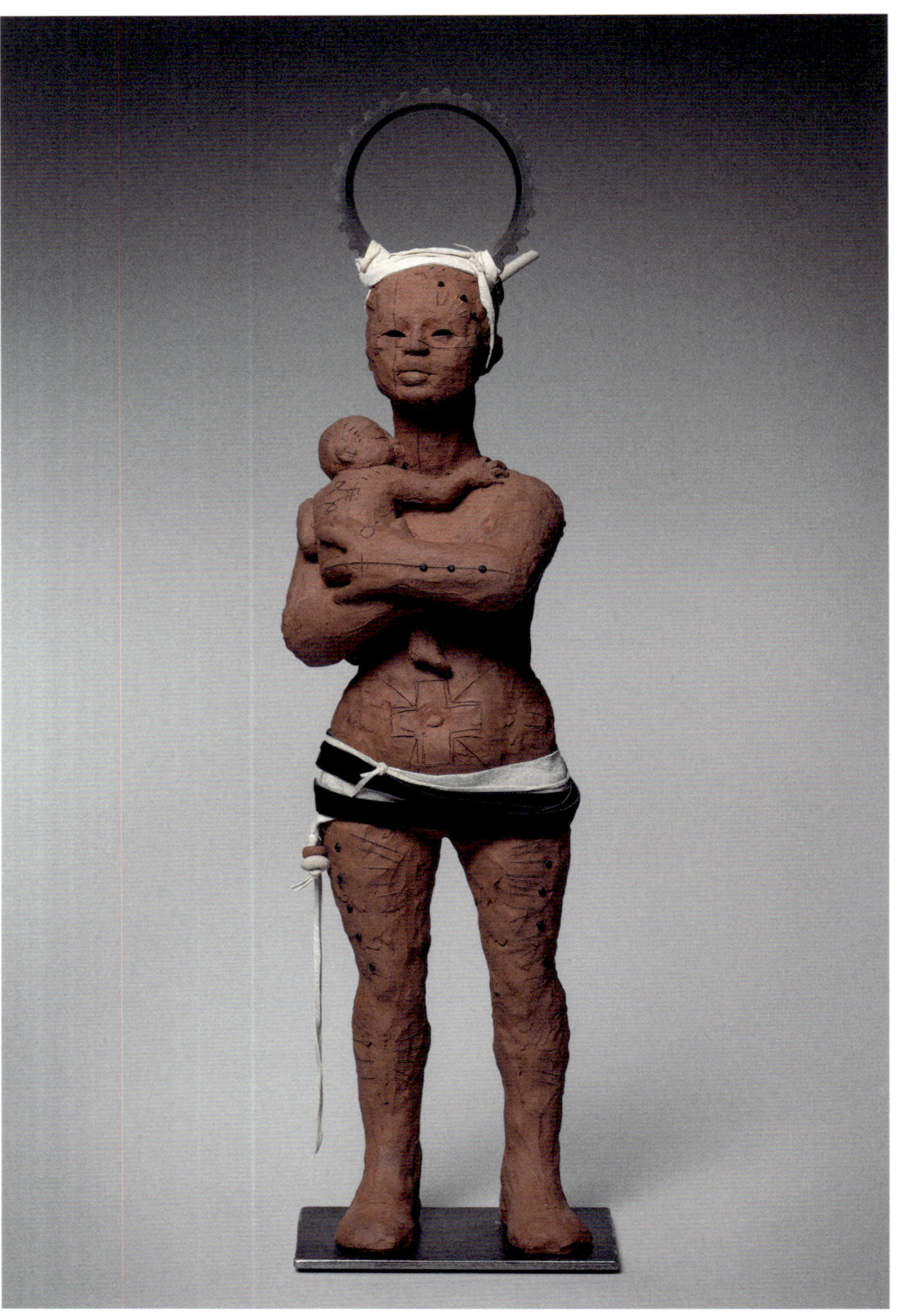

which wear protective clothing and gear as if suiting up for battle. Yet having become a mother, her approach shifted to one of repair, focusing on the world she is building for her child and her descendants. In the artist's words, "I have somebody that I want to have a beautiful, wonderful life."[10] Similarly, when Simpson's figures have open eyes, like the mother in *Genesis*, they "remind people that they are being watched."[11] Like sentinels, the artworks stand guard to keep humans on their best behavior.

The figures in *Genesis* have etched markings on their bodies and metal bolts suturing areas of the arms and legs. The body scars—a plus sign, an X, and animal tracks—are signs of pride, denoting experience and protection. In a 2023 article, Simpson explains that "the plus sign . . . is the star for guidance; the x . . . is for protection," and the animal tracks suggest "the path we're on."[12] In 1989, Swentzell created *Tattooed Woman*, a female figure whose body also features painted emblems and designs. Of this work, Swentzell writes, "I think of this woman as existing in a spiritual reality signified by her

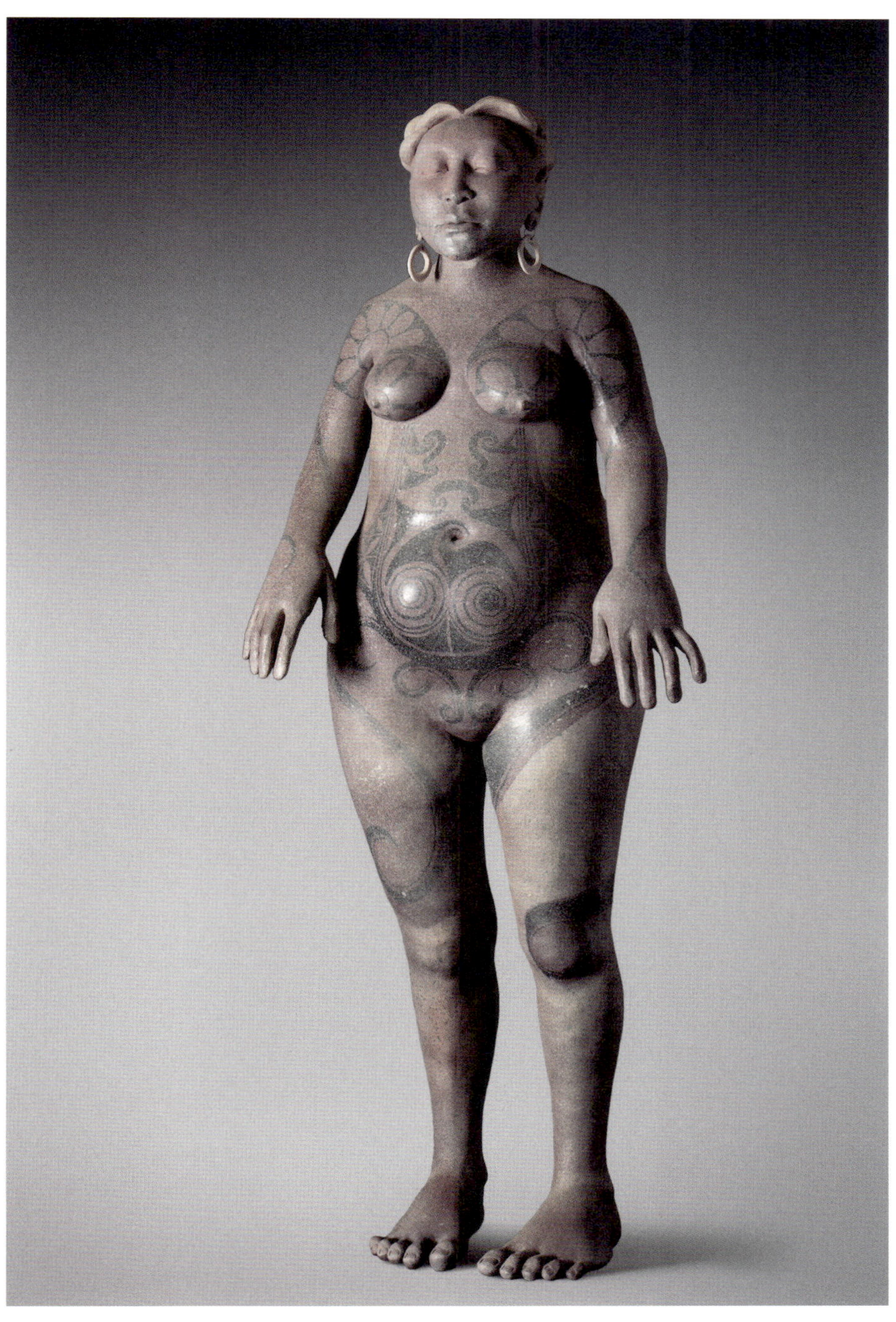

Tattooed Woman, 1989. Roxanne Swentzell (Tewa, born 1962). Original clay; 110.5 x 44.4 x 30.4 cm. Hood Museum of Art, Dartmouth, Purchased through the Virginia and Preston T. Kelsey 1958 Fund and the Robert J. Strasenburgh II 1942 Fund, 2019.4. © Roxanne Swentzell. Photo © Denver Art Museum

tatoos [*sic*] in which her senses have been heightened. She is aware of more than what can be seen or felt."[13] *Genesis* carries forward a similar sentiment—the mother stands in her power and proudly wears the markings of her wisdom.

PUEBLO WOMAN: *MARIA*

Simpson is from Kha'po Owingeh, one of the six Tewa-speaking pueblos of New Mexico. The pueblo is adjacent to Española, a city known as the lowrider capital of the world. Growing up, she admired the tricked-out, customized lowrider cars with their sleek and stylish bodywork but not the sexualized images of women draped across them. In be-tween earning her MFA in ceramics from the Rhode Island School of Design and her MFA in creative nonfiction from the Institute of American Indian Arts, Simpson completed a certificate in automotive science from Northern New Mexico College. She was the only

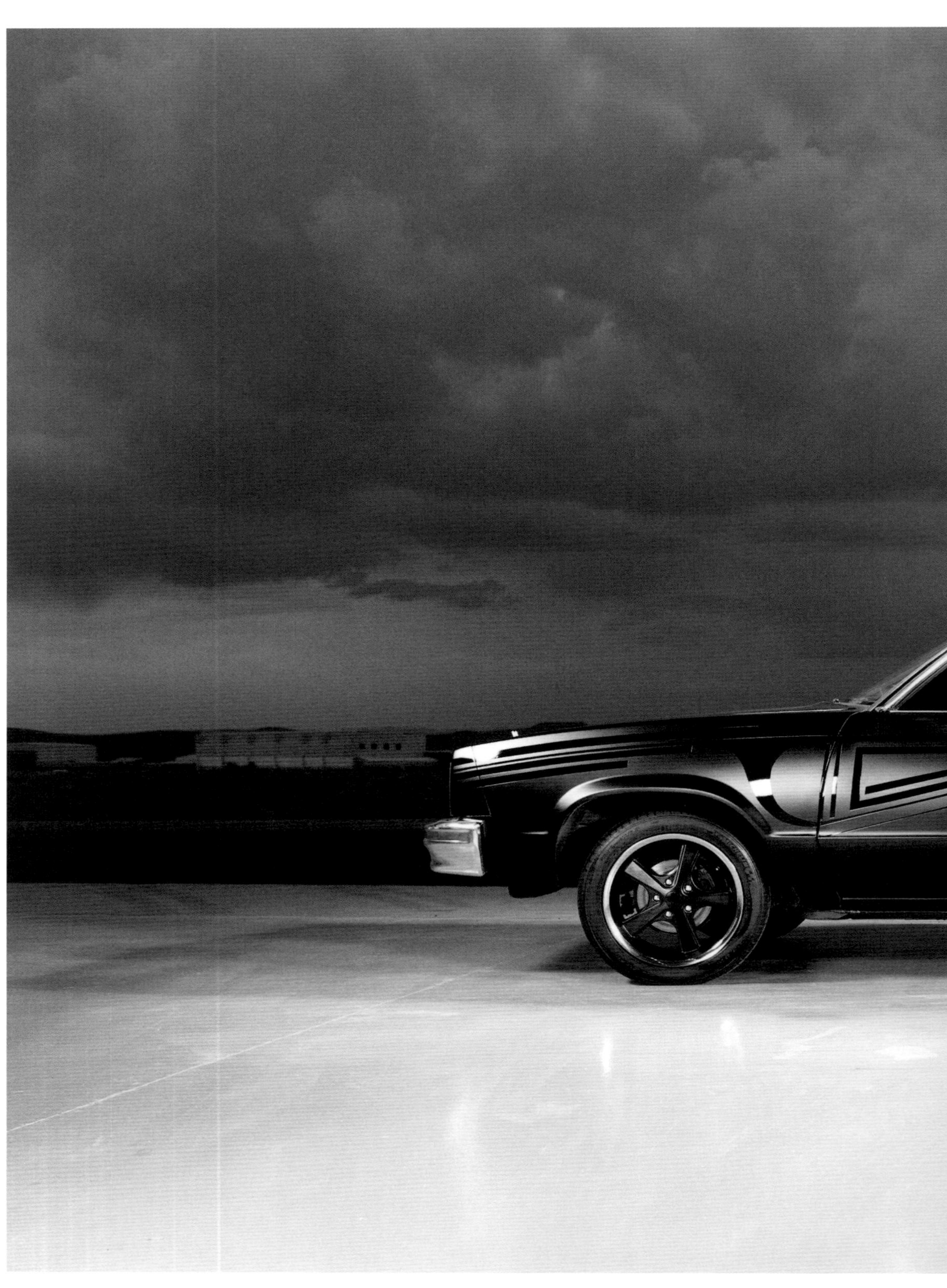

Maria, 2014. Rose B. Simpson. Collection of the artist. *Maria* is a 1985 Chevy El Camino customized by Simpson.

woman in the program. "Part of the reason I was there [in the program] is because I am a Pueblo woman," Simpson explained, adding, "It was my mom under the car fixing the starter. It was my mom with the chain saw. It was my mom who owned the tractor. And that's how I was shown that it's possible, and that's cultural."[14]

Merging her automotive knowledge with her cultural upbringing as a Pueblo woman, Simpson in 2014 created *Maria*, a customized 1985 Chevy El Camino painted with glossy black geometric designs over a matte black exterior (see p. 40). The designs are inspired by Tewa black-on-black pottery, and the work is named for Maria Martinez (1887–1980), the San Ildefonso Pueblo ceramicist known for revitalizing the blackware technique (see pp. 44–45). For Simpson, the connection between automobiles and pottery came from working with her mother in the fields of Kha'po Owingeh. Like Pueblo pottery, an El Camino is a sleek, utilitarian vessel holding, transporting, and safeguarding cargo;

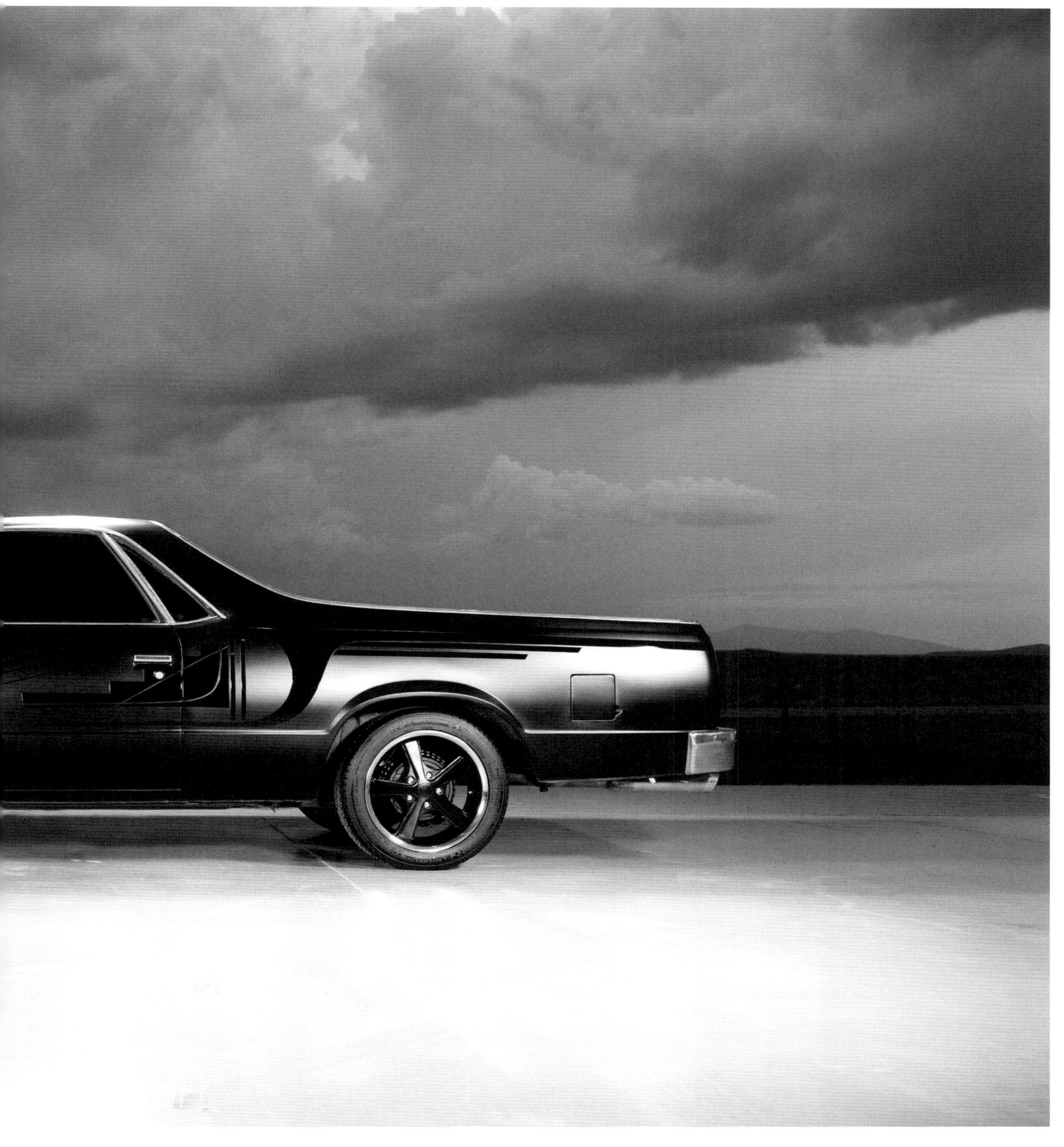

(Untitled) Jar, 1923–37. Maria Martinez. Earthenware, clay, paint; 16.5 x 19 cm. National Museum of the American Indian, Smithsonian Institution, R.E. Mansfield, 26/4199. Photo by NMAI Photo Services

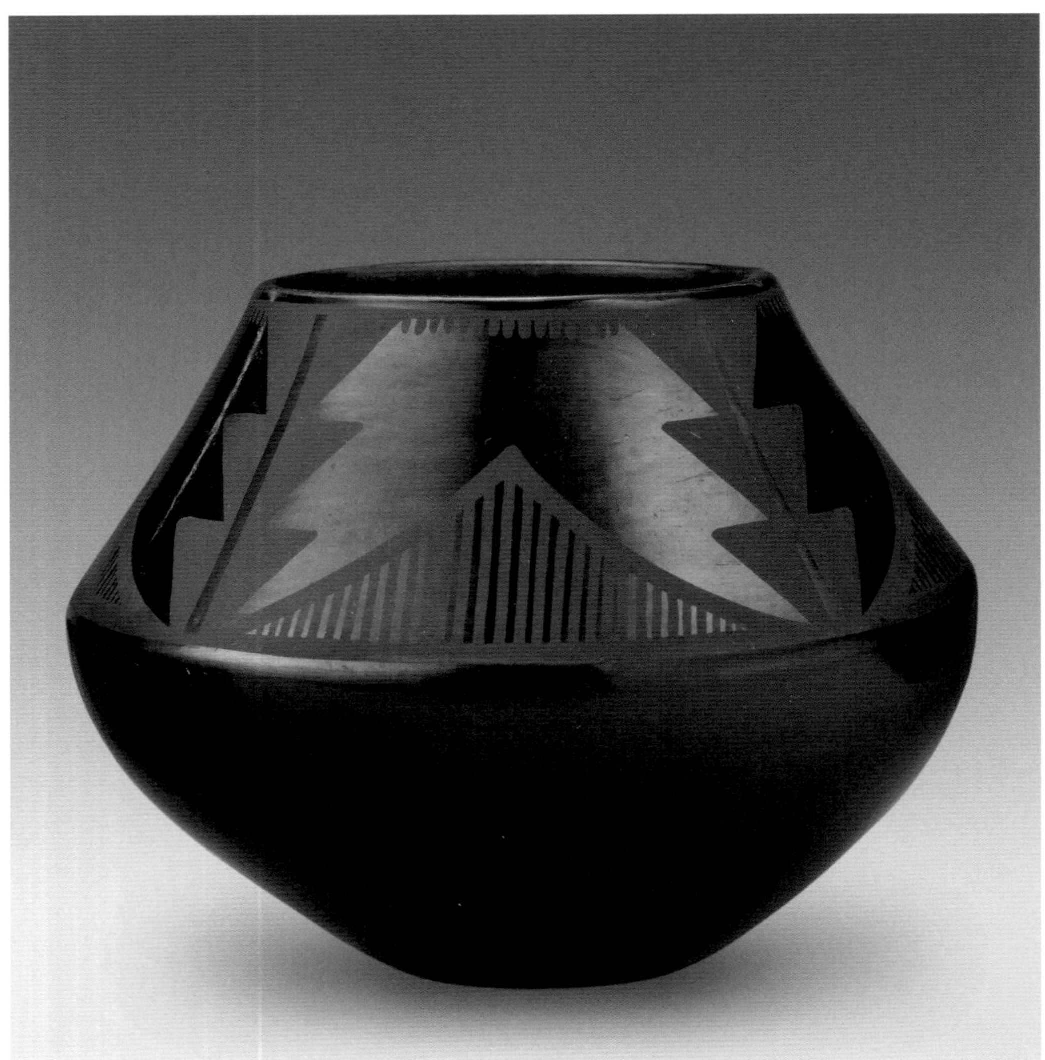

with its tailgate and bed, an El Camino easily lends itself to hauling items to and from the field. In conceiving *Maria*, Simpson thus imagined "an empowered vessel," one that "demonstrates, expresses, emphasizes, and builds up the power of Indigenous women."[15]

More than a simple reference to the maker of famed blackware pottery, *Maria* honors its namesake as an icon of female empowerment. For Simpson, "Maria Martinez was the matriarch . . . . Her husband [Julian Martinez] did the painting, but it wasn't his name that was being sold. She was the businessperson and person in charge. She exemplifies empowerment in Native women, and specifically Pueblo women."[16]

Martinez is among the most famous Native American artists of the twentieth century, the subject of monographs and documentaries.[17] She traveled and exhibited her work at world's fairs, and her art may be found in museum collections across the United States, including the Art Institute of Chicago, the Denver Art Museum, the Museum of Modern Art, and the Smithsonian American Art Museum. Besides the recognition outside her community, she was active in the pueblo. "I took care of my people, and other people . . . . After I finished my work I went over and took care of old people when I was young and strong."[18] Martinez also taught the blackware technique to younger generations of her family and to students at the Santa Fe Indian School. Pottery continues to drive economic development in many pueblos.

Around the same time she completed *Maria,* Simpson was an artist-in-residence at the Denver Art Museum. There, she constructed seven "post-apocalyptic indigenous warrior" outfits, made of leather, metal, and found objects and symbolizing the seven directions.[19] She also undertook a public performance with *Maria* "to challenge the stereotyping of indigenous identities, deconstruct gender roles, transform the relationship of objectification of women in car culture, and consider the re-application of relational aesthetics."[20] Simpson selected Indigenous people, mainly women and queer-identifying individuals, to wear the warrior outfits in the performance. As Simpson slowly drove *Maria* up the museum's entrance plaza, the models walked on either side of the vehicle. Along with the hum of the engine, the 1,000-watt car-speaker system blasted the sound of a heartbeat. Simpson has replicated the *Maria* performance in other locales, particularly in Santa Fe, where Martinez famously sold her pottery. In addition to the performance, *Maria* speaks to the paramount role of Pueblo women in their communities as protectors, providers, and creators: the heartbeats of their culture.

INDIGENOUS WOMAN: *TRANSFORMANCE*
Simpson's art is often presented outside northern New Mexico, in the homelands of other Indigenous peoples. In 2021, she had a solo exhibition at the Nevada Museum of Art that included a residency at the Nuwu Art + Activism Studios in Las Vegas.[21] Founded by curator and artist Fawn Douglas of the Las Vegas Paiute tribe, Nuwu Art + Activism Studios combines art, education, and activism through exhibitions, classes, studio space, and community programs.

Nevada is the homeland of the Nuwu (Southern Paiute), Numu (Northern Paiute), Newe (Western Shoshone), and Waší·šiw (Washoe). While there are thirty-two reservations and Native communities across the state, tribal land accounts for only 1.6 million acres, or 2 percent of the total acreage. Las Vegas is Nuwu land, and as more and more white settlers entered the area in the 1850s, the Nuwu were removed from their territories, water sources, and ancestral villages. Until 1983, the Las Vegas Paiute had only ten acres of land.[22] Las Vegas is often portrayed and marketed as a resort destination and an adult playground in the desert, not as a city with a thriving Indigenous community.

In her residency at Nuwu Art + Activism Studios, Simpson asked herself, "How do I, as a guest in [Douglas's] ancestral homelands, help support her community?"[23] The artist recognized the importance of acting like a guest in someone's homeland—practicing care, respect, and good intention. Simpson worked collaboratively with Douglas and other Indigenous people of Las Vegas to create a performance piece. In undertaking the performance, Simpson and Douglas pondered such questions as "What does empowerment look like? What does Land Back look like?"[24] They considered how, as Indigenous women, they could prioritize Indigenous sovereignty, ancestral knowledge, and practice respect toward the land and its beings. The performance that resulted, *transformance,* was a collaborative, community-centric, and land-based work highlighting Indigenous presence in Las Vegas.

For two weeks, Simpson and Douglas, with local Indigenous people, engaged in the acts of making and community building. They sewed dresses, constructed moccasins and leather belts, and made jewelry while talking, laughing, and eating together. They created seven sets of regalia, representing the seven directions. The bottom trim of each dress incorporated a row of plus signs—a motif that, as discussed earlier, Simpson regards as a star, a symbol of guidance. Seven Indigenous women participated in

Maria on Canyon Road, Santa Fe,
August 22, 2014. Rose B. Simpson drives
Maria up Canyon Road, as Razelle
Benally, Freyr Marie, Ailani Swentzell,
Carmen Selam, Stacy Brossy, and
Micaela Maestas walk in front.

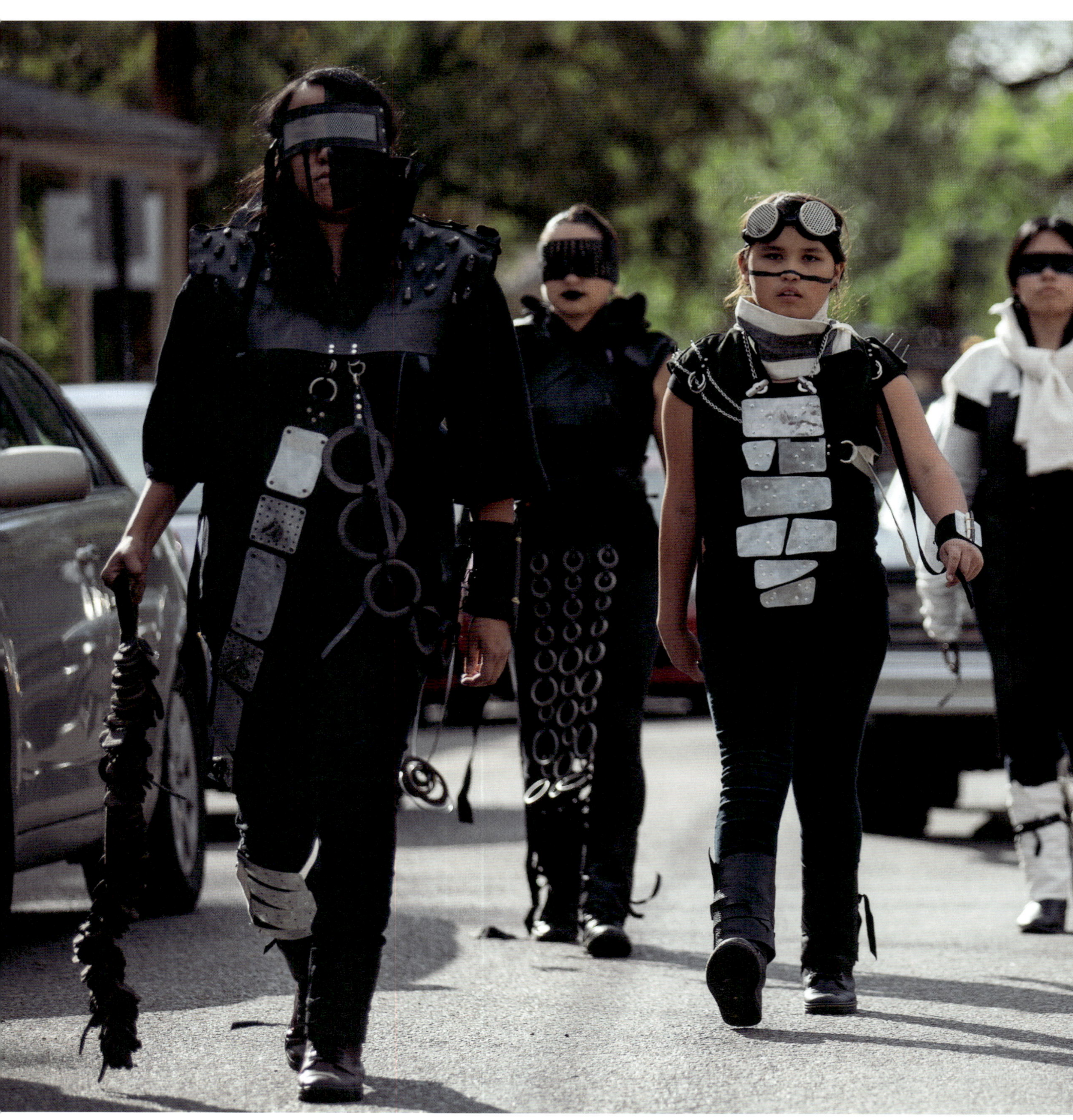

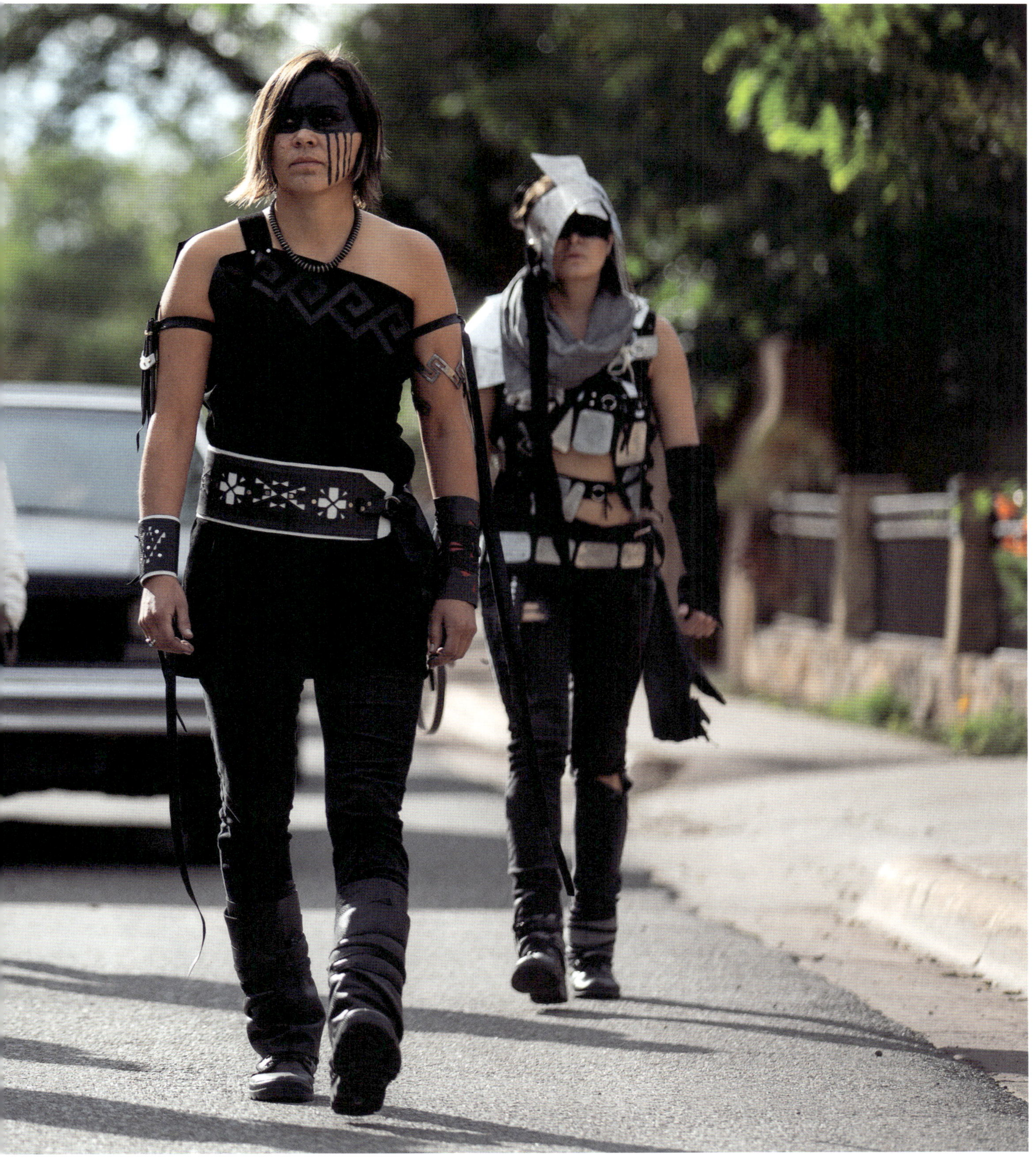

the performance; the group included two families, Simpson with her daughter and Douglas with hers. On the day of the performance, the women and girls donned the cloth dresses, cinched with leather belts, and wore moccasins and strands of necklaces. They formed two lines, and each person picked up a black bandanna with the word "remember" printed on it.

Standing in front, Simpson and Douglas led a solemn procession, lasting about sixty minutes, along South Maryland Parkway, a busy Las Vegas thoroughfare. They walked in unison for twelve steps, then stopped for twelve seconds, and continued at the same pace of twelve steps followed by a twelve-second pause for the rest of the procession. Despite the raucous sounds of car engines, horns, and other street traffic, none of the women spoke. At one point, they encountered a plastic orange barrier that Douglas cut, allowing them to continue. The procession ended at its starting point, the Nuwu Art + Activism Studios.

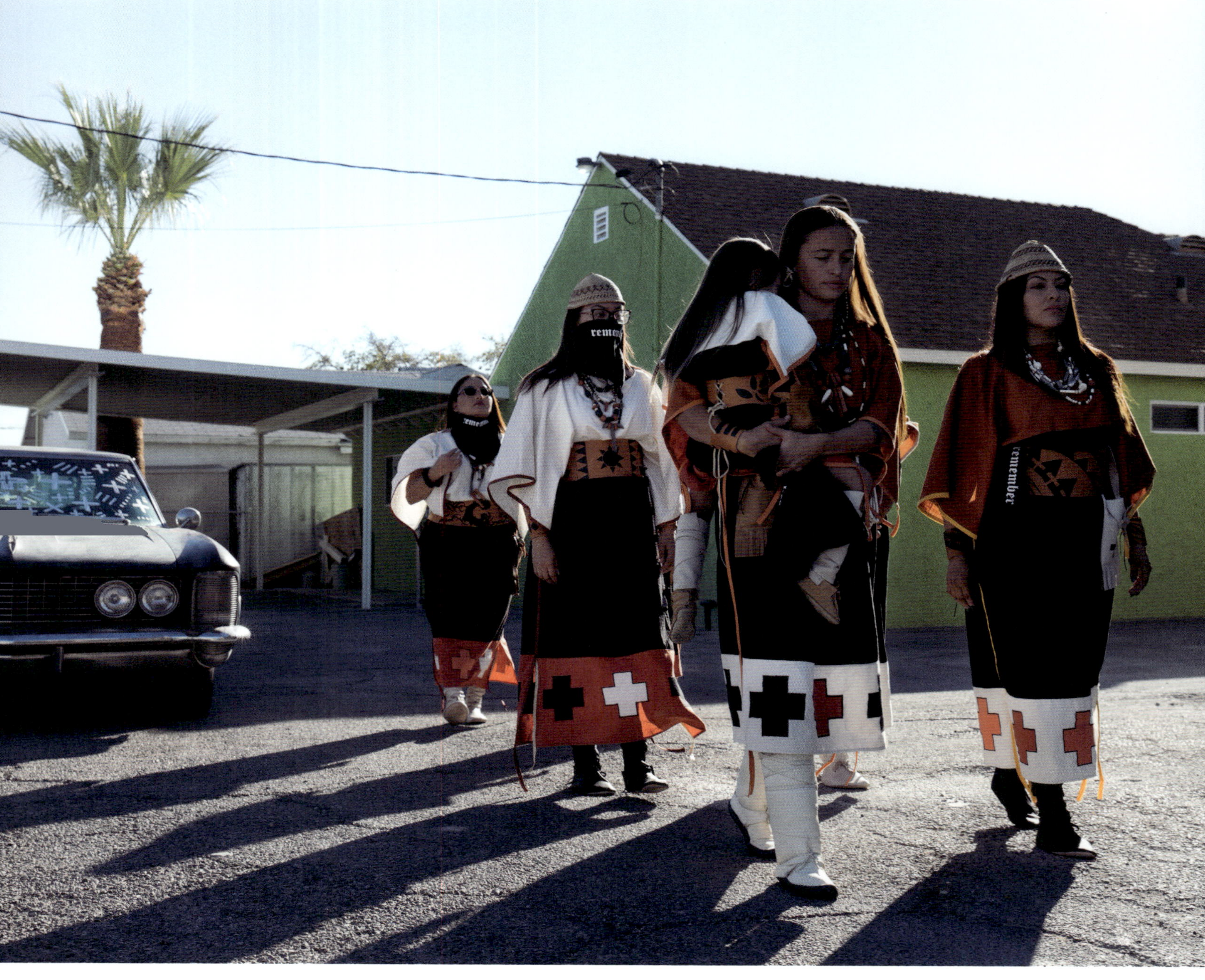

Performance of transformance presented by the Nevada Museum of Art, 2021 Art + Environment Season, South Maryland Parkway, Las Vegas, November 13, 2021. Rose B. Simpson. Photo by Mikayla Whitmore

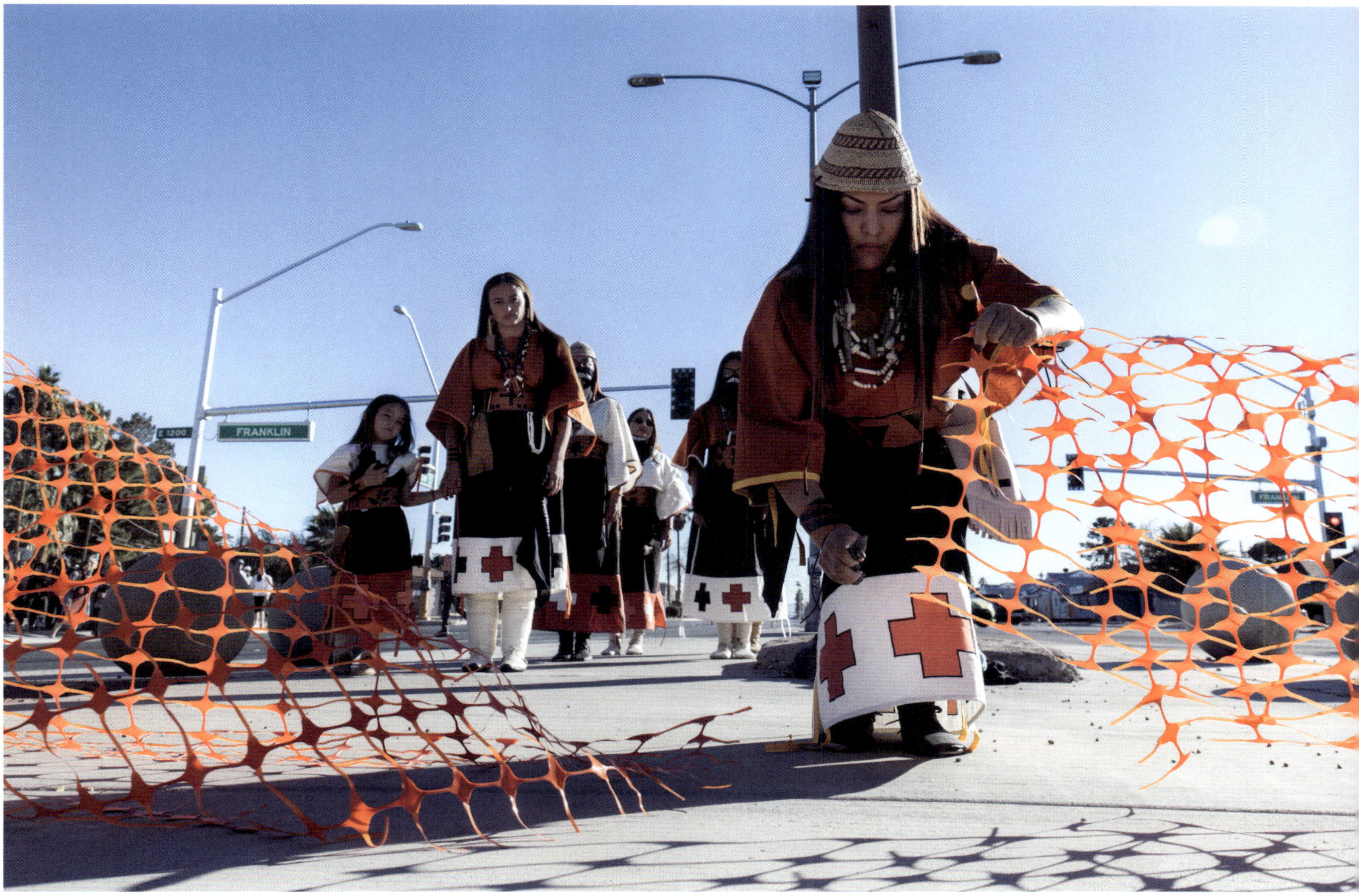

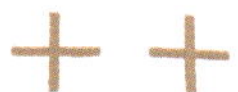

Performance of *transformance* presented by the Nevada Museum of Art, 2021 Art + Environment Season, South Maryland Parkway, Las Vegas, November 13, 2021. Rose B. Simpson. Photo by Mikayla Whitmore

transformance was a quiet, solemn performance. Although no words were shouted or even uttered, the women made their presence known. Taking their time and not rushing, the group walked together as one and then stood in their collective power. Simpson recalled, "The feeling of empowerment was so much stronger than anything I'd ever felt before."[25] *transformance* was not a solo vision but an act of co-creation between Simpson, Douglas, and the other Indigenous women. With their collective effort and trust, they empowered one another.

+ +

Simpson's artworks emanate from personal experiences and from her worldview as an Indigenous woman. They also emphasize relationships—relationships to community and place and between multiple generations of family. Works such as *Timeline Necklace*, *Genesis*, *Maria*, and *transformance* speak to Simpson's identities as a daughter, a mother, a Pueblo woman, and an Indigenous woman, identities that are not discrete but closely intertwined. In a 1991 interview, ceramic artist Tessie Naranjo (born 1941), Simpson's great-aunt, described her pottery making thus: "it has to do with femaleness in a big way. Femaleness, femaleness. My community is female. My culture is female. My art-making is female."[26] Having been born and raised in a Pueblo community, Naranjo's art, self, community, and womanhood are all connected. Nowadays, this intersection of gender and Indigeneity is termed "Indigenous feminism," articulated by Chiricahua Apache scholar Nancy Marie Mithlo as "a gendered assertion of identity tied to place, process, and community."[27] As a Pueblo woman, Simpson's art and culture are firmly connected.

While Simpson's artworks are manifestations of her experiences, she understands that they live another life outside her home and community. In 2022, she explained, "My work is research into a very personal space, into my relationship to process and to a spiritual or psychological journey. The objects are the result or the by-product of that investigation. It's what comes from the journey. These things are kind of like the wake of it, that can ideally go out into the world and help other people, maybe, in their own investigation, their own journeys."[28] Simpson creates as part of her life journey, but by revealing herself, she makes others more cognizant of theirs.

1. Rose B. Simpson, "My Mother, the Builder," *New Mexico Magazine* (June 17, 2020), https://www.newmexicomagazine.org/blog/post/my-mother-the-builder-rose-simpson-roxanne-swentzell/.

2. Richard Nilsen, "Talent for Pottery Runs in the Family," *Arizona Republic*, January 25, 2009, E4.

3. Rose B. Simpson, "Sourced: Inspiration, Innovation, and Material," National Council on Education for the Ceramic Arts, September 25, 2023, YouTube, https://youtu.be/9i8unoddSv4?si=5xGkMe7yBycYGyCk.

4. Morgan Freeman, Roxanne Swentzell, and Rose B. Simpson, "On Lineage, Place, and Futurity," in *Form & Relation: Contemporary Native Ceramics*, ed. Jami C. Powell (Hanover, NH: Hood Museum of Art, 2020), 51.

5. Chad Scott, "Rose, Rina, Roxanne and Rose B. Simpson: Four Generations of Santa Clara Ceramics at Norton Museum of Art," *Forbes* (March 21, 2024), https://www.forbes.com/sites/chaddscott/2024/03/21/rose-rina-roxanne-and-rose-b-simpson-four-generations-of-santa-clara-ceramics-at-norton-museum-of-art/?sh=57479a95f2ad.

6. Simpson, "My Mother, the Builder."

7. Freeman, Swentzell, and Simpson, "On Lineage, Place, and Futurity," 50.

8. Simpson and her mother have collaborated on three major works. They include an early sculpture that is about Simpson's birth and that she refers to as "Horned C-section"; it was created by Simpson, Swentzell, and her father, Patrick Simpson (born 1952).

9. Simpson, "Sourced."

10. Simpson.

11. Simpson. Elsewhere in this volume, Simpson discusses the theme of watching, both in *Strata* and in other works. "Molded by Life: A Conversation Between Natalie Diaz, Rose B. Simpson, and Dyani White Hawk," this volume, 98.

12. Ariana Marsh, "Indigenous Sculptor Rose B. Simpson Makes Otherworldly Beings to Reconfigure Her Neural Pathways," *Harper's Bazaar* (March 30, 2023), https://www.harpersbazaar.com/culture/art-books-music/a43454340/indigenous-sculptor-rose-b-simpson-makes-otherworldly-beings-to-reconfigure-her-neural-pathways/.

13. Roxanne Swentzell, "Tatooed [*sic*] Woman," https://www.roxanneswentzell.net/Pieces/rox_clay_tatoowoman_r.html.

14. Dyani White Hawk, "*Maria*, Rose, Empowerment, and Indigenous Women Rollin' Hard: A Conversation with Rose Simpson," in *Hearts of Our People: Native Women Artists*, ed. Laura Silver (Minneapolis: Minneapolis Institute of Art in association with the University of Washington Press, 2019), 84.

15. White Hawk, 84.

16. White Hawk, 84.

17. Publications about Maria Martinez include Alice Marriott, ed., *Maria: The Potter of San Ildefonso* (Norman: University of Oklahoma Press, 1965); Susan Peterson, *The Living Tradition of Maria Martinez* (Tokyo: Kodansha International, 1977); Richard Spivey, ed., *Maria* (Flagstaff, AZ: Northland Press, 1979); Diana F. Pardue, *Maria and Julian Martinez: Shaping a Tradition* (Phoenix, AZ: Heard Museum, 2003); and Diana F. Pardue et al., eds., *Maria and Modernism* (Phoenix, AZ: Heard Museum, 2023). The documentaries are *Hands of Maria* (1968, dir. J. Donald McIntyre) and *Pottery Techniques of Maria of San Ildefonso* (c. 1965, dir. Stuart Roe).

18. Lea S. McChesney, "'Carrying On': Gender and Innovation in Historic Pueblo Pottery," in Silver, ed., *Hearts of Our People*, 91.

19. The seven directions are the four cardinal directions along with up, down, and center. Rose B. Simpson, "Selected Performance and Installation," https://www.rosebsimpson.com/performance#:~:-text=In%20the%20spring%20of%202013,found%20objects%2C%20and%20ceramic%20components.

20. Simpson.

21. The exhibition was titled *Rose B. Simpson: The Four* and was on view from April 24, 2021, to April 17, 2022.

22. In 1983, the US Congress returned four thousand acres to the Las Vegas Paiute tribe. Called the Snow Mountain reservation, it is located eighteen miles away from the original reservation.

23. Simpson, "Sourced."

24. Simpson.

25. Simpson.

26. Nancy Marie Mithlo, "A Real Feminine Journey: Locating Indigenous Feminisms in the Arts," *Meridians: Feminism, Race, Transnationalism* 9, no. 2 (March 2009): 1.

27. Mithlo, 2.

28. Rose B. Simpson, "In the Studio: Rose B. Simpson," Joan Mitchell Foundation, July 8, 2022, https://www.joanmitchellfoundation.org/journal/in-the-studio-rose-b-simpson.

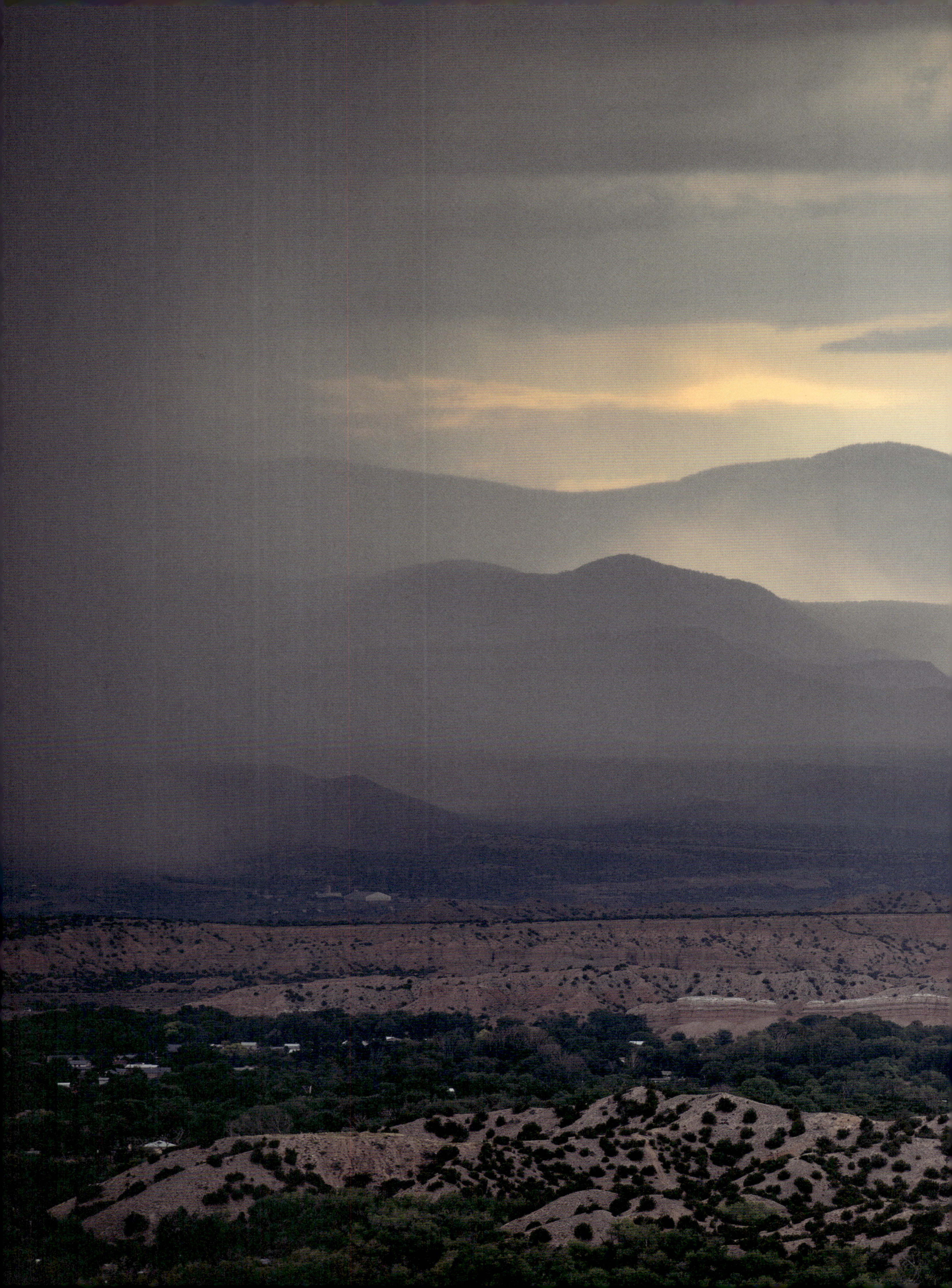

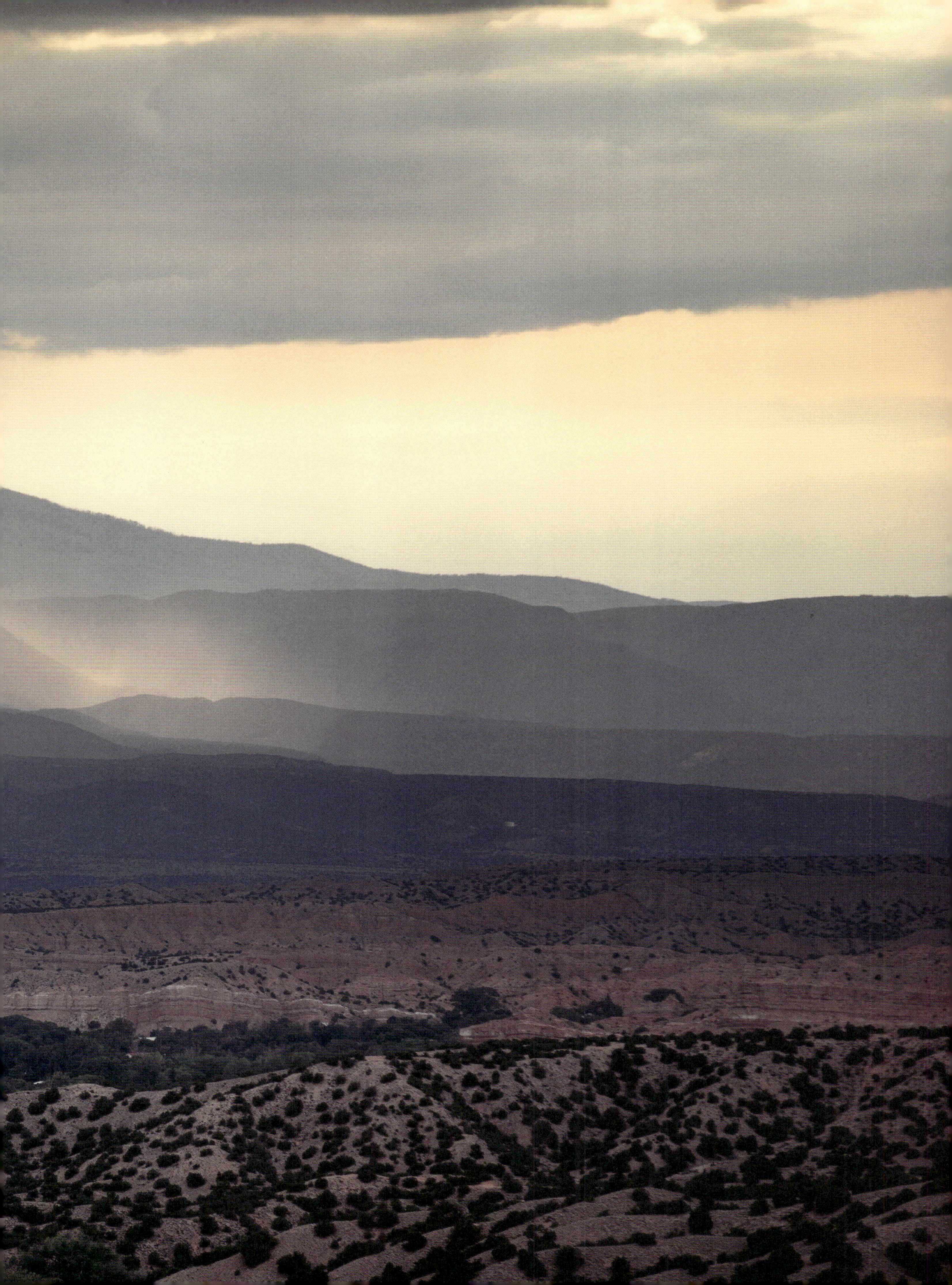

STRATA

Rose B. Simpson

HYPOTHESIS
Here I begin a time for words.
My mind bounces from earlier to later, and there are words and they worry, and I think the word is "fret." So many things to do, so many, it feels like books leaning their way off a bookshelf, and I'm trying to stay busy while propping the books with my body, my head, maybe my shoulder for a minute, then my elbow, all to keep them from tumbling, tumbling down on me. So many words. Words upon words are in those heavy books.

Sometime soon I will parse through and identify those that are worth keeping, and those that just need to be dropped. Maybe they will stack and become my legs, my stomach, the pages and pages that I have read, that I have written, that I have absorbed and helped pray me into being.

Like in any beginning, I am self-conscious. I wonder about words, about my words, and I see them in piles in buckets for me to pick through. I want to know who they are, greet them and ask to employ them respectfully, find reverence for their being, be responsible for the community they will join—the family that they will eventually be beholden to. Words are like sculpture. To build. To bring together. To mold and form. I feel the pressure of responsibility, of cause and effect.

In a dream, I traveled through my body like Ms. Frizzle and the Magic Schoolbus, but without the teacher and the bus and the students. I saw all my internal parts big and I could go deeper and deeper into the quantum-molecular nature of my physical being, and when I did, I found communities. I found my consciousness in a neighborhood of sorts; there were little sectioned-off places that felt like rooms or homes, and thorough-fares where travel could happen, and vertical appendages that resembled lines of poplar trees. The colors were unfamiliar, the shapes were blobby and unidentifiable, but there were beings, things of consciousness, with names. They traveled around and within each other like any tight community, with relationship dynamics, families, and personalities.

There was a shocking realization in this world—dead cell-beings lay around everywhere, interrupting the flow of the community, and because of all the death there was a deep melancholy saturating everyone and everything. There were loved ones laid out in living rooms, along the roadsides, and they were treated with solemn reverence. There were so many that there were seldom spaces where joy was able to shine.

When the dream ended, it was clear to me that I needed to do something. On a strange morning of synchronicities and conversation, I learned about how intermittent fasting

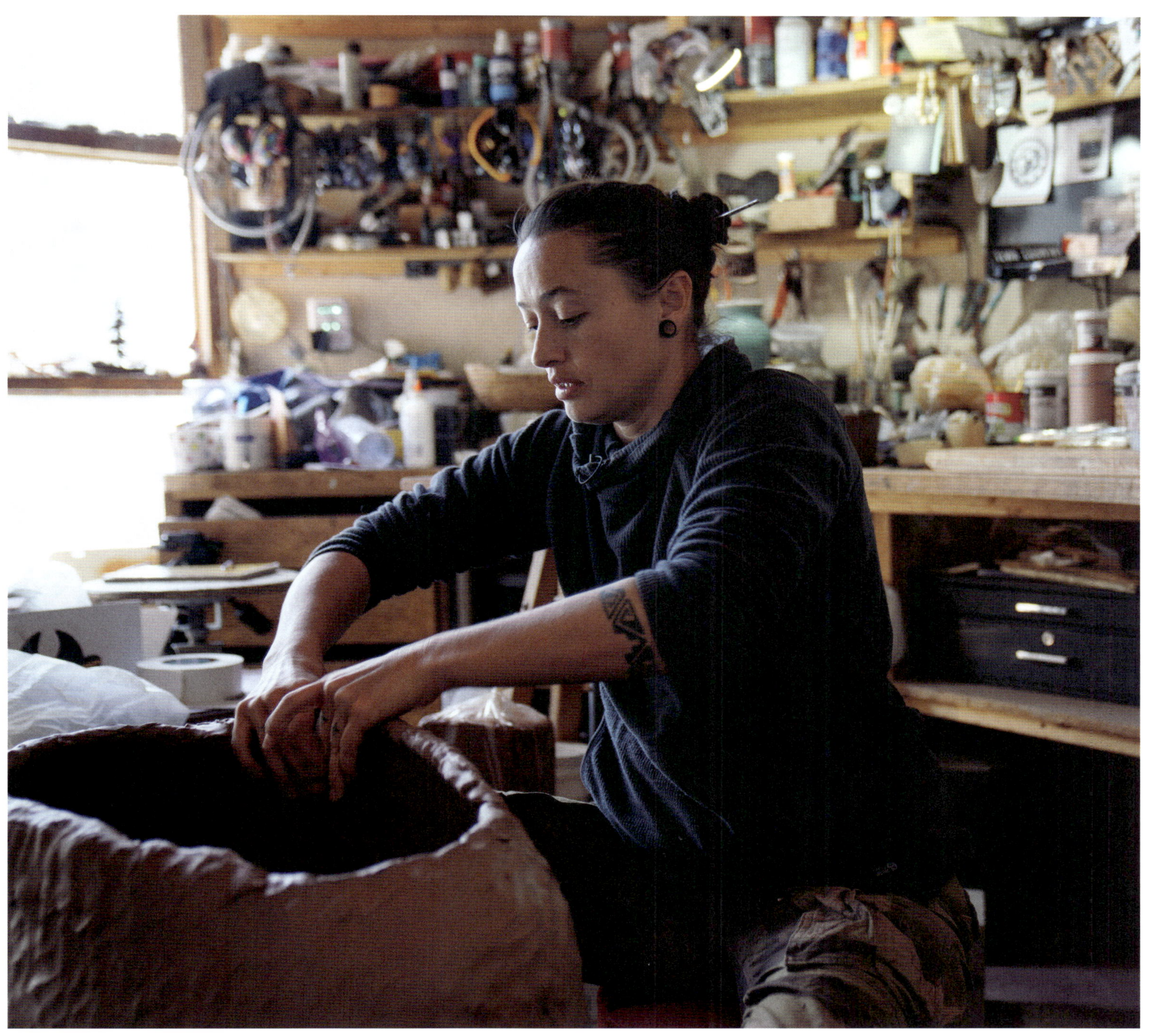

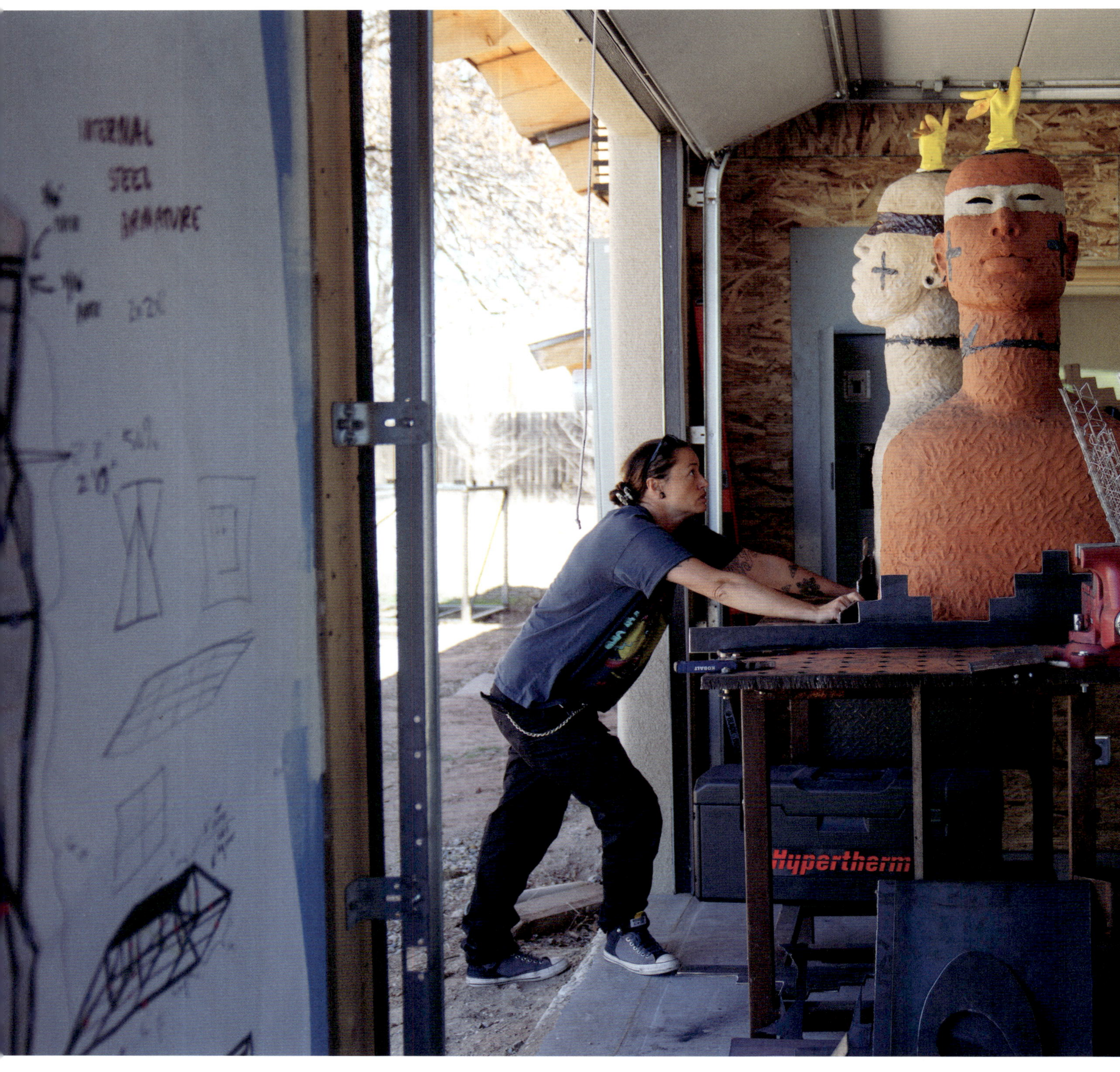
INTERNAL
STEEL
ARMATURE
Hypertherm

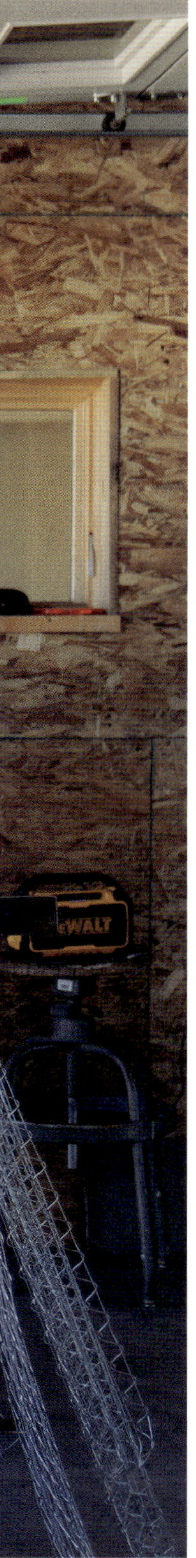

for a certain length of time pushes the body into an autophagic state wherein the system is forced to process "ghost cells," or cells that have died and are still hanging out in the system.

It isn't easy to take action, or to feel regret, or to realize that my actions would hurt someone else. So many someone elses. So many. (Someone else?)

Maybe all those cells are the letters, they are words of the dense book that is me—they are that which calls forth and becomes the worlds we see. Who am I ("Rose," the voice I hear tossing around between my neck and my crown) to these cell-beings? Are they aware of me? Do they have a name for me? And if they do, are they annoyed or frustrated with me, or maybe they think of me as some sort of Almighty Being? Did they pray that I become aware of their circumstances, and my presence and action answered their little calling voices?

When I visited the quantum version of my physical being it was as if, in their world, no other world existed. All the beings were going about their lives as normalized as we do on this plane. It makes me think we are the cells of a stupendously large being in another reality watching us do our thing, marveling at the simplicity of our awareness.

And here I am, irritated by the thought of tax money getting spent on bombs and stop-lights controlling emptiness at midnight; I feel crushed by the pressure of what I have deemed as adulting. Is there someone like who I was in the vision, wandering through our humanity world and listening to our yearnings? Or knowing how to fix something we can't even see as wrong, as it is "just how it is"? I think so.

Run your fingertip along these words. Feel the texture of the paper, listen to her sound. This is sculpture. This is creation. It's a deep responsibility. Maybe there are words within the molecules of the ink of the letters on the paper, and those molecules are words, too . . . and they are aware, or not aware, of their being as a letter in a book on a page in your hands, traveling up through your eyes and into a voice in your head.

Open some technology, here in the year 2024, and you will find millions of words, images, sounds that are visceral and internal. We have all become capable of infecting our shared cyber-world with our thought-beings. We are co-creating a reality. I don't know about you, but when I spend some time in the cyber-world, I leave feeling like I've been running around a paintball course being shot with every kind of emotional paint-ball bullet. I put the phone down and look away, smeared with a thousand emotional colors. This experience leaves me feeling spun-out, disregulated, and depressed. I miss myself. I wonder what the cell-beings think when their Almighty disappears down a social media bender.

We are affecting, effected, infecting; we are creators of a physical, psychological, and emotional reality. What if I can't know how and who I'm affecting, what if I can't be in control of the entirety of my influence? What if I will inevitably make mistakes and I really don't want to be that person?

I must be so deeply in denial to be unaware of how many beings are hurt because of the decisions I make daily. Every hour. Every minute.

Oh, to be aware; to know how, where, to listen. Oh, to know. Oh, to know. Oh, to know.

Both the magnitude and the minuscule overwhelm me. This is where I begin my search. This is the hypothesis.

DEPTHS

In the winter, the sun is still far behind the Sangre de Cristo Mountains when I rise. I lift the blinds, and the moonlight is still glinting off patches of snow—the negative of yesterday's persistent shadow.

On the deep windowsill that hugs the floor is where I set my hot clay tea mug. The steam starts a slow and stable dance. I cross my legs and settle myself on the round pillow that's been waiting. I wrap my shoulders with a shawl and tuck the ends at my waist. I might take a sip.

Here is where and when I enter wonder. I wonder my breath, body. I wonder my balance, thoughts. I wonder space between thoughts until they are sparse. When I let my body tell all body needs to, I begin to wonder energy, psychic spaces, the ethereal. I begin with the space above my head and I hold "IS-ness" for her, for purple. There is a sucking feeling up, up, and then peace. I move to my forehead; I ask for IS-ness in my Knowing. There it is, indigo. I move down—my blue voice, my green heart, my yellow joy, my orange creation, my red strength . . . I leave space for wonder, for listening. I ask, "Is there anything you want to tell me?" and I listen for a feeling, or a word, or an image, or a silence.

I look for growth beyond work, where listening is action and speaking is action and action is no longer. That there is just as much to know when settled in being. This is how we want to be heard: that there is no work to do, that there is a silent knowing, and that there is where it all is, and all can be known.

Then I let go and it rises, on its own, like a bubble, through each and all, leaving a wake of delicious energy I have to trust, and it rushes above purple and rolls back down all around me like a waterfall running around a big me-bubble and as it runs down it turns red-violet and the world washes clean of bullshit like a receding wave has washed the world clean and all that is left are the boulders, and I can smell the raw truth; it has all been cleansed, and the world is anew. It is fresh and wonderful, and I don't ever want to leave this feeling.

I let it go. I let my identity wash down through me into the floor, and it, whatever "it" is, is gone. I empty.

One morning in a pause from this state, my eyes rose again out onto the yard and there I beheld a chair. One chair. Empty. Un-sat-in. Was it waiting, was it busy, was it doing something? There was the roof of my truck over the wall, waiting. The identity of the chair, the truck, was in relationship. There was no moving, or doing, unless it was engaged with. There was something about the stillness of a tool in disuse, an empty chair. It was no longer a chair; no longer for sitting, no longer soft, or scratchy, or comfortable or not. It was only itself. I felt the chair, I imagined being the chair. In that moment, I became matter. I felt the simplicity of just being a piece of creation, sans identity. The ultimate freedom of stillness. I was the boulder that was left after the wave. I felt the stone in me. I was it all. I was wood, I was fabric, I was made, I was raw. I was no expectation, no judgment, no desire, no identity. I was okay.

I'm still learning to accept good things, so my body can only handle this for so long; every day it seems to hold for just a little longer.

Inevitably my thoughts return, and it is time to pray aloud with my voice, and I close my eyes and hold my hands out to amplify my words and feel the intention viscerally. I speak my gratitude, I speak my truth. I know there is that which listens to the words I choose.

Then I press my head to the floor.

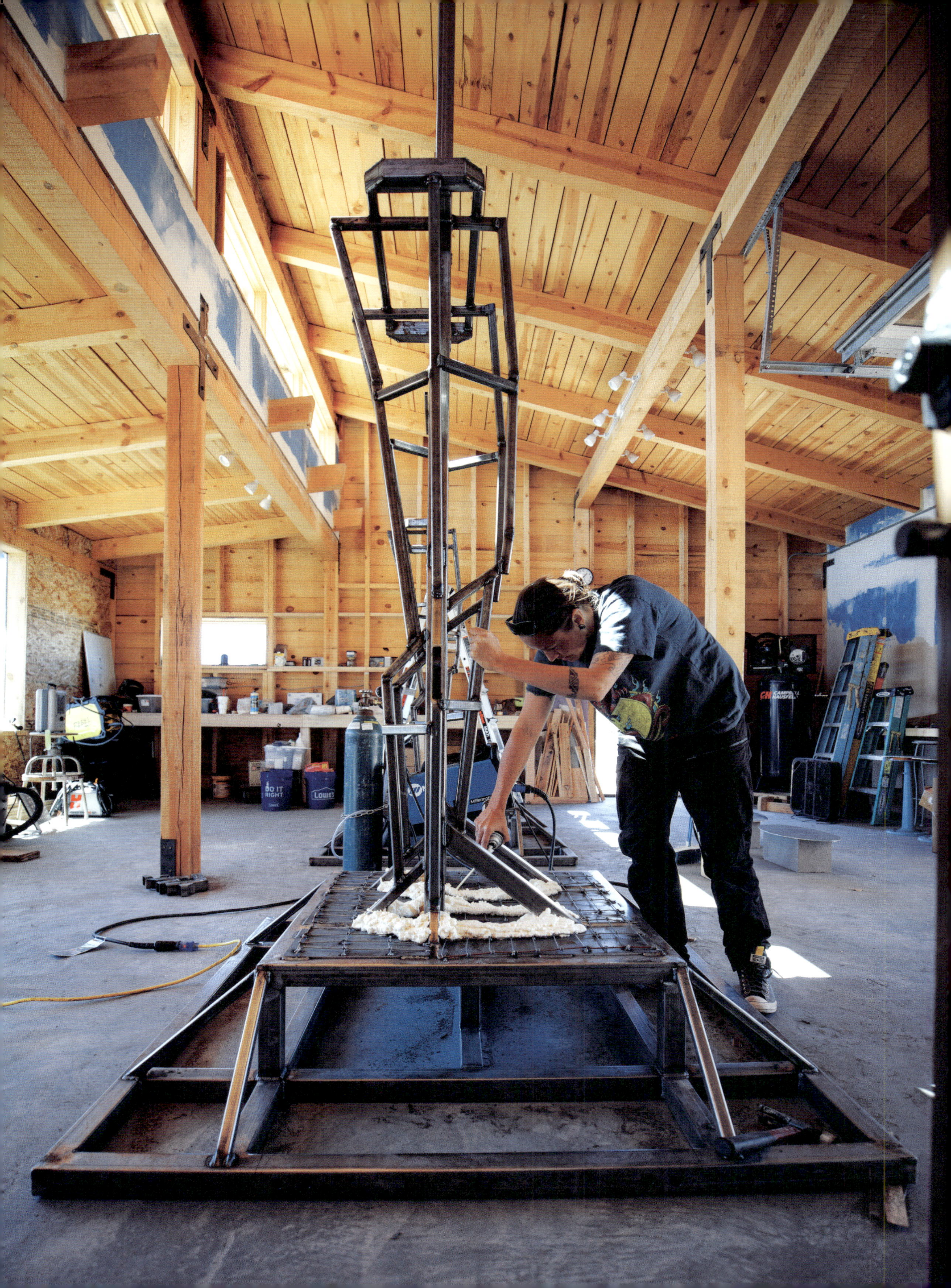

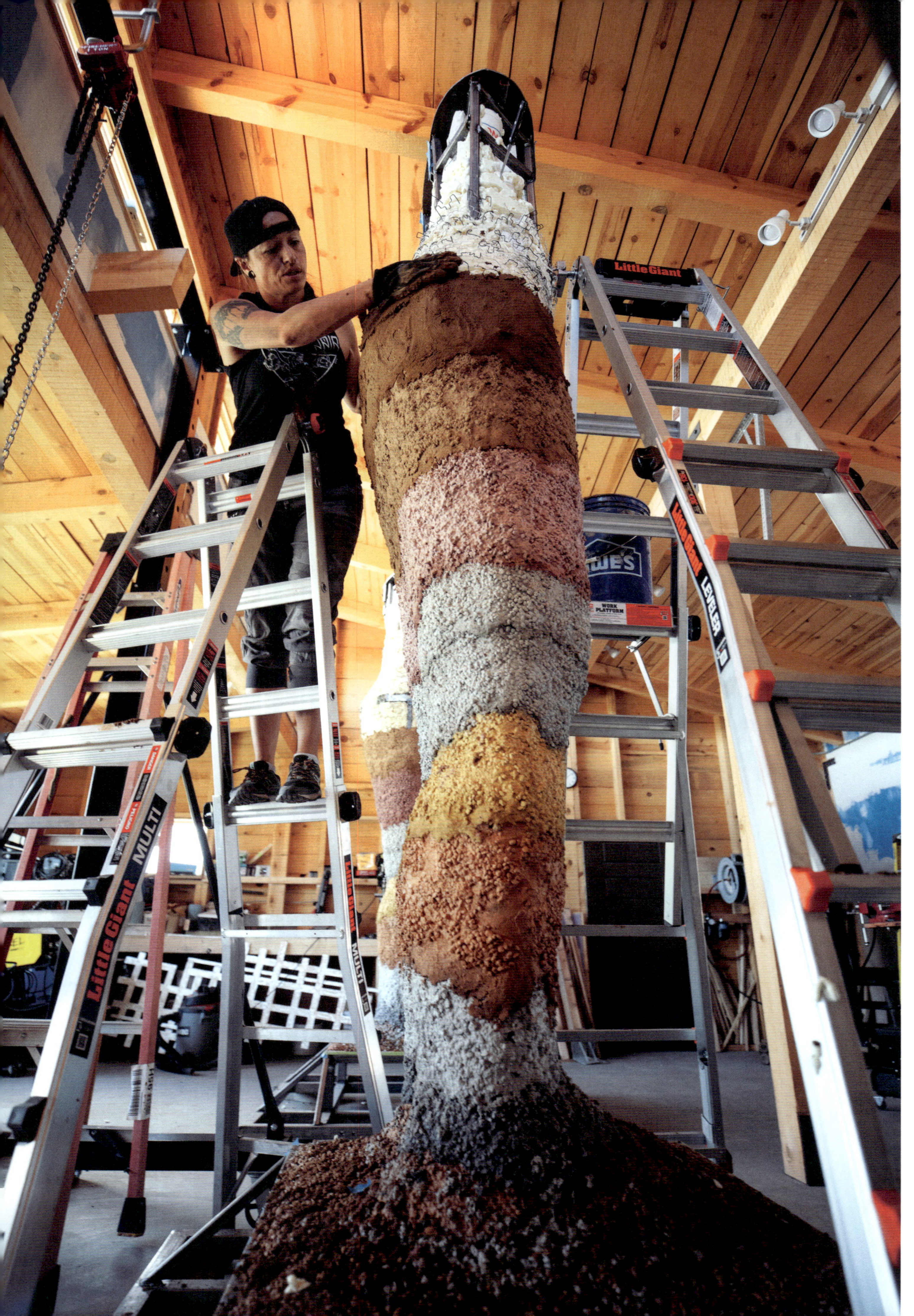

FOUNDATION

"Mama! Are you there?" And I listen. My legs are still crossed, and the center of my forehead is against the cool wood floor. The protection necklaces I was gifted by holy ones dangle to the ground; the bear fetish stands on his little black stone feet.

My eyes are open but blurred, I feel-gaze deep into the ground. I have done the dance, the one of her Flicker Fox, so she remembers me. I wait. There Earth-Mama is. She is in there, deep. She is stirring. I'm glad for this. It is when she is still that I worry.

Sometimes it seems like she's on a long, heavy phone call with Sun-Father; when she hangs up, she cries and cries. Sometimes I find her facing out, like she's standing in her doorway, hands on her hips, critical look on her face, readying herself for something—I'm not sure what. I feel something coming, something from deep down where she is, where she's been, wrestling with her own demons.

Today, she is busy. She doesn't notice me. It feels like she is organizing canned food on her pantry shelf or something like that. That kind of fussy busy. Maybe she is getting her home set up nice so she can begin a journey. You never know. Maybe I'm projecting because this is what I've been readying myself for. I am anxious-patient. I know it is coming because when I lift my nose I can smell it in the wind. Maybe they've been preparing for something. Planning, if that's what you call evolution.

I feel like I'm pacing the steps on her front porch, patrolling her walkway, sleeping restlessly in the bushes, startling at every sound, waiting for it to begin. I'll keep checking on her. I'll keep checking in.

Her Earth-rumble is coming, and I am ready.

LANDSCAPING

Most times I have forgotten that I am the wind. Most times I brace myself and feel irritation as the wind whips my hair across my eyes, sticks to my lips. I grind my teeth at the constant roar by my ears; I ache for stillness, for silence. Too much movement. Too much . . . until I feel it sucking through my teeth as my body flows boom-boom down a desert dirt road. I feel it fuel my heart, cling to my blood, make me lighter and lighter; it moves me. I go.

What about the long game, the etched stone—slowed down until the wind is sculpting the being that I am. Stretch it out, slow, and it becomes a massage where granite is clay in weather's hands.

Most times I have forgotten that I am the water. At the crest of a waterfall, I stood reading the Morse code of glisten-pops as the water yearned faster and faster toward the sucking edge. It pulled me with it. I projected my fear onto all those water-consciousnesses, as the roar of the edge, the fall, the crash, the boom was nigh. Do they know they are headed to the edge? Or do they know and are releasing—readying themselves for the inevitable? Do they ride gravity in faith, knowing, as water, this is only one chapter in All That Is?

I imagine I am at the edge of that cliff, the slip at the top and the roar echoing from below, and instead of resisting or dreading this plunge, I open my glistening heart to the sun, spread my arms wide, and deliver myself backward into the abyss. As I fall, I remember, "This is why."

And crash—I am mist, and as a rainbow I float. I am the sculptor of stone, sculpted by stone, I love every temporary boundary as I am the shape-shifter.

Most times I forget that I am fire . . . then I feel it peeling down my upper arms and out my pinky fingers and it bounces off me—sparks, just the very teeny beginning of my capacity to flame. The sparkle glinting off a grain of sand.

Melt stone, crack and jump and play. I got this from my Mama. Mama knows fire.

Watch out now.

ARCHITECTURE

Recently, I was lying in a morning bed with my seven-year-old daughter, and she looked down at her feet and said, "Mom! Mom, look! My feet are so far away!" I put my leg next to hers. "Your feet are just gonna get farther and farther away." I wonder if we grow to miss them . . . the identity of who we are as bodies gets normalized and familiarized but in that, the lack of sensationalism makes the parts of us strangers.

At forty years old, I am still trying to understand this body, wondering if she is me or if I'm a visitor in her being-ness. That I see my father in my hands, my mother in my toes, and I wonder who was in the position of agency at the choosing of this life. This being. This vessel.

New Mexico landscape

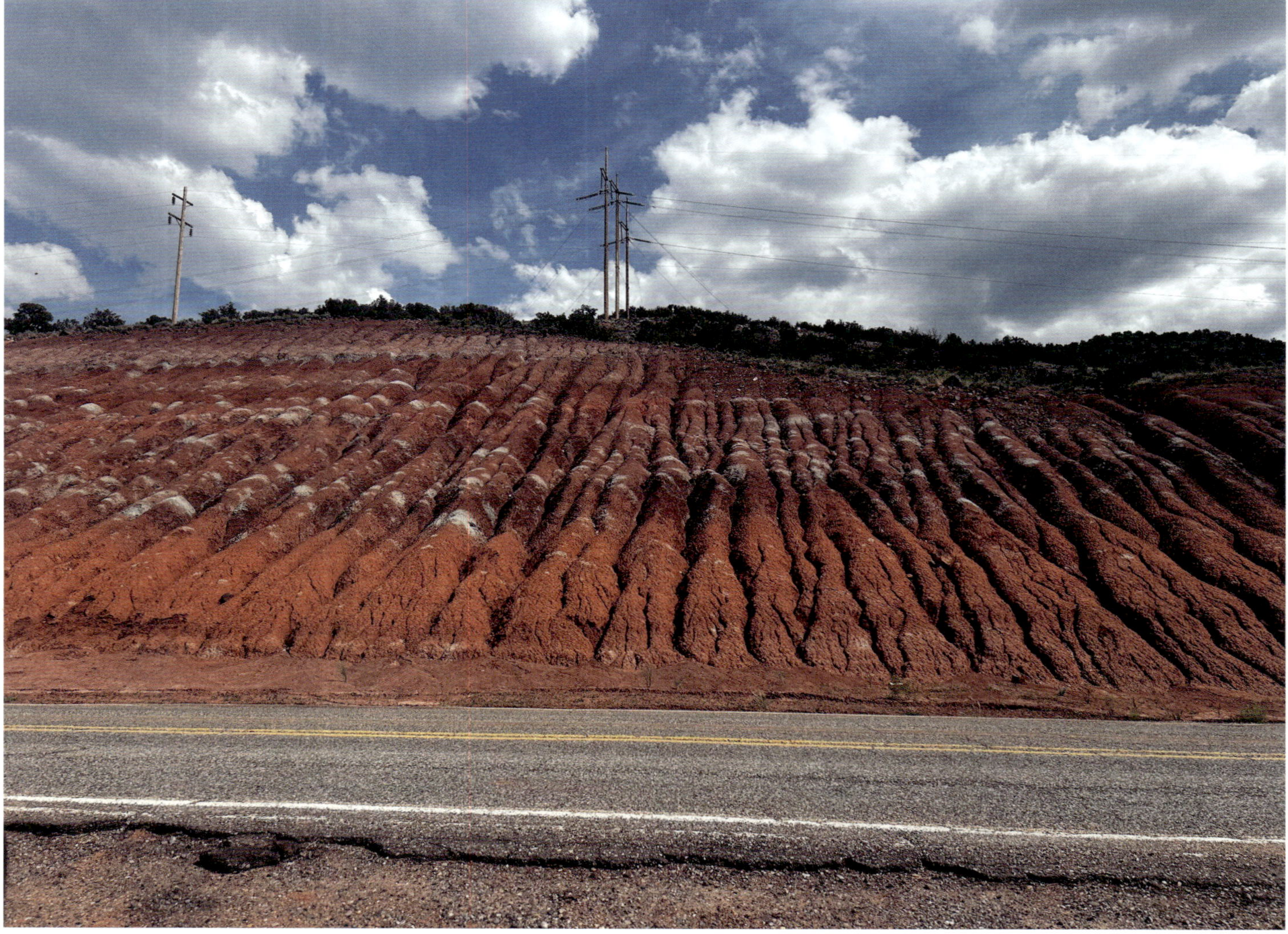

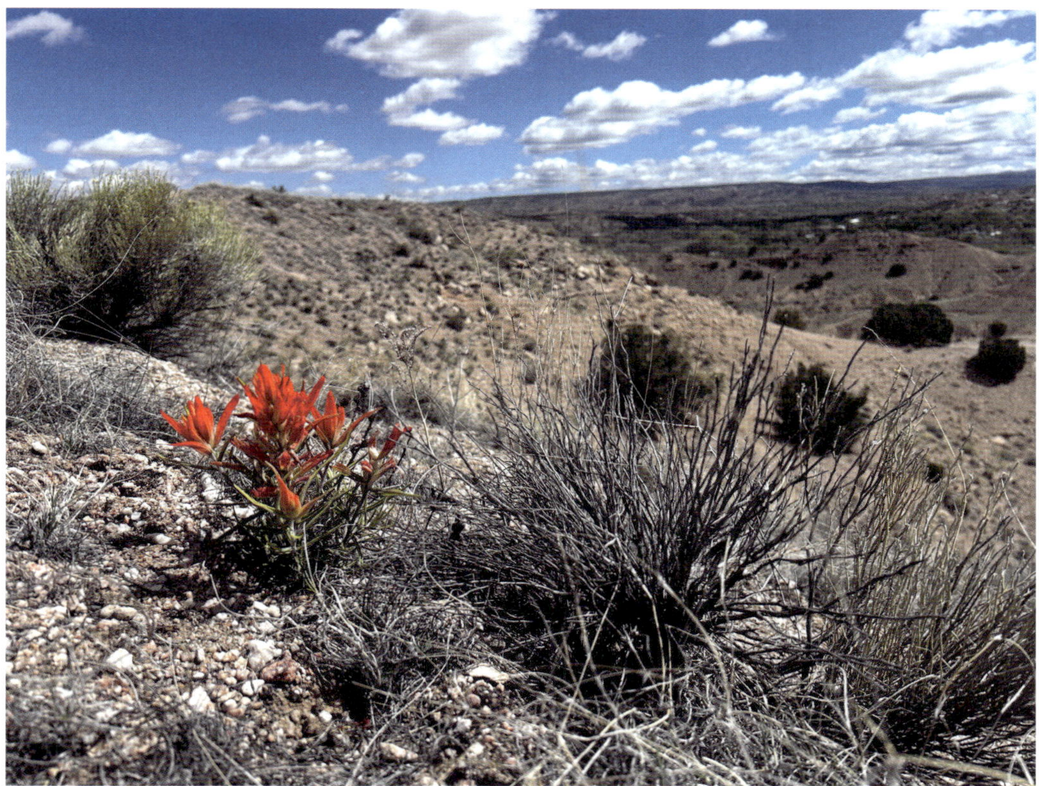

In meditation and in the long, dark minutes before sleep, I wander the rooms and hall-ways of my body, my being. I could spend a lifetime just asking questions of my fingers, the nape of my ankles, the hairless space behind my ears. This is that lifetime. I wonder about the soul and if we are given a body, and then it bends and shifts to match the light within. I see my daughter change as she grows, wondering how it was that she changed as a baby to look like me; maybe she didn't see a father to mimic, so she made me as much of all of her as she could.

In my newfound love I yearn for immortality—I pain that the touch, the smell, the abso-lute ache for this tiny person's closeness would ever end.

I watch as old houses that were loved into existence crumble back to the Earth, or burn, or demolish. Old cars abandoned on the side of the road. They are someone. They lived as long containers of story, in relationship, in love. I choose the clothes I wear; they be-come my skin. I inhabit the rooms of my dwelling; it becomes my shell. The car is journey, my power, my friend. They speak, too, if listened to. We shape-shift into one another, we become the spaces we are in; the spaces hold us from spilling over until we are ready to and we splash through the door and out into the world.

Are our bodies the clay vase that holds the water and flower of spirit, the container that gives and gives and gives and gives and gives and gives . . . have "I" been unaware of the giving, and in the taking it tires, it degrades, it makes do? Would immortality be possible if I could reach the constant awareness of what the body needs and be actively acquiescing?

Oh, my god. I pray for her forgiveness. I scratch my apology in stone, for how I have not yet known how to be good, I've been unbelievably cruel. I'm sorry, body, I'm sorry. Show me the way, I will listen better. I will heed. Closer and closer and hopefully in time.

DREAM

I've heard that in the beginning, there was the word.

Word.

Isn't it amazing? Amorphous blob willed itself self-aware, and in noticing itself as separate—there was someone else to speak to, to hear—a voice was born from the need to call out. The desire to call out—born of yearning, to feel moved to express. That which could define emotion, define the yearning, it sculpted experience through intentional manifestation.

Here I am, with word in hand. Here I am, a sculptor. In this life I was given clay, wood, steel; like family members, I know them. My mother handed me the clay and the mud, showed me how to speak, how to build the word in hollow human forms, invested, intentional. My father gave me metal and wood, and I've built ladders of sentences and homes for prayer. I am responsible and accountable to these gifts, these manifestables.

These-here words, here to define the dreams I love to have. Here to call.

Dreaming, for me, is delicious. At night I close my eyes, excited; maybe I will be gifted an enlightening metaphor. In my night-dreams and daydreams I am given visions as thought-forms. These are translatable in many languages. They are messages, perhaps—if I trust their source as that which is connected to all things. I feel we are all responsible for the conscious editing of their manifestation. When I am in my power, clarity, and agency, I am able to sift through these thought-forms and choose which ones get to flow through me as voice, as sculpture, as written word, as action. It is wild, isn't it, to be the one that gets to curate? (And to try to do so not with judgment but with intu-ition—judgment feels like someone else's thought-forms from another time co-curating in order to override that conscious truth of the present.)

In my dream we witness, from a place of deeply rooted connectedness to all things, we witness the connection in ourselves, through one another. We see that we are of the same. We see the power, the particles, the layers, the long histories of transformation, and that we humans are only a tiny chapter in a being-ness that is wondrous beyond anything we are capable of imagining. That humility is faith, it is trust, it is deeply okay.

This dream boils up from the depths of the past, the below, through the strata of landscape that we find ourselves in, right through the sensual, visual, spiritual, physical, emotional anthropomorphic identities we inhabit to interpret and experience, right out through our fontanels, and bursts out as a rain cloud—a word, an intention gathers and spills, dripping the blessing of nourishment and transformation onto the known world.

We will keep knowing bigger, and broader—I (and we) will be shown ever humbling and expansive perspectives.

Feel it changing. It is. Change me.

There. I said it.   :)

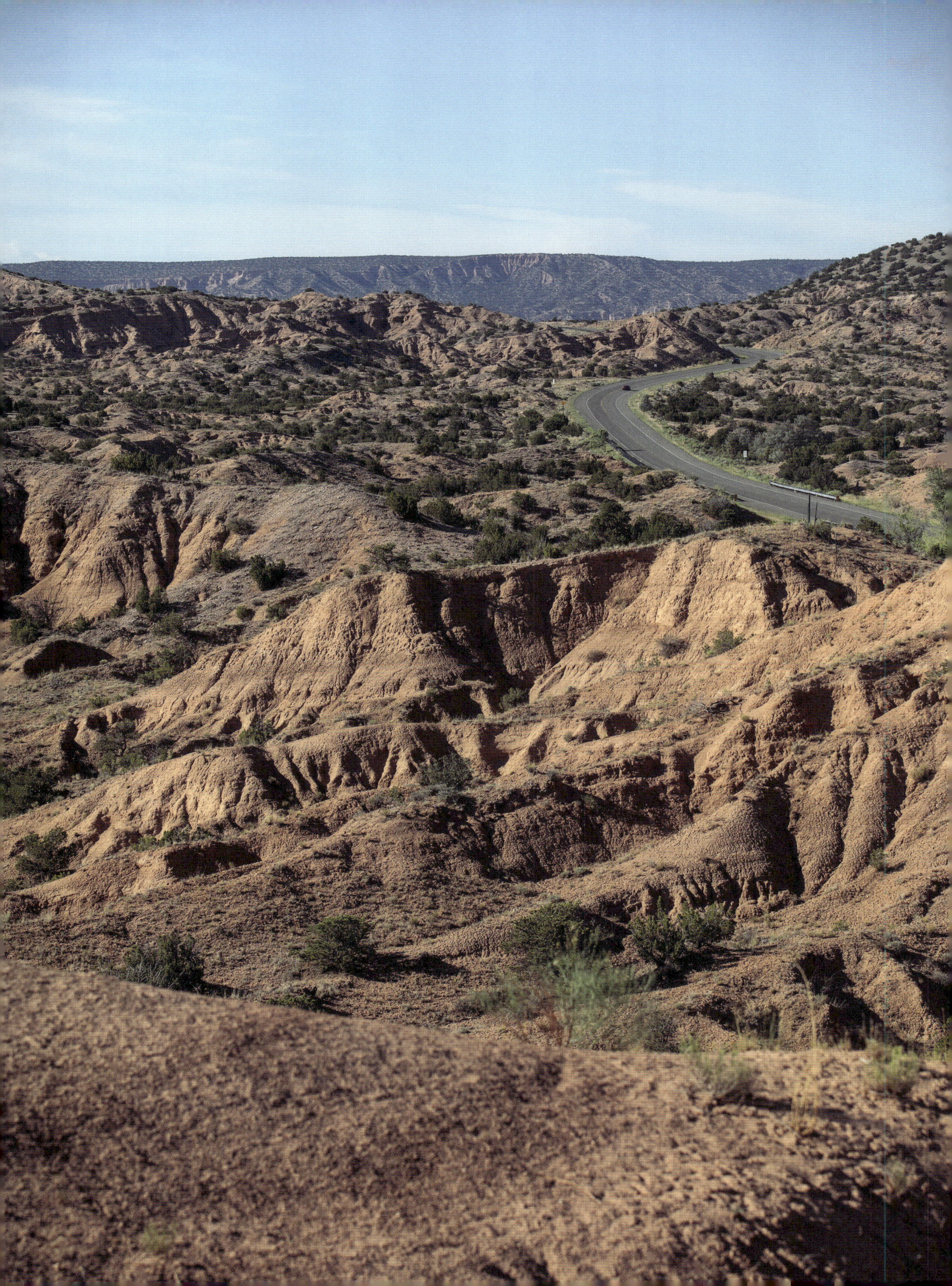

A Dream House

Karen Patterson

How to make a home for dreams . . .

There is a small field in New Mexico's high desert that lies idle, dormant. It is deep into January, which is a time for the soil to restore its balance, to remain as it is, to rest and regenerate. In just a few months, the garden will spill over with corn, beans, squash, and chiles.

Until then, the land rests—and dreams—and in doing so, she gathers her strength.

There are seven buildings. All of them surround this half acre of land, and they each protect and nourish it in their own way. They need this land, they provide for this land, and they too are in their own seasons of becoming. Each building, with its own cadence, timbre, and pitch, is waiting to come to life, in its own way, this year.

> *She once dreamt that she was in a boat with three other people. It was another life-time, another universe, and it felt like something catastrophic had just happened. She was responsible for holding these rocks, or maybe they were seeds. She was holding them so tightly they were leaving imprints in her palms.*

A view of the field that sits at the center of seven buildings that fuel Rose B. Simpson's practice

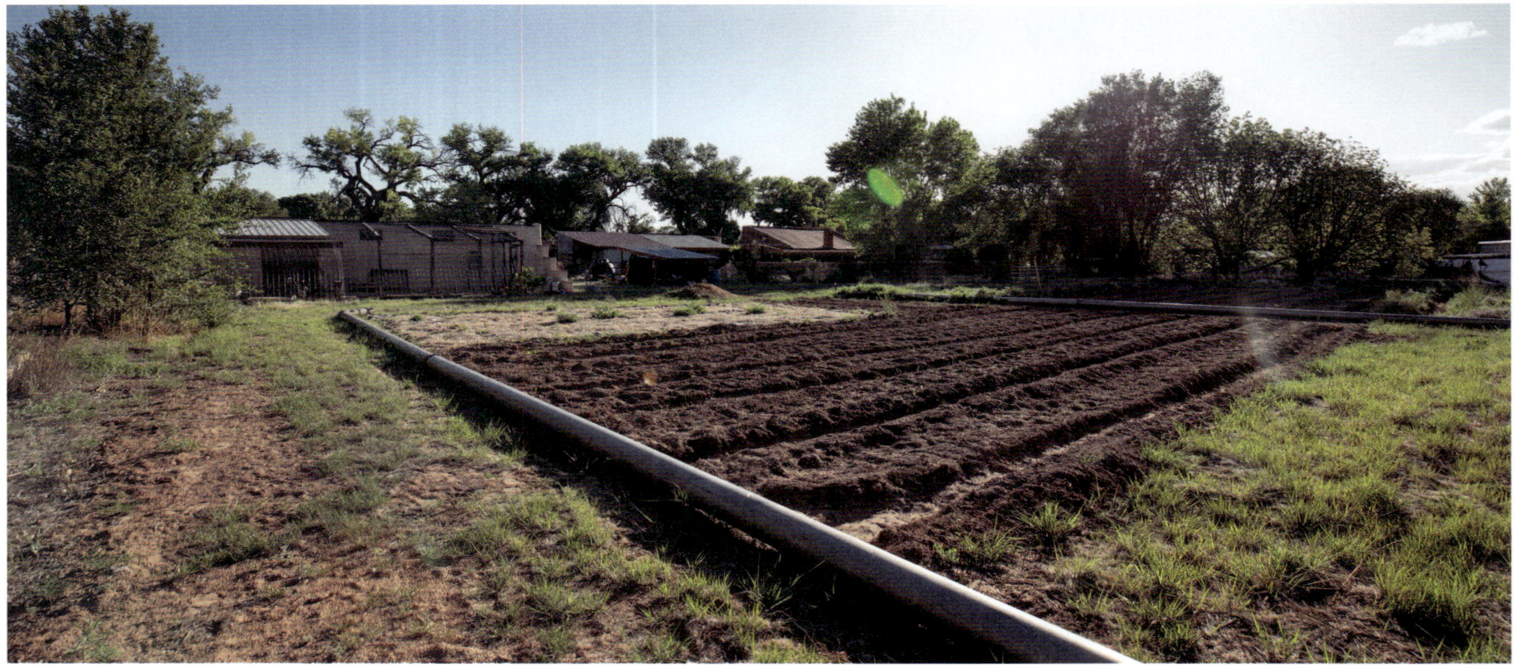

"

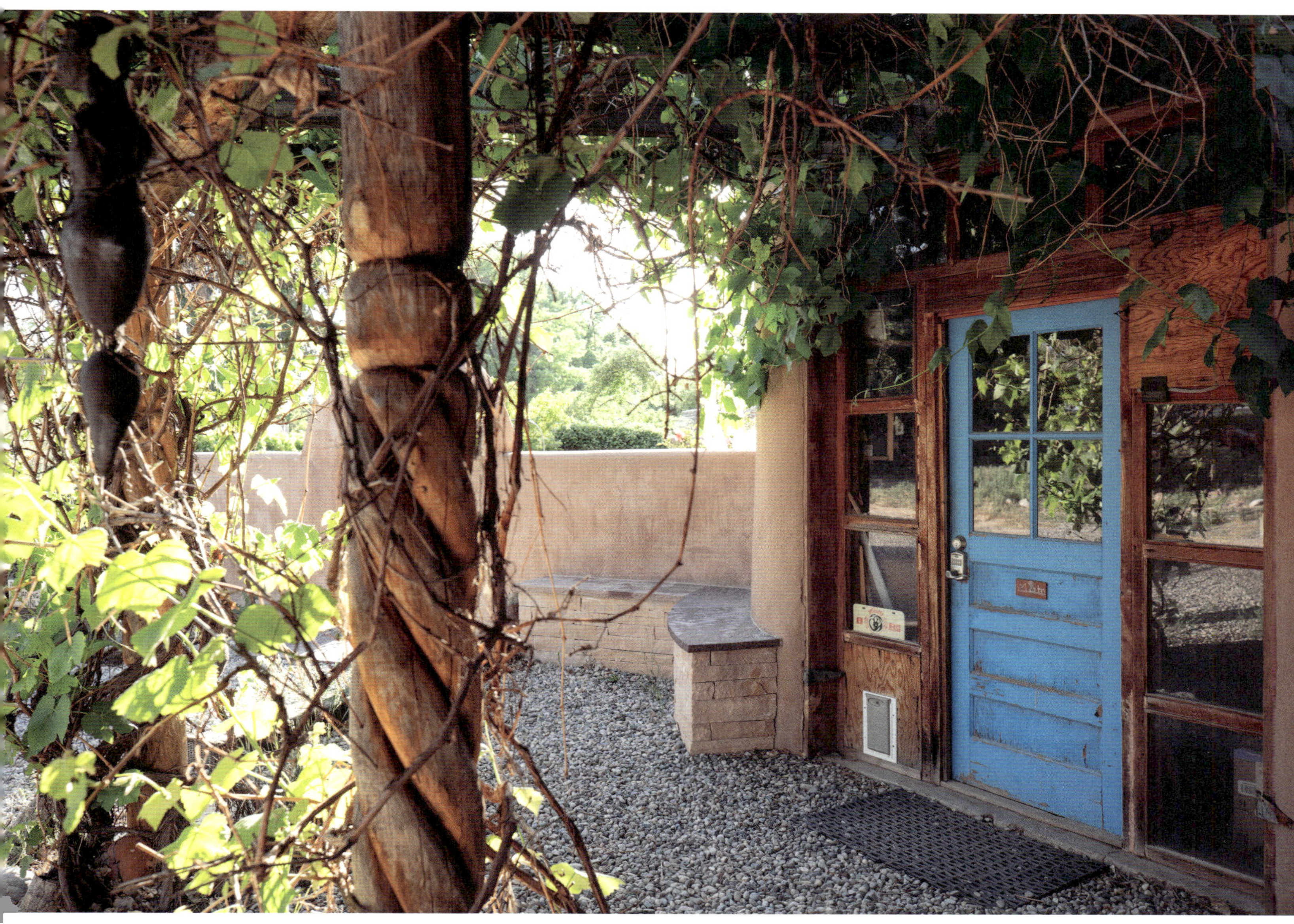

The door to Rose's old studio

You can't see the buildings from the road; they are tucked away behind a high adobe wall, at the end of a long road off the highway. I nearly missed the entrance.

The largest one might be the first you see. It is a two-story adobe home, and it has already started to rustle, to come alive, in the early-morning hours. Women stay here, and, every day, they learn the intricacies and temperament of growing something. To tend to the fields and maybe also to themselves while they are here. The kitchen has a tempo you can count on. It's like a metronome—the steady pulse—for the land and its residents, with a warmth you are completely reassured by. The slow roll of tea brewing every morning, before the day starts.

Across from the house, along the dirt road, is a greenhouse with seeds germinating. It sits next to a small shack where Pedro, the goat, lives. This humble wooden building looks dark inside and it feels moody; it doesn't ask for anything. It has only stood here for eight years, but the inescapable desert sun has weathered it.

"It ages you," she says.

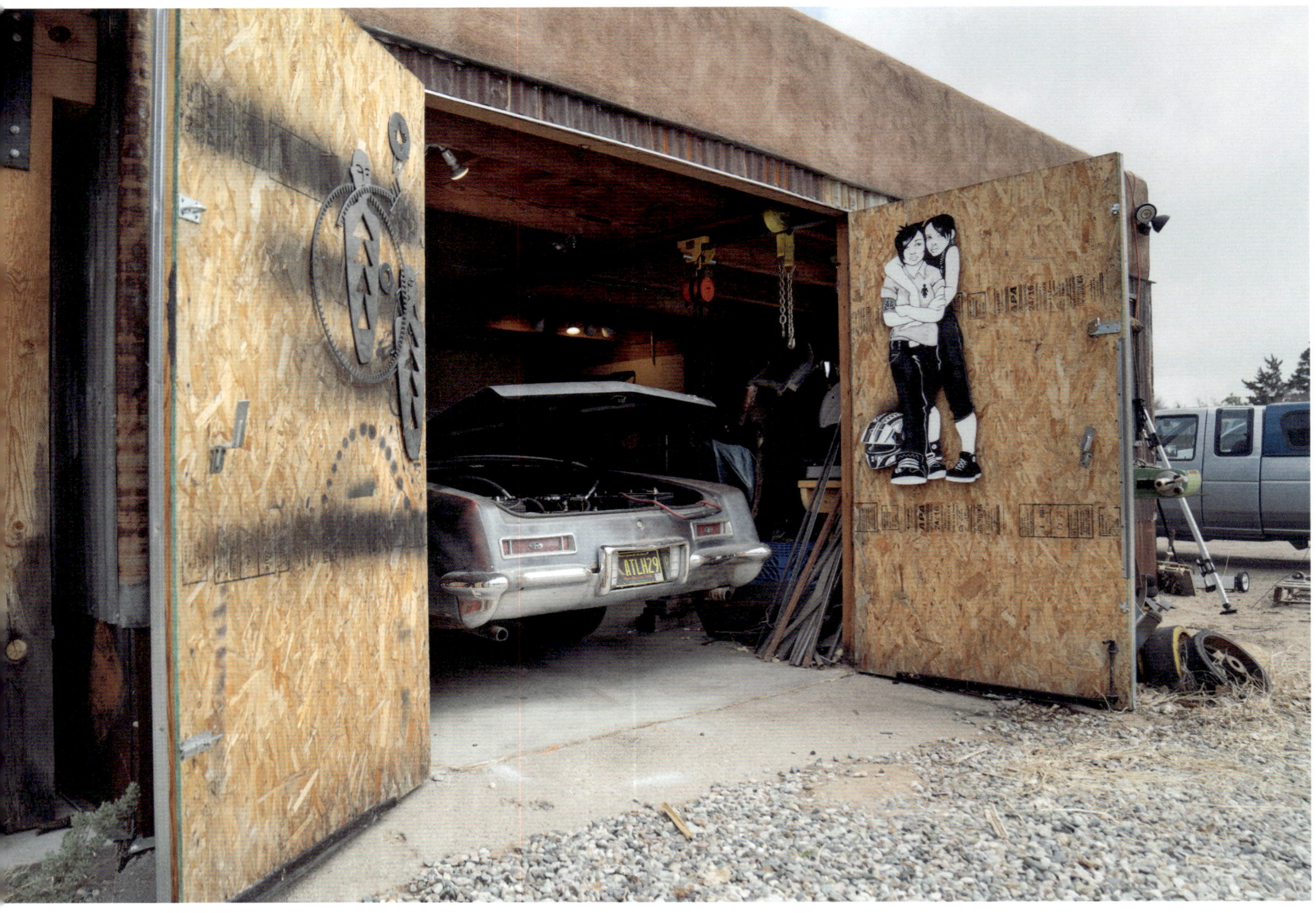

The garage with works in progress

So, it creaks in the heat and bends with winds. It is rooted here and withstands the elements alongside the soil it provides for.

We didn't spend much time at the shed or the greenhouse; there was an issue we needed to investigate.

The garage is directly across the field and currently sits with its lights out. Even in the stillness of the morning, as we walk toward it, the shop glistens. Light bounces from car hoods to spray-paint cans and along racks of tools and engine parts.

As soon as you go through the back door, there is a palpable sense that something— someone?—is eagerly waiting for us. She is giddy and ready to perform.

As we come upon the '64 Buick Riviera on a jack stand with her hood open and with parts lying about, I learn of major change coming. Maria will soon have a sister. Rose walks around her and tinkers with the engine, possibly fixing something, likely just letting her know that she's here now, and it's time to get to work.

"This is going to be a fun one," Rose says with an equal measure of mischief and seriousness.

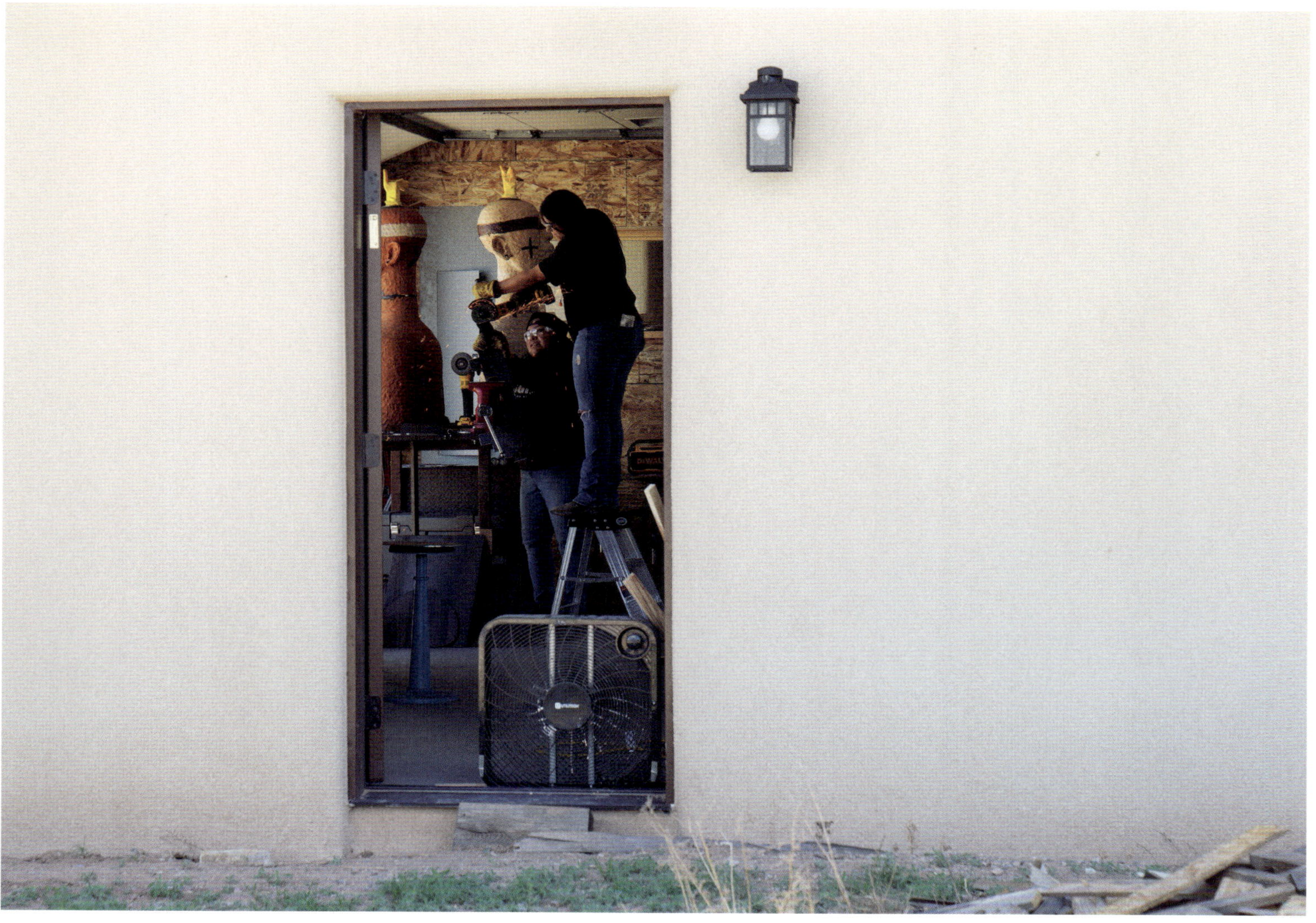

View of Rose's studio

The other two buildings in this homestead are both studios, and they are the reason I'm here today. To see how Rose's dreams morph into physical spaces.

One studio lies hushed and calm this afternoon, while the other is buzzing with the noise of metal grinding. The first, awash with a golden warmth of clay, is teeming with natural light from the open door. There's a small piece of paper, curled and blurred from use and age, with the words "Baby sleeping."

She will keep that.

The cool, curved walls have masks and pictures, but it's more sparse these days. Some things are getting packed up for the move.

Cool to the touch, this studio is smaller and cozier than I imagined. With all the work that has been made here, I envisioned it to be massive, endless. But the scale is snug and lived-in. Drawers spill over with glues, tools, and half-used odds and ends. Bags of clay sit slumped on worktables, next to baskets of beads and rope.

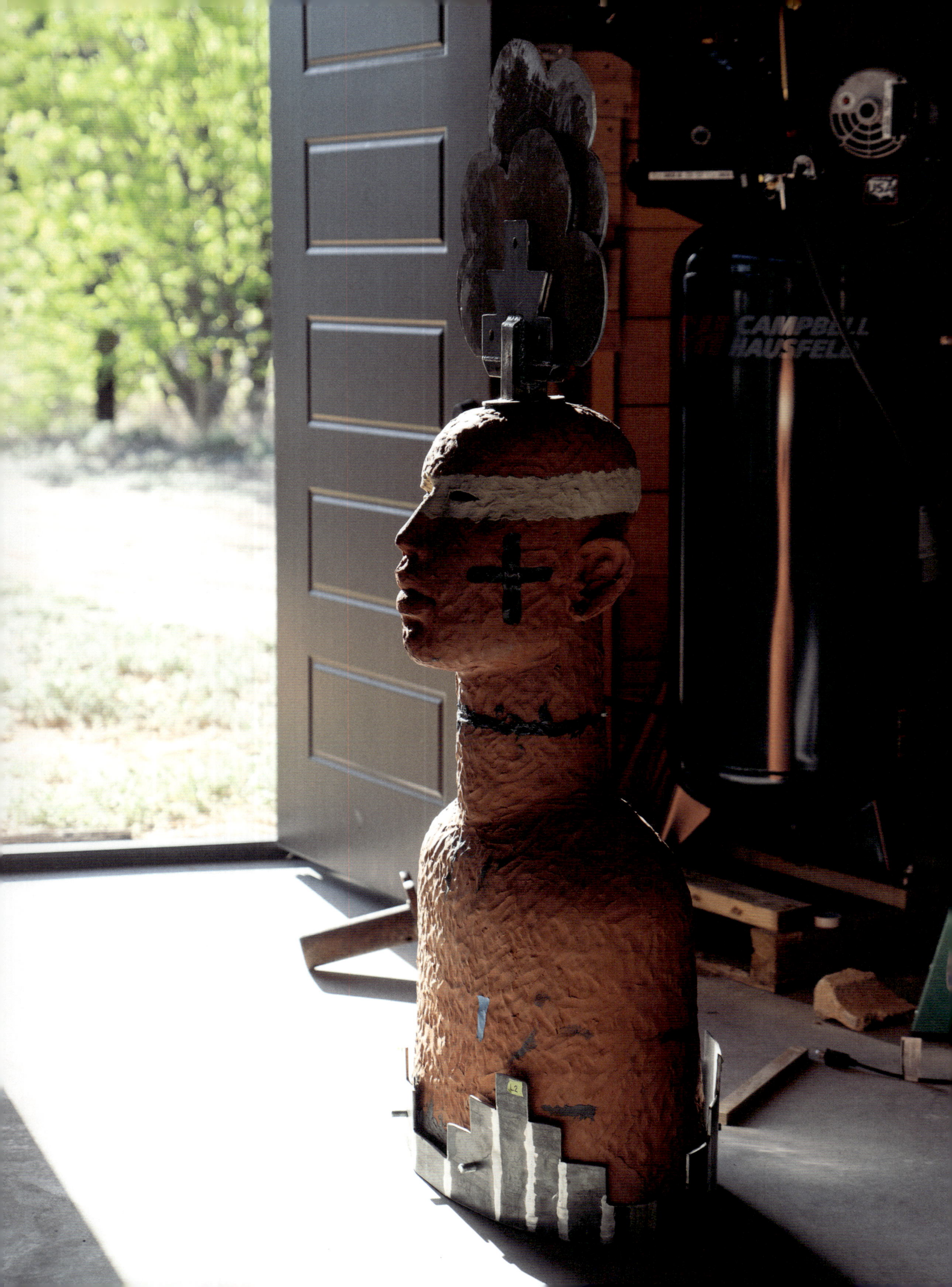

This was Rose's first studio after art school; she started working here more than ten years ago. It used to belong to her great-uncle Michael Naranho, and soon it will become a new studio for her mom, Roxanne Swentzell.

> *She gets out of the old car and starts running as fast as she can. But she doesn't run fast enough or get far enough away, and three shots are fired in rapid succession. This is not the first time she has died in a dream.*

> *"It happens a lot. Sometimes I wake up and I can feel where the wounds are."*

All these things—the mud, the amulets, the memories, the big plans, the bolts of leather, the Hot Wheels lined up along the window, her collection of rusty bent wire, Nugget's baby shoes, the sweet sign on the door—will start their move this year. Some things will come with, some things will be let go.

But first, this new studio needs to be ready. Rose has to find a pause in her steady pace of projects, which is not on the horizon. So, this soon-to-be-old studio, with its amber hues and nested knowledge, sits and waits.

Parts of the new studio are already in production mode, even in its unfinished state. The glass-faced building sits further down the road, behind the garage and in front of an abandoned building that everyone says is haunted.

Rose, Wanda, and Celestial are all here in the studio today, hatching plans and assigning stations for a full day of welding. Wanda is cutting metal into puzzle-like pieces, Celestial will grind them, and I will round the edges before handing them off to Rose. She then welds the pieces onto six four-foot-tall masks. Each mask will have more than fifty individual pieces and will be placed on top of seven towering figures, slated to commune as *Seed* and watch over Madison Square Park in New York City this summer.

Rose is the only experienced metalworker in the studio today, but she teaches and shares, and we all do our best. For her. We move seamlessly from laughing to learning and settle into the quiet rhythm of our floating thoughts. An elementary school teacher, a young student, Rose, and me.

> *She once dreamt she was a fox with nowhere to burrow. She was roaming in the foothills and couldn't find a place to tuck in.*

This move to a bigger studio is a profound life shift that is both physically demanding and psychically supercharged. She is carving out her own space—her dream house—and it is slowly coming into focus, brick by brick, intention by intention.

The project Rose worked on with the Fabric Workshop and Museum in 2022 was a first step in this journey to build a place all her own. Before she creates anything, she travels inward and explores her own psyche, to try and understand the hopes, to turn over the secrets, to follow past lives, and to listen to the voices.

She intentionally created the installation as a way to locate her inner self and to give each part of her a room to live in. With its narrow corridors and long shadows, she made sure that it had spaces you can experience and rooms with thresholds not to cross. The constructed labyrinth offered, and it withheld. *You can't have all of her.* You can watch a video of the rushing Rio Grande from behind a window, but you cannot go in. You should look up as you walk through the hallways; the bricks smell of earth. There is a workroom with just one table, with just one chair, and with just one cup. Three large faces watch over the table.

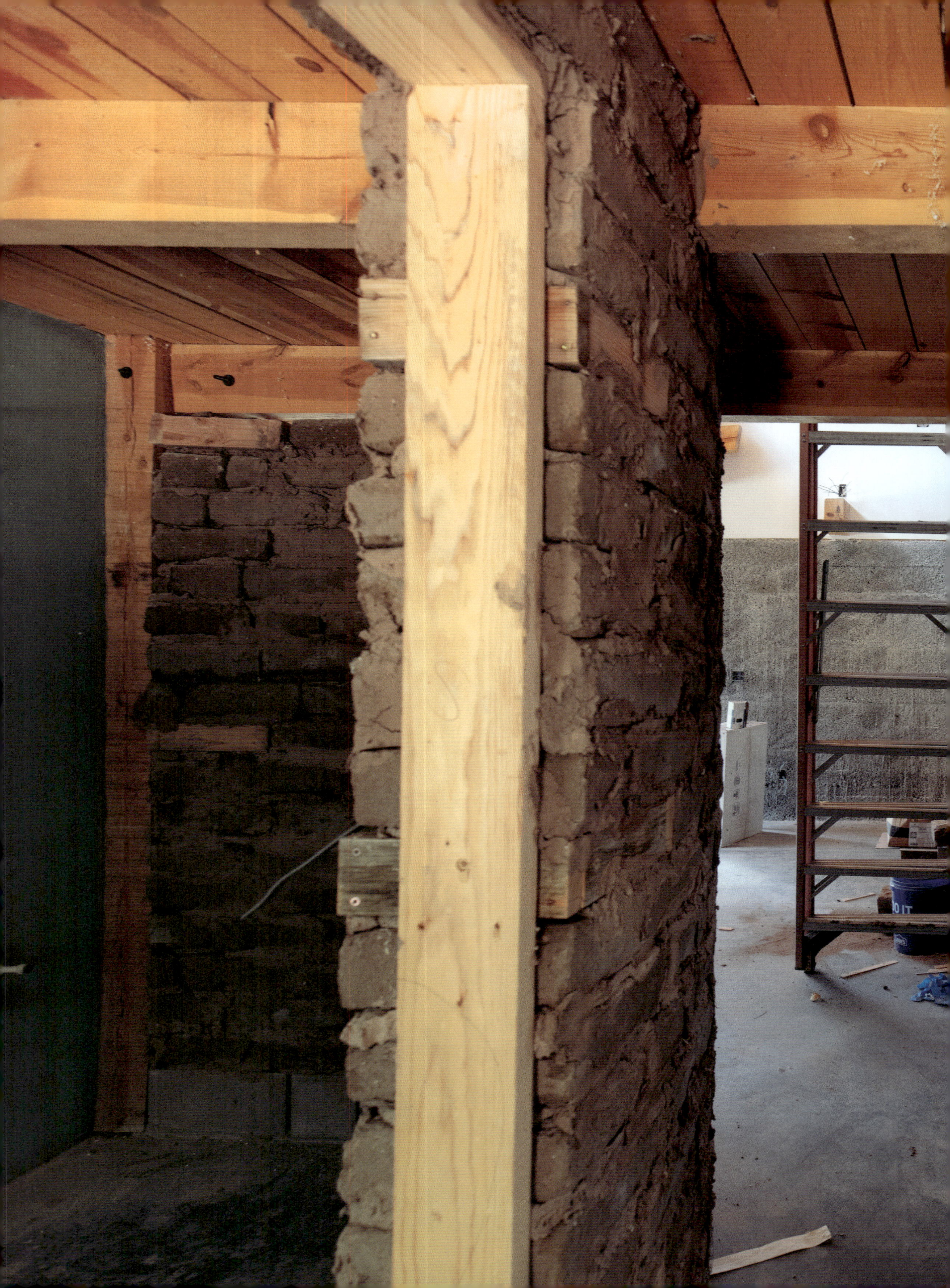

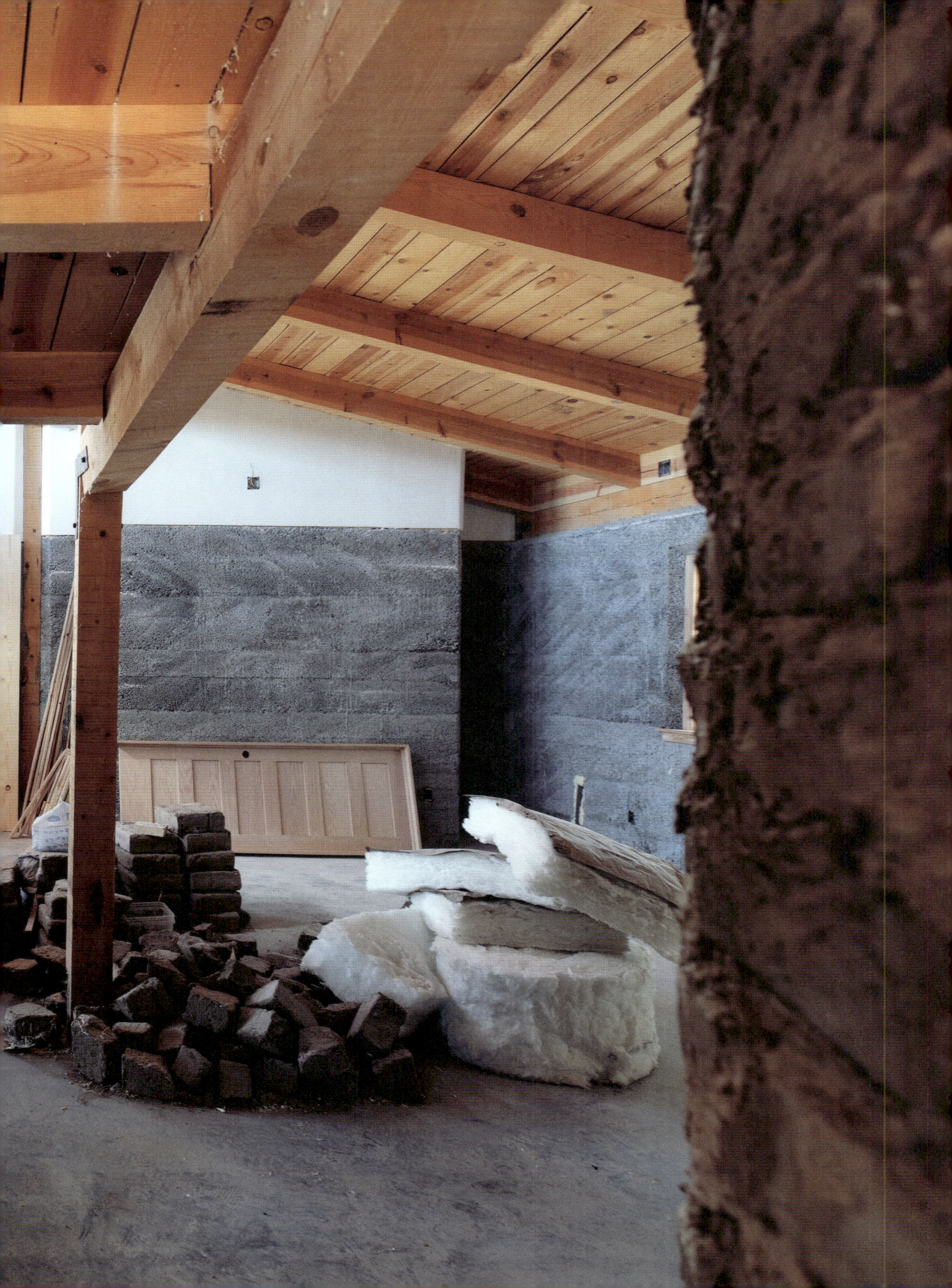

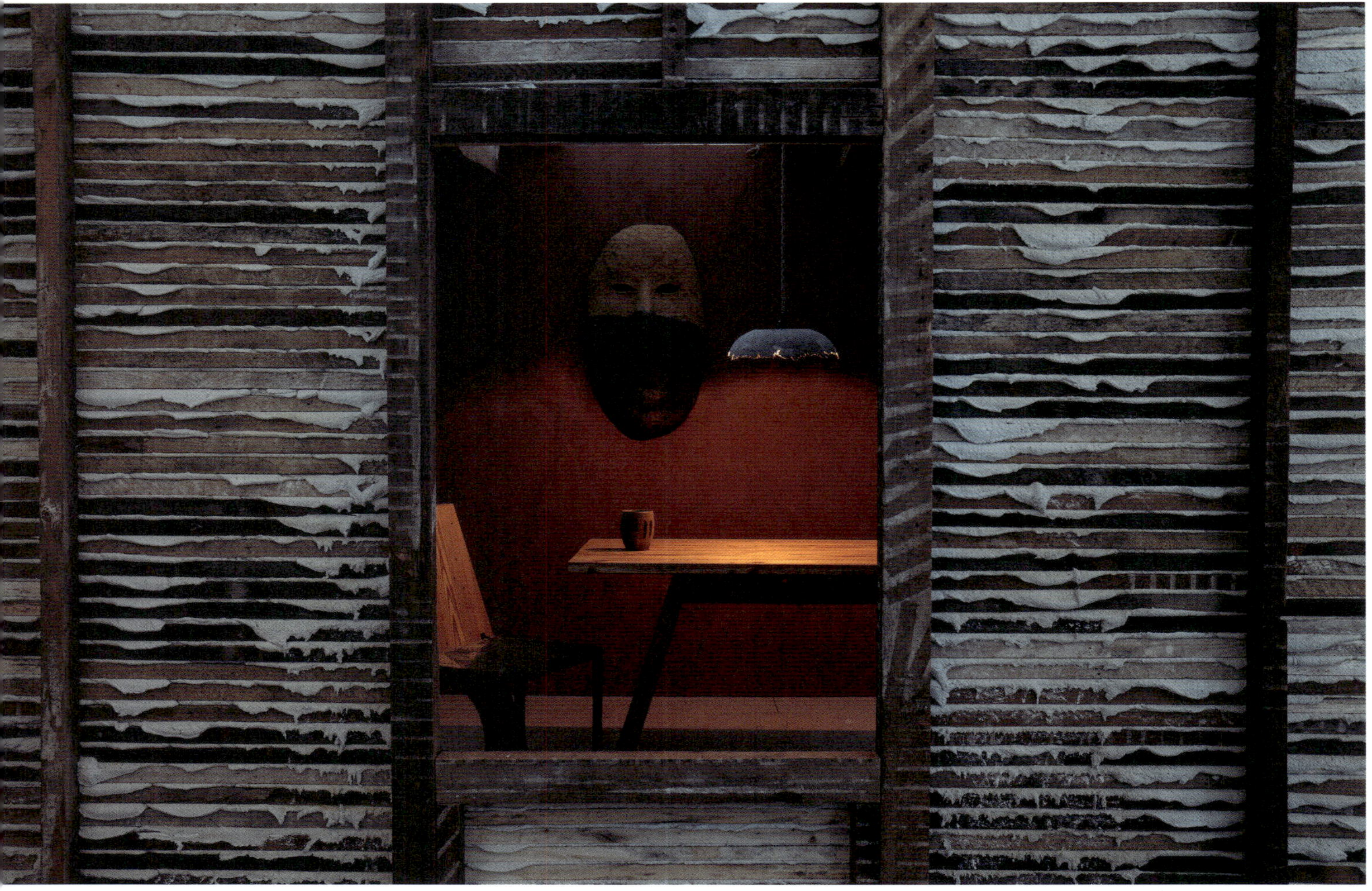

You're not sure if you should walk here or if you should give it room to breathe.

The last room invites you to sit on soft cushions with your swirling thoughts, nestled below inky stars painted on soft paper baskets. There are seven spaces in total.

Rose has always used dreams as a blueprint for her life. Her practice is fundamentally about visualizing and manifesting a dream. Sometimes these visions jolt her awake. Any sequence of dreams can collapse time, unsteady her footing, move through her body, and take her breath away. There are dreams for whom she feels responsible, for whom she is grateful, and to whom she feels beholden. The women who run wildly are deeply rooted, are close by, or just out of reach.

Her journeys through her subconscious are mythic. Here, she can remember what somewhere used to look like, can see what hides behind the feeling, can know how hard this is, or can feel how overwhelmingly beautiful it might be.

She whispers prayers and then can't sleep.

The unfinished part of the studio, next to the metal shop where we are shaping steel puzzle pieces, is made entirely of adobe clay. It feels both cavernous and light-filled, as though we are underground peering upward. It will have a kitchen, a sewing area, and a perch for her daughter to play. Soon, after all the pieces come together, she will start working in clay here.

Once, two months after Nugget was born, Rose was feeling overtaken by the sleeplessness and the helplessness of caring for a colicky baby. She felt lost in it, overpowered,

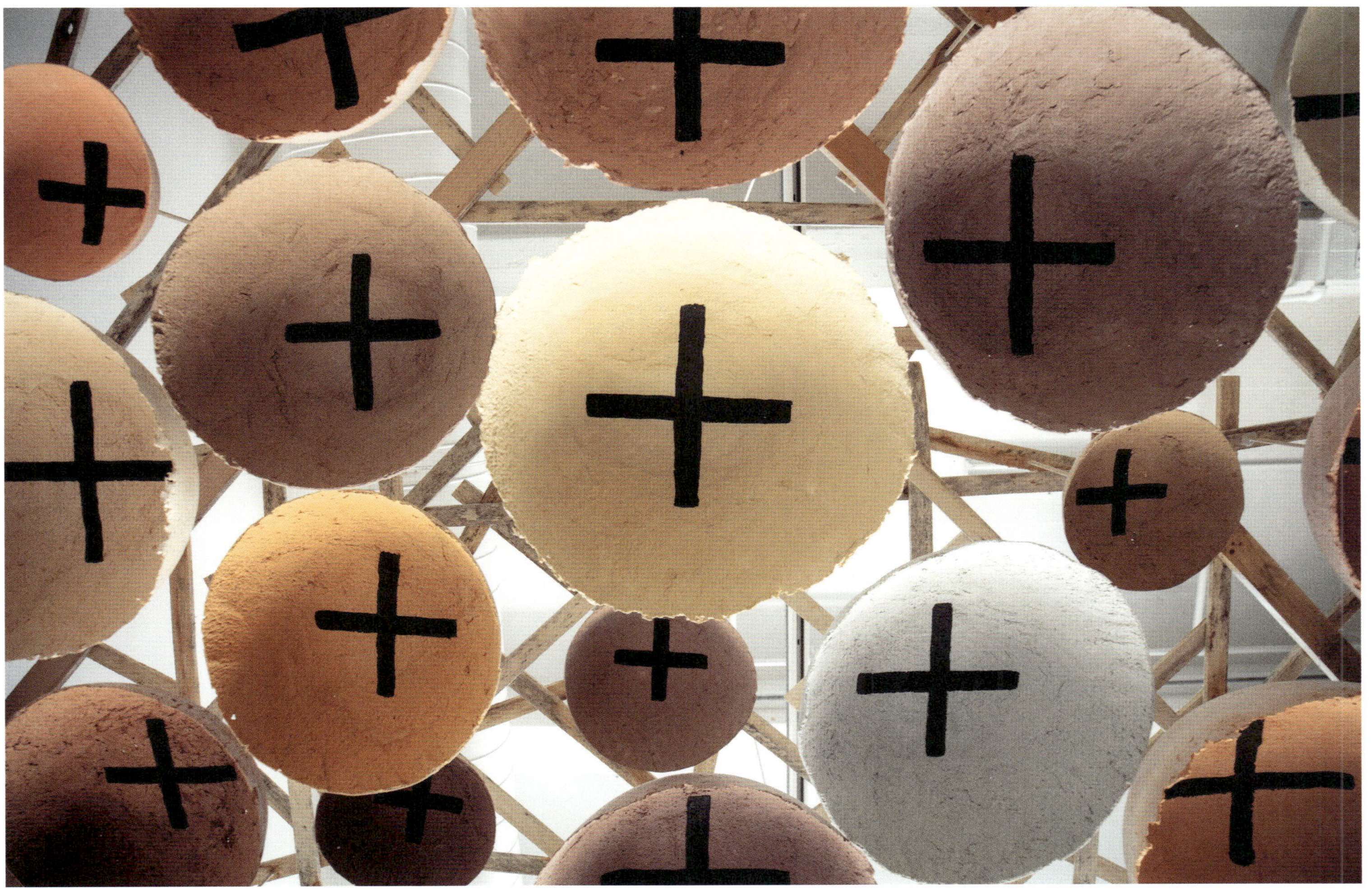

Looking up at baskets made of paper installed on the ceiling of the *Dream House* installation at the Fabric Workshop and Museum in Philadelphia, October 7, 2022–May 7, 2023

and the walls were closing in. She wanted to go for a ride. So, she bought herself a brand-new yellow motorcycle and brought it up to eighty-seven miles per hour in ten short, heart-racing minutes. When she got to the end of the road, she jumped off the bike, called her friend Tony, and said he could have it.

Her world was different now.

These dreams are storms brewing, swirling with competing expectations and contradicting desires. Stirring with the things you want to do and the things you must do, with the people here and with those who have passed, with elders and with young girls, with lowriders and with art openings.

Rose is at home with her dreams. They can offer infinite possibilities or they can remind her to steel herself, to brace herself for what's ahead. These are the sleeping stories and these are the waking moments, all at once, all the time. She takes it all in and breathes it all out. Sometimes she might try to hold on to those fleeting ones with a tender, knowing squeeze. She lets them take her and acts on their behalf.

As she has been building this studio, the dreams have become especially vivid.

Rose has moved a lot of her energy into the world lately. Over the past four years, she has built, adorned, and sent more than sixty figures into the universe. She sends them out as prayers as they leave Santa Clara Pueblo for their new homes.

"They are strong," she says. "I have faith they can handle this. I worry. For them. For us all, and I also have faith."

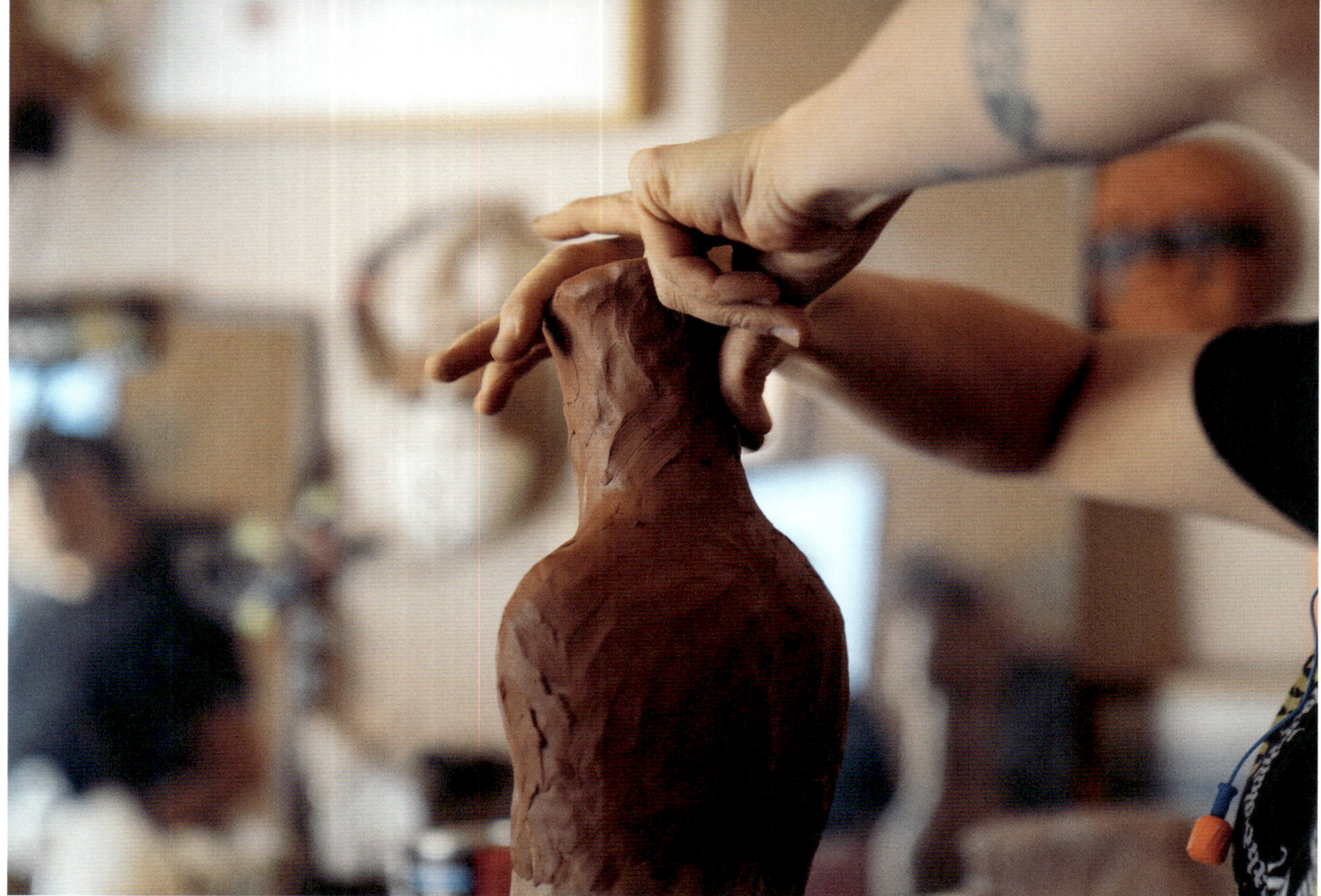

After a morning of welding, we drive a half hour to Ojo Spa resort, to soak in the healing waters of the thermal pools.

Everyone in the dream, including Rose, is speaking fluently in Japanese. She is sitting with two people that she doesn't recognize but she clearly knows them deeply. She has been traveling with them for a long time and she feels as though they are working together. They are sitting next to the creek, and Rose is aware of tension brewing. They are tying fabric into knots; maybe they were going to dye fabric. Lots of knots to make lots of patterns. There was a sense of power around them, and they could feel that there was danger in that power.

They had to keep the calm. The man with them was an incredible fighter, and they knew that. He could snap easily, so they had to keep him relaxed. Tying the knots was both a way to make patterns and a way to make some sort of magic that kept him at ease. So, they kept tying knots. But suddenly there was rage, and he erupted.

And then they died.

Again.

The Pueblo Revolt was a revolution against Spanish colonizers and is widely understood as an early and successful Native uprising against a colonizing power. In 1680, after decades of torture and oppression, Pueblo people organized a revolt. To coordinate the timing of the rebellion, Po'pay of Ohkay Owingeh sent runners to all nineteen pueblos carrying knotted cords, each knot representing the number of days until they would take action. A knot was to be untied each day, and the revolt would begin once the last one was unbound.[1]

The resort's parking lot is busy; the resort has become a sought-after winter destination for wealthy retirees and bachelorette getaways. We weave through the crowds to secure our spots in one of the hot pools. From our vantage point, we can see that they are constructing more pools, and that the resort is expanding for more visitors. I learn that, before it was a resort and spa, this area used to be a free community pool for the surrounding pueblos, for kids and families, and for birthday parties.

On our way out, I stop to buy a bottle of water at the gift shop, and Rose points to *Bless Me, Ultima*, a book by Rudolfo Anaya, an early and important writer of contemporary Chicano and New Mexican literature. His novel is set in the 1940s and is about a young boy struggling with competing expectations in his home of rural New Mexico.

In a 1987 interview, Anaya said that the greatest breakthrough in finding his voice happened when he was writing late at night, as he was struggling to bring the story together. "I felt something behind me," he said, "and I turned and there was this old woman dressed in black and she asked me what I was doing. 'Well, I'm trying to write about my childhood, you know, about growing up in that small town.' And she said, 'Well, you will never get it right until you put me in it.' I said, 'well, who are you?' and she said, 'Ultima.'"[2]

For Anaya, this message from his subconscious gave him the mentor he needed and a spiritual guide to take him through a lifetime of writing.

> *I don't seek characters; they seem to come to me asking to tell their stories.*

We are now trying to make a left turn onto the road that leads into her pueblo, but the steady stream of oncoming after-work traffic coming from the Los Alamos National Laboratory—the birthplace of the atomic bomb—is unrelenting.

A letter from Rudolfo Anaya to Rose, November 1, 2018. © 2021 by The University of New Mexico Foundation, Inc.

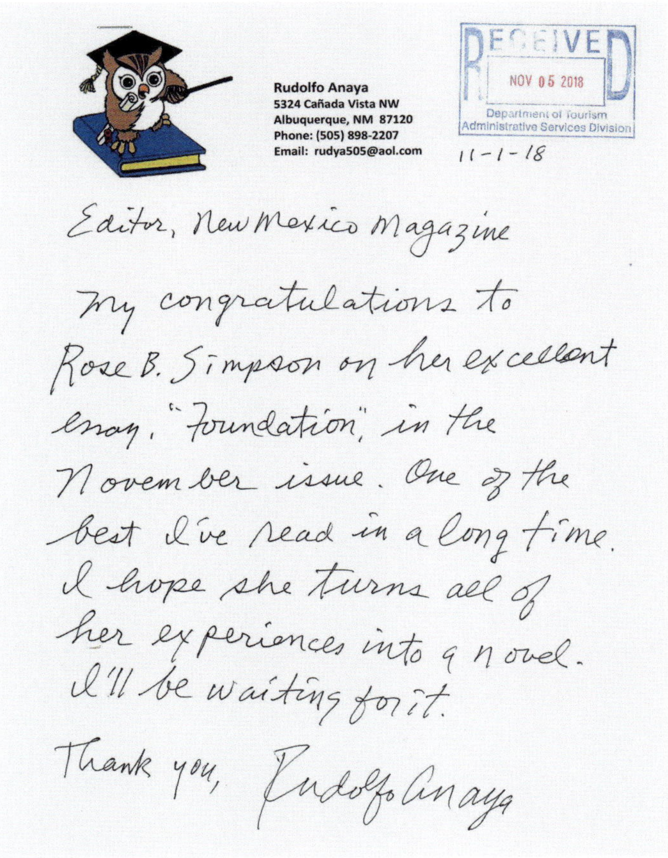

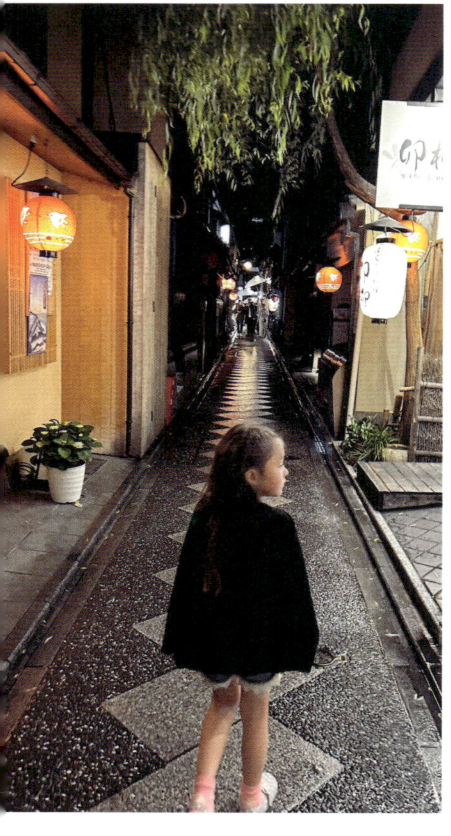
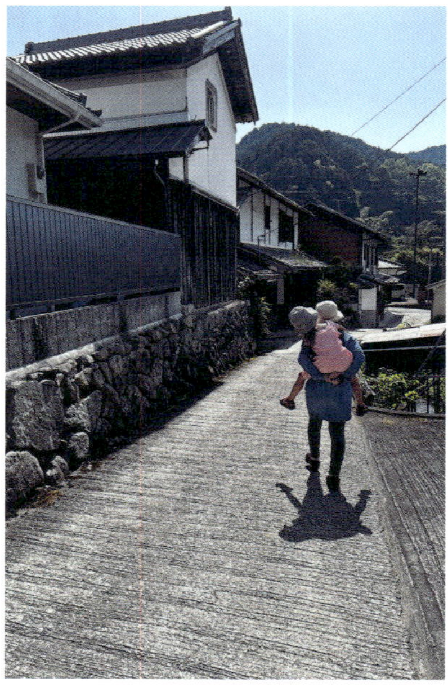
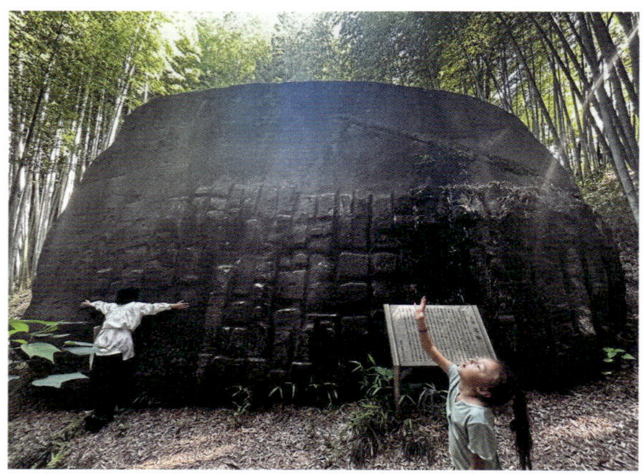
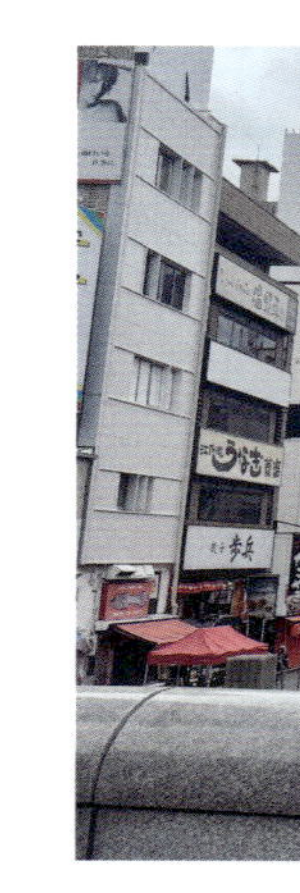
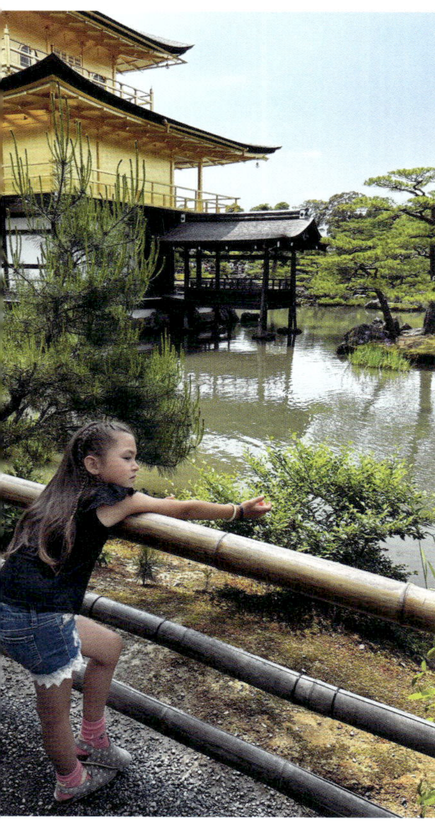
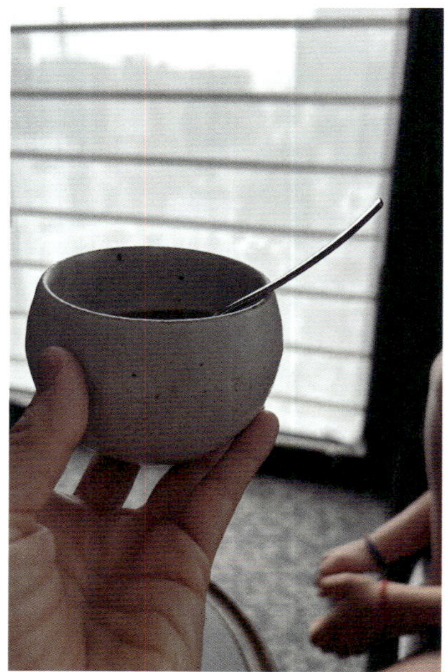
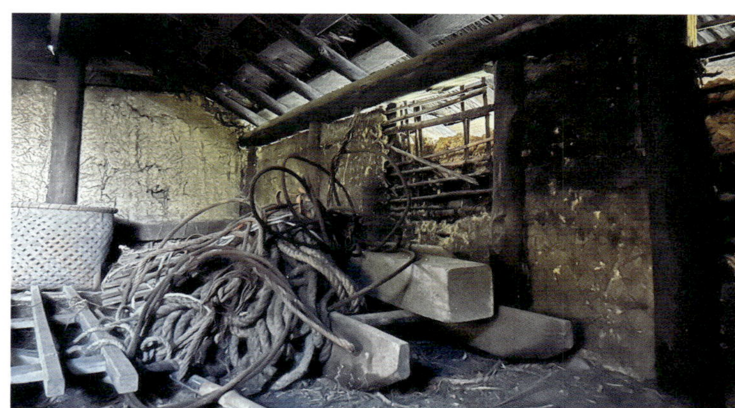

Photos of Rose's recent travels to Japan taken on her phone, 2023

Rose lives with these layers and moves through jarring lifetimes and watches as they topple onto one another.

She is back in Japan, in a small rural town that eerily reminds her of her hometown of Española. She remembers seeing monkey tracks in the snow and how she pulled prints outside in the cold, behind an old building. She remembers that the kiln was keeping her warm. There is a long road that is so familiar to her, it has definitely been in her dreams before. As she walks along it, everything feels recognizable. She knows where neighbors hang their laundry and who has chickens roaming around. It is the same road in every dream.

She has tried to find this area on Google Earth before.

Maybe her dream twisted it.

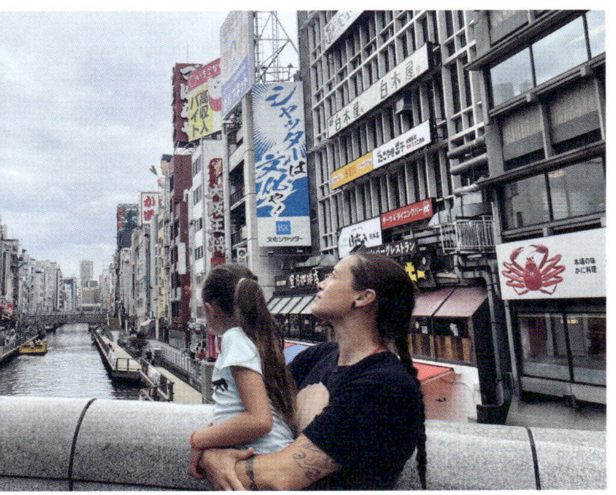

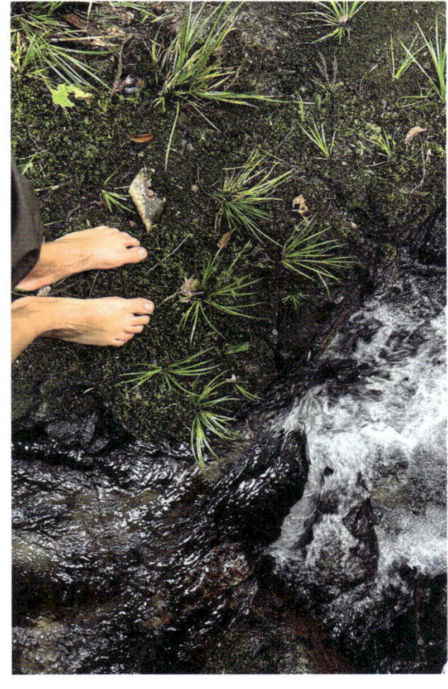

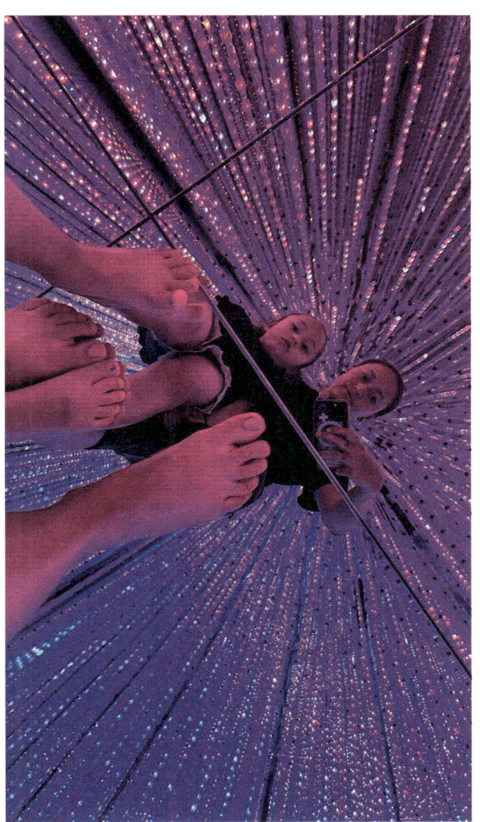

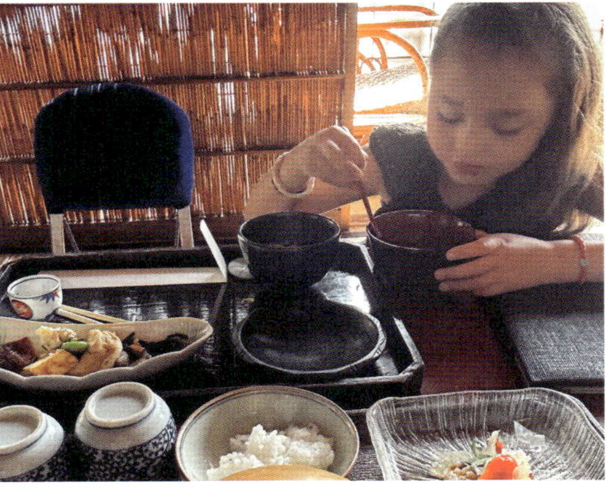

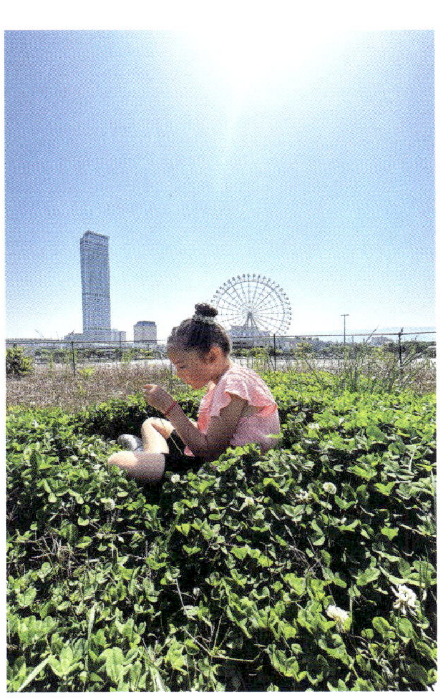

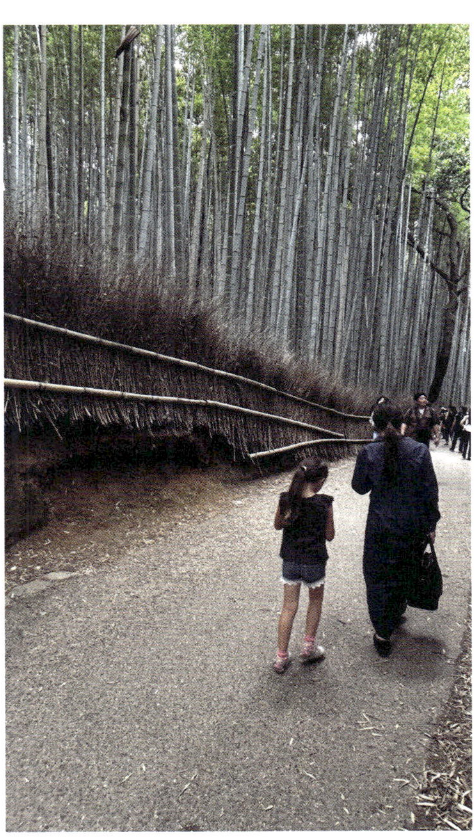

But now she is back here and she is thinking about the prospect of Bunrako puppets animating her figures, giving them movement. She is with her daughter, and they are driving further and further up a deep, winding canyon.

They are tired, so they sit to have tea. Afterward, they decide to go for a walk into the canyon, following the creek. They are scrambling now, jumping from rock to rock. This is where the dragons first came out of the water, and she feels like it is time to pray.

They arrive at a house in the small town of Kayanomori. The home has missing walls, and you can see through the thatched roof to the sky. It sits between two creeks, which adds a thrilling layer to the house the first time she sees it.

It is thundery; you can feel it in your chest, in your feet.

"Who are you?" she asked as she stood in its doorway. Wooden shoes and old motorcycle parts on the floor. The tattered banner hanging outside has a phone number on it. It is for sale, but no one has ever called. She decides that they will work on this house; it will be an art piece, a backdrop for the puppets. The stage is set. Another dream house is underway, and they will come back to bless it with a ceremony this summer. The pieces fall into place.

I don't know that I'm the one that is making any of this happen. When you get this type of feedback, you know you are on the right path.

How do we make sense of this? Of these buildings, of these dreams.

As she is giving her speech at Madison Square Park to welcome the sculptures to their new home, it starts to rain.

I am grateful for this lesson.

Let's live within what she has made.

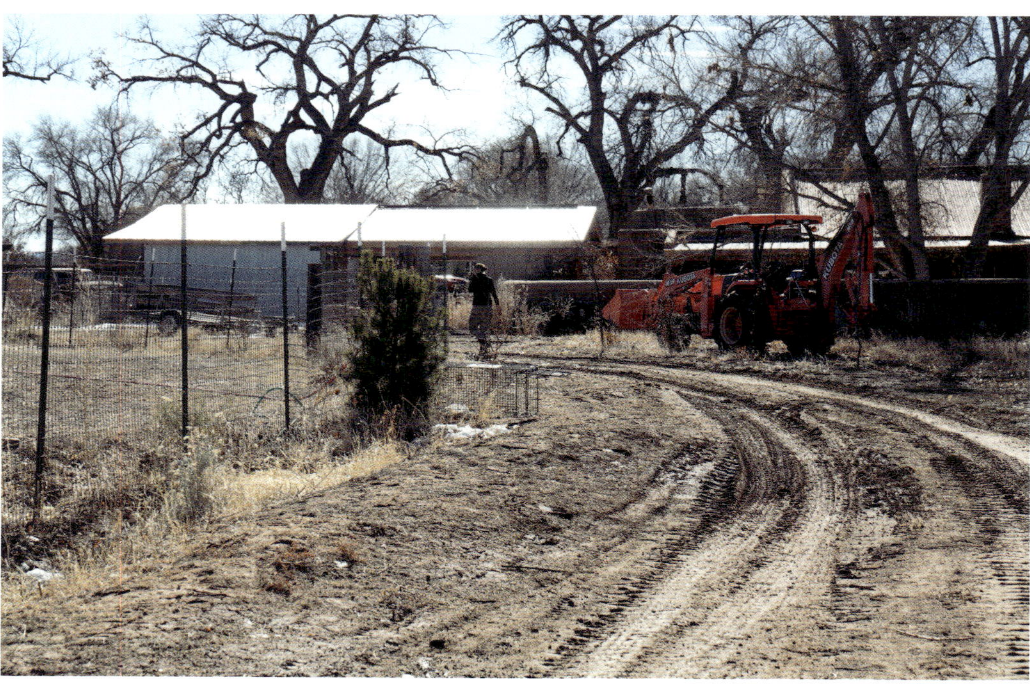

Flowering Tree site between the artist's old and new studios

1. *Nah Poeh Meng* (Poeh Cultural Center, Santa Fe), exhibition text. See also indianpueblo.org/revolt/book-club/.

2. Rudolfo Anaya, "An American Chicano in King Arthur's Court," in *Old Southwest / New Southwest: Essays on a Region and Its Literature*, ed. Judy Nolte Temple (Tucson, AZ: Tucson Public Library, 1987), 113–18.

1. *Nah Poeh Meng* (Poeh Cultural Center, Santa Fe), exhibition text. See also indianpueblo.org/revolt/book-club/.

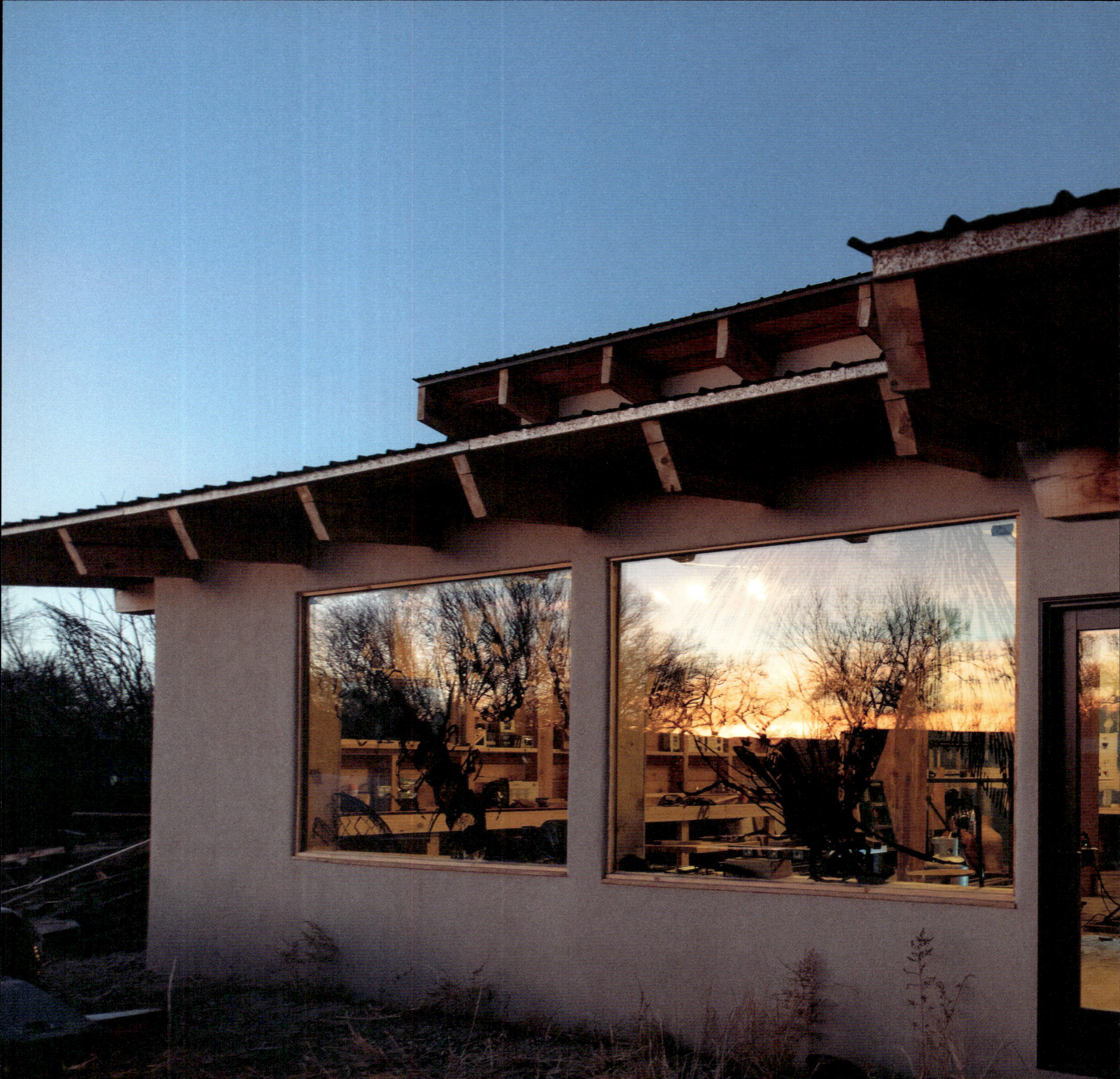

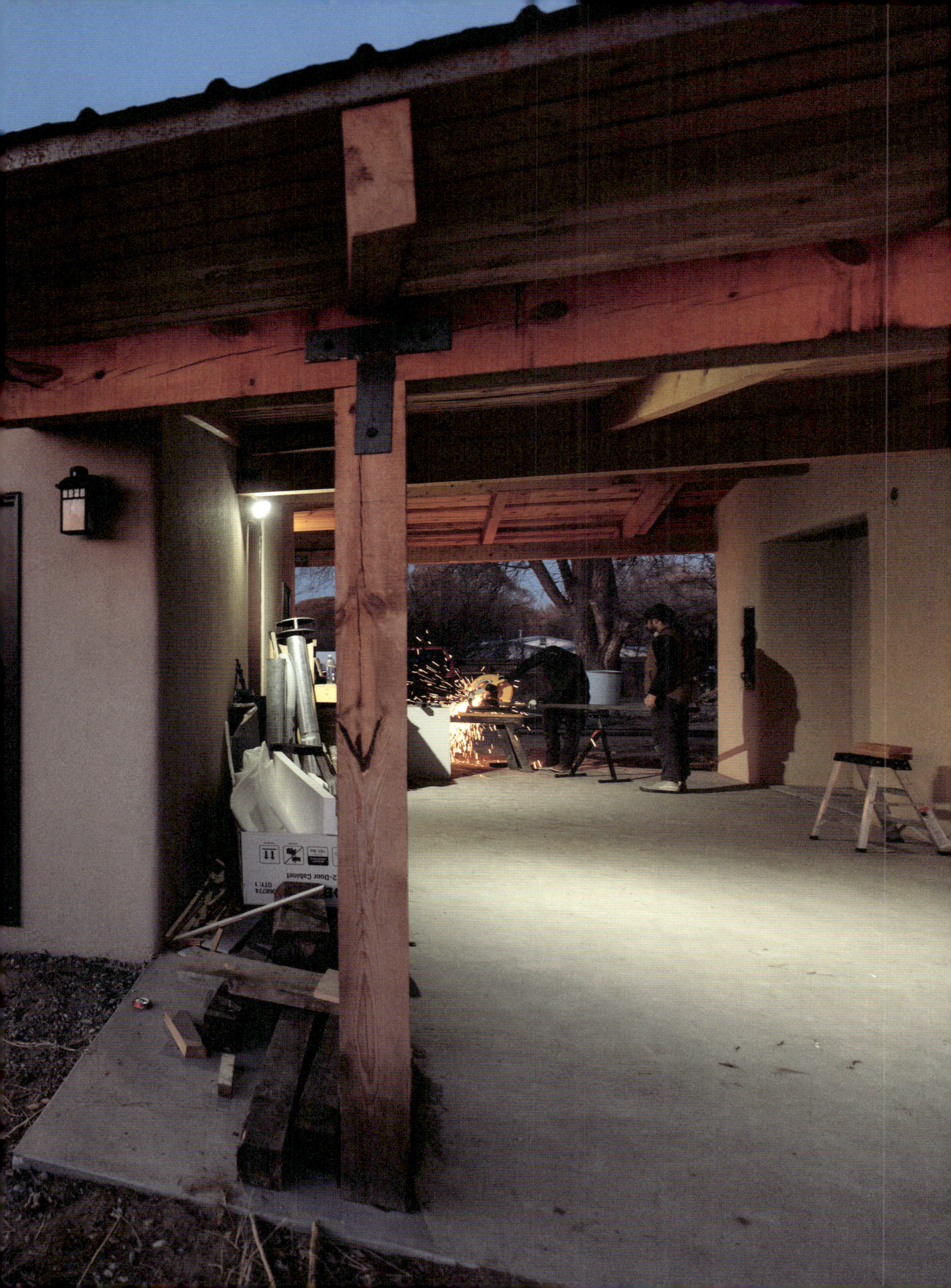

Molded By Life: A Conversation Between Natalie Diaz, Rose B. Simpson, and Dyani White Hawk

Rose B. Simpson: Thank you all for making time for this; it's really, really special. You're all special people to me. I feel really blessed to be in this squad [*laughter*].

Natalie Diaz: This is a good squad.

Dyani White Hawk: I feel the same.

RBS: I want to begin with a couple of things that have been on my mind. This piece is called *Strata*, and it's basically two beings, super earthy. They have these really big, chunky, solid bodies with clay busts, and they're witnessing each other. They have these big cloud headpieces, kind of like aircraft aluminum. And what I've been thinking about with it is self-awareness. A lot of my works are either witnessing each other or they're building a relationship with the viewer. The intention is to give consciousness to the inanimate because we've disconnected from that. Because it's *Strata*, in a sense it's about history, it's about something bigger than humanity.

In the mornings, I pray. I put my forehead to the ground. I look through to the center of the Earth and I talk to Our Mother. It feels like this incredible thing. I look down and say, "Hey, how it's going? How are you today? I see you. How are you feeling?" And I feel like the Earth herself and nature and that deep, deep history of our very three-dimensional experience on this world is how we build self-awareness and reverence.

Hence, the scale of *Strata*. Hence, the impact in space. Those things were important to me when I considered this piece. Fun fact about the Cleveland Museum of Art is that it's right next door to the Cleveland Museum of Natural History, and that might have had something to do with it, because me and [my daughter, Cedar] had a really, really awesome morning at the natural history museum. Looking at those fossils is unreal. And seeing—I don't know, just like when you realize your own experience of life in a larger context. We are so small, we are so tiny, and there are so many billions of consciousnesses happening simultaneously.

And I think, how do you view that holistically but also responsibly and with accountability and consciousness? Those are some of my initial thoughts about this piece.

ND: You mentioned the scale, the size of these clay bodies, these busts. In thinking of strata, that immediately opens literally layers, and it's kind of moving us out of the usual measurements of time. Americans love a centennial. They love one hundred years of something, whereas we think generationally. The title challenges and unravels or unfolds that temporal-spatial relationship.

As you're talking about self-awareness, and as you say you touch your head to the ground, to the Earth, to see into it, I think there's something really beautiful and incredible about the ways you view your work with clay. So, in some ways, again, it's like a refusal of time.

One of the ways I was coming to it was as a gift of understanding the self without the colonial ego. I say that because it's a place where the body of earth is becoming in your hands—the literal act of sculpting the clay—and your body is also returning to one of its first forms, like a form of possibility that doesn't exist in a way that this colonial world thinks of the body, the human, the self. The act itself, the sculpting from clay, is a touching and an acknowledgment of the energies we came from but also that we carry. So, there's a way of thinking of this as a life force, thinking of the clay and these materials as a life force. You're a poet as well, so I don't think this feels too far-fetched, but I imagine the clay knows you and also feels a kind of return to a home in your hands.

I'm wondering if you and Dyani can talk about what it feels like to work from a material, a body of earth that you are of, and then to shape it?

RBS: Clay is one of the easier mediums to build a relationship with and to have an empathic response with, because it's similar to a body. It's so similar to a body, and working with it is very intimate. It's like skin; you're covered in it, you're with it, you're interacting with it directly. Whereas I'm working right now with steel, and I'm doing a lot of welding. There's going to be concrete in *Strata*, too. And those are all different types of relationships to material, and there is an entirely different language that you have to speak with them. With steel, the energy in the studio changes. And the way you approach things changes, and I feel like you almost have to transform yourself to speak its language. It's hard for me to switch gears from welding in the morning and then working in clay in the afternoon. I've gotta start my day welding and end my day welding because I'm almost shape-shifting into that relational experience with that material.

I feel like the more conscious we can be about that, then the better we can channel or *translate* material. We listen to the material, we ask it what it wants to say, then we try to honor its voice in the third dimension.

DWH: It's interesting, one of the things I'm thinking about is on the point of material. It would be fun to just nerd out and have a longer conversation about how we think about material. Knowing you're choosing your material, especially in relationship to scale, Rose, I'd love to hear you talk more about why you chose these materials for *Strata* in particular? How much is practicality and how much of it is the history embedded in the material?

For me, a lot of times I'm choosing whether a piece needs to be done in paint, if it needs to be done in beadwork, if it needs to be video, or if it needs to be installation. And then what I'm thinking about is if it needs to be an intimate piece, or if it needs to take up space and why, and what statements are embedded in all those things. I'm thinking about the history each of those materials brings with it. It's part of the guiding decision, coupled with my desires for how I want to move in the creation of something.

So, there are many factors that guide material choice. But I'm often thinking about whether it's directly the material itself or if I'm referencing a material via color or texture. I'm often thinking about that material's relationship to the land, our relationship with it, and it helps me dig in and tell the stories that I want to share through the work.

RBS: *Strata* is actually partially pumcrete, and pumcrete is a new material that I'm building my new studio with, and that's how I got inspired by it. It's a mix of pumice and concrete so that it's not so heavy. I think about honoring material and honoring the environmental impact of art making, and how we take so many resources and gifts from our world and natural resources, natural gifts from the world, and turn them into these metaphors that we put into the world. How do we, in a sense, be conscious about that and still do it justice?

One of the reasons that engineering is super important in my work is that I want the work to get as much *work* done as it can, and clay is inherently fragile. So, I put in a steel infrastructure so that it won't break in shipping. That, to me, is more honoring of its integrity, because it's going out in the world to do work and I need it to make it there. I don't want it to be gifted back to the landfill. It needs to get as much voice and communication from those materials to hopefully make change and do right by the materials that were taken. To make something this tall is a lot of engineering, and the pumcrete is light, so it's not as hard to move. We don't use as much fossil fuel to get it from point A to point B. When you mix concrete with larger particles of pumice, which are about one-half to one centimeter in size, those particles give it a rough and textured body.

But to return to scale: they're big. The space is very large. When I went to visit the Cleveland Museum of Art, I saw that the atrium is massive. But it also has this incredible light, and I felt like I wanted these vertical forms to cast shadows and to have these kinds of headboards. The roof has this incredible glass ceiling with the glass panes set into rectangles, and it makes these really cool shadows that move across the floor throughout the day. I wanted to add to that, and part of the headpieces were inspired by the filtration

of the sky into the architectural space. The pieces are in conversation with and inspired by the architecture itself. The Cleveland Museum of Art's atrium was a collaborator in the becoming of these things. It spoke to me with its beauty, and I pulled that in and then included it.

DWH: Was there something beyond the atrium and its architecture that guided your choices as well?

RBS: The atrium is the entryway into the building. You enter into a very contemporary space and then see the original facade of the 1916 museum. So, there is a path through that space. I'm captivated by the space between two objects or two beings that are witnessing one another and how there is visceral tension between them, and I wanted all the visitors to walk between the two sculptures in that path, and to sort of pluck the string of consciousness as they enter the space.

Hopefully, that allows all the viewers to begin to feel the influence of intention in artistic objects in their own bodies. So, perhaps they are transformed by that, and they will witness the rest of the museum in a different way. By seeing artistic creations as beings rather than objects.

ND: I wanted to return to materials. I'm thinking about the pumice stone, other than the way we know it in the Indian way, which is for our heels—no, I'm just kidding [*laughter*]. Pumcrete is a new material for me. First, I was like, are they using pumpkin out there? What's going on [*laughter*]? Leave it to the Pueblos; they put pumpkin in the concrete.

RBS: It's a secret recipe [*laughter*].

ND: And afterward, you can eat it [*laughter*].

DWH: The most aromatic concrete.

ND: I'm thinking a lot about the volcanic activity around New Mexico, and this material as created from a very fiery, intensive volcanic action-reaction. One way of looking at it is that it has a negative impact. It's resisting concrete in a way, which then makes the concrete more abundant. It can be moved and worked with more abundantly.

RBS: I wouldn't know about pumcrete if pumice weren't abundant here [in New Mexico], and our volcanic activity. It's hardened, volcanic ash. It goes back to the natural history museum, and the pumice being like the transformation of carbon-based life forms like trees, then turning into fire, and then turning back into a hard object.

We also use pumice as a temper for our clay, because it doesn't expand or contract since it's already been through the heat; it's already gone through that. It creates stability for the clay that keeps it from exploding when it goes through the fire. So, it almost holds the clay's hand back through the heat. You could put it that way. That's what the temper does.

ND: Beautiful that stability would come from what it has been through. Like, maybe a better way of saying survivance, or all the things we've tried to say over time about Indigenous peoples and our Native peoples and our lands is to say because of everything it's been through—the fire, down to its ash—suddenly it has strength and stability.

RBS: I love that. Yeah, it really is.

DWH: But it also has stability through longevity. There's stability in a long-term perspective. There's stability in long-term knowledge. It comes through age. It comes through experience. I like that analogy a lot, Natalie, and I feel like there are a few different ways to look at that.

It's interesting to hear about your working relationship with pumice, Rose, and the ongoing relationship with the land base, where you're at. That speaks to Indigenous knowledge and those historical relationships, which then leads back to what you're talking about, Natalie, the ability to have stability because of that maturity and understanding. A long-term understanding of something and that relationship and the workings of a place and community.

ND: I'm thinking about the ways we tend to think about the object of art. I think of what your hands must go through and endure. I think, too, about the ways each of your bodies are poised in the different works you do, whether beadwork, paint, clay, welding, or concrete. You have all these skins of making. As you were saying, Rose, you have to develop a different relationship to each one. I'm thinking a lot about where you hold your "making tension" and imagining how you feel even your own bodies as you're making.

These figures are a continuance of what was before, not only ancestrally but also in your works now and what you made before this, before arriving here. I don't have children; you both do. You're both mothers and makers of life in this way, from your children to the objects you make. So, I'm wondering if we could open up a bit of a portal about the ways you think of the marks you leave? I mention this because I think there is something about who you make for. I know this is the art world, but I've heard you both talk about that. You're not making for the art world first. You're making for the world that you live in, and that your beloveds live in, and the struggle in it and the joy in it. I'm wondering if you can both speak a bit about that.

DWH: One hundred percent. The thing that comes to mind foremost is about intentionality, care, and a dedication to extending love. That is part of being a mother. It's part of being a community member too, though, regardless of whether or not you have children. As an Indigenous person, we're taught about the importance and significance of community and the well-being of one another. And, that is one-hundred percent amplified once you become a parent and you are then responsible for life, making sure that the child survives this world not only physically but mentally and emotionally, and you're tasked with all of that for their whole life. That doesn't stop at eighteen.

Some of the thoughts I had when you were talking, Natalie, were about the title *Strata*, the way we're able to see the strata in the way that it's constructed. And when you were talking about skins, it made me think about the way our bodies become stratified through becoming a mother, through the changes to our bodies, through aging, through experience, through the way that we care for our bodies or the way that the circumstances we live within allow us varying levels of being able to, or not being able to, care for our bodies.

I also keep thinking about the way the sculptures face one another and, Rose, how you were talking about their engagement with one another. And that's something that, to me, is at the core of why Indigenous voices are important in the art world. And why so many of us are being asked to shut up right now when voicing our compassion for and understanding of those that are suffering from the destructive forces of colonization. Our value systems have taught us to see one another, have taught us to recognize one another, have taught us that the health and well-being of the person standing across from you is related to you. That the health and well-being of your child and your community, of your neighbor, the person you haven't met yet, is all related to you.

One more thought. I was with my oldest daughter at the Denver Art Museum and made sure she got to see [Roxanne Swentzell's] *Mud Woman Rolls On*. I stood in front of that and said, "Look, baby, do you remember Rose?" She said, "Yes." I told her, "This is her mama." And then, to be able to round the corner and say, "Look, and here's Rose, and this is her family."[1] I keep thinking about

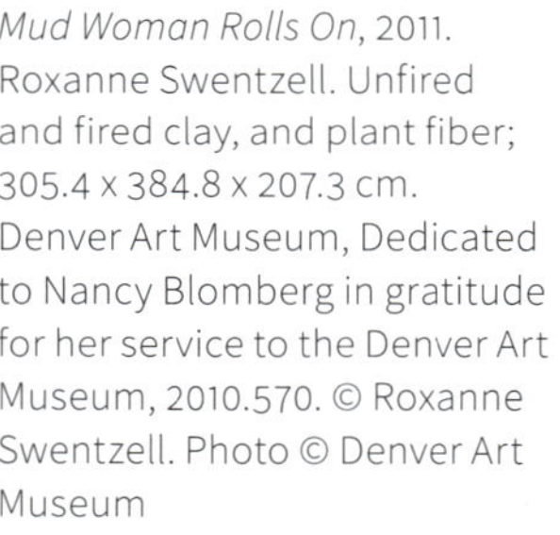

Mud Woman Rolls On, 2011. Roxanne Swentzell. Unfired and fired clay, and plant fiber; 305.4 x 384.8 x 207.3 cm. Denver Art Museum, Dedicated to Nancy Blomberg in gratitude for her service to the Denver Art Museum, 2010.570. © Roxanne Swentzell. Photo © Denver Art Museum

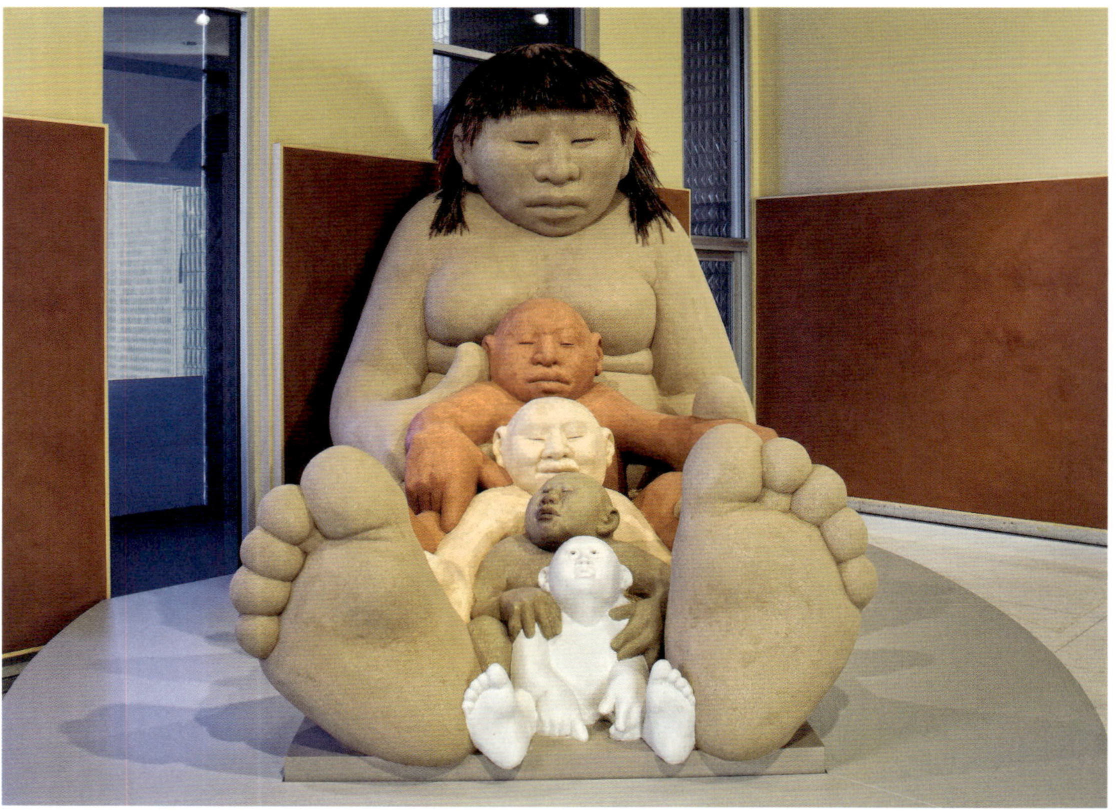

Mud Woman, and after looking at *Strata*, the figures serve a very similar function. They're different but their scale and intentionality around nurturing are aligned. *Mud Woman* is such a beautiful illustration of getting to watch time play out through the nurturing of generations in your own family and the way that nurturing and those lineages are continuing, and the way that we are blessed by the act of nurturing and the act of care and the act of cultural continuity and intentionality of thought and creation. And now we get to interact with these sculptures, which are in a way both asking us to feed and nurture one another.

RBS: I love that. I didn't think of that relationship but I helped my mom build *Mud Woman*, and that's an important piece. Natalie, addressing your question about time and future and this idea of future: I think an investment in anything, whether it's physical or conceptual or prayerful, is a consideration of the present and the coming present. And I think that Dyani's reference to my mom's piece—I've been thinking about what makes art powerful, what makes it strong, what makes it persist, and I think a lot about maturity. Maturity is persistence.

So, if we look at Dyani's work that she's getting recognized for now, versus her works from undergrad—because we went to school together—as well as mine, it's that we didn't quite know how to push further past the discomfort into where it becomes rich. And I see young artists, and they don't know yet to *attend* to that baby's coughing and crying all night long and to stand there and rock that baby, rock that baby, rock that baby past the point you ever wanted to. You get past your own physical discomfort and you get past that moment when you want to stop because it's no longer easy, and you push through to the other side and you take a deep breath and you look and there's something that is mature.

ND: These objects are never static. They're imbued with, embodied with, embedded with life, with all the marks that have been made on them, with all the marks that they've made on you. Rose, this for me is a really beautiful way of thinking of maturity in that this *Strata*, these beings are always capable of another layer, another bit of growth. The same way you said the volcano is all that it's been through, down to its ash, and can make something new. It can make concrete new. It can make your own making new.

I want to talk a little bit about the word "witness." I know you're using it in a very different way than we tend to use it in this Western way of relationships, like witness as evidence or witness like, "I can't do anything about it." But one of the other ways you're thinking of the word "witness" is that it also means "to come to know," and I think it's really challenging and displacing what knowledge means. This work that's going into the museum's atrium, the fact that these two beings are witnessing one another: they're also coming to know. But coming to know doesn't mean that they're just going to stand there. You said a really beautiful phrase about how you're imagining the tension in between them—seeing, witnessing, being. Being alongside, with, or of one another. In some ways, one is creating the possibility for the other by being there, by doing the witnessing; then the other can also be witnessed and therefore within the space.

In terms of marks—making marks, or leaving marks: when you see someone's work, you also feel someone's body or feel your own body. I wonder about the work you're doing now, Rose, the work you're doing now, Dyani, and what marks the works have made on you. Whether it's a scar here or there, or another way you're able to see the world through that work.

RBS: I think about transformation a lot and how we can be open, be pliable in a sense, where we are molded by life and what's around us and keep changing and not become stagnant. In that sense, I feel like I've been taught by my work. It has shown me myself and given me so much information about the world and about my direction and how to self-reflect. I feel like as much as I'm working with it, it's also working me.

There are layers and layers of that shifting happening, and I really like that the piece itself has a consciousness. Like, the layers stop and then there is the being that is witnessing, and then that clay will turn into the next layer. It's generational and it's relational and it too will melt and something new will be, and it will become the groundwork for what is next, like we all are in a sense. We pray and hope that whoever we become a foundation for next in this world, that what they have will be so much more brilliant and so much more beautiful than we could ever possibly imagine.

It's a reminder that we don't exist in a vacuum and we are in constant relationship and in constant influence with one another. And when we forget that and we think we are independent beings that are not

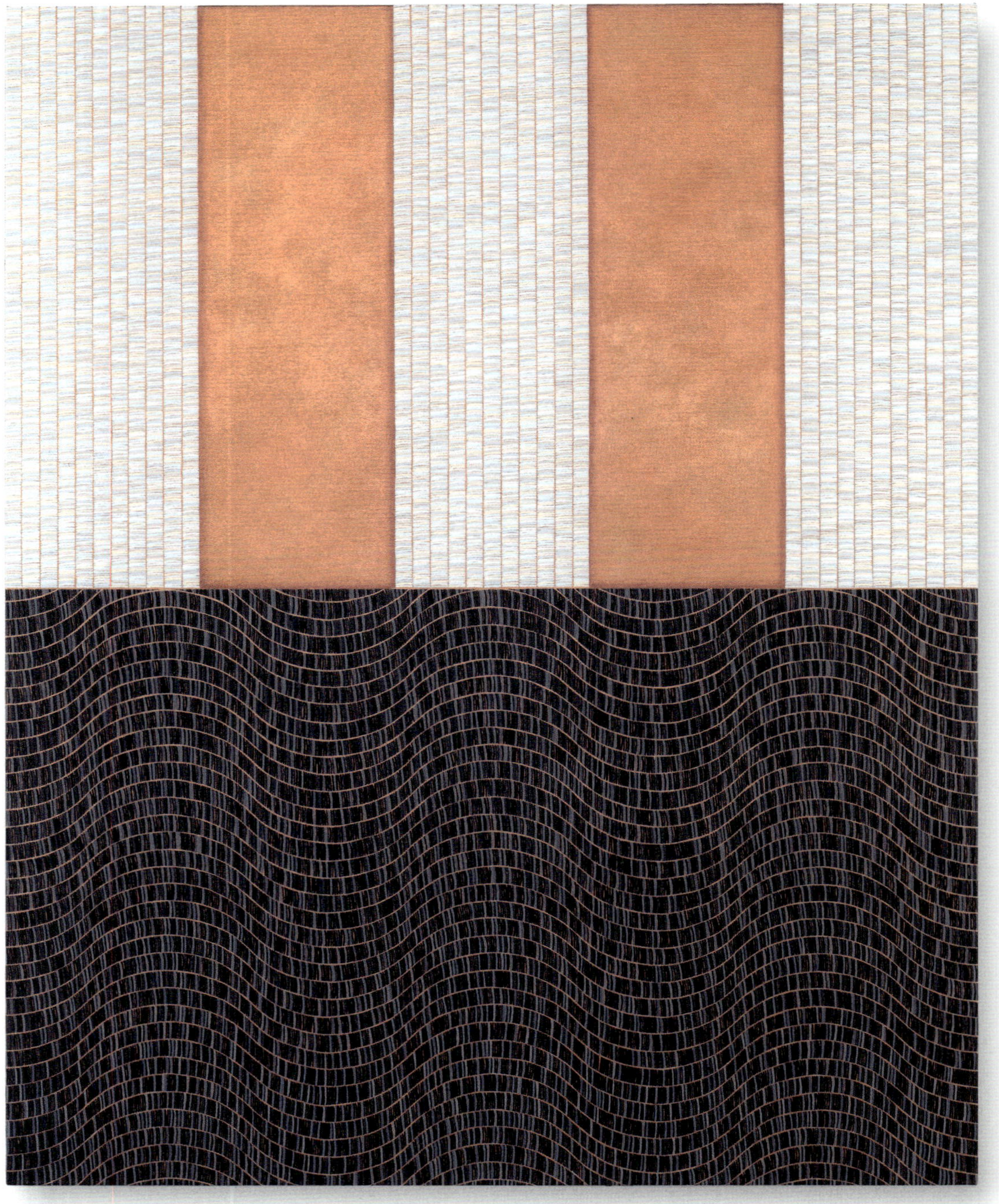

She Gives (Quiet Strength IV), 2018. Dyani White Hawk (Sičáŋǧu Lakota, born 1976). Acrylic on canvas; 152.4 x 121.9 cm. © Dyani White Hawk. Photo courtesy of the artist

accountable to the world around us, we stop feeling and we stop witnessing—we stop being witnessed, because it's both ways. I think about living in the community, and everyone's watching me and what you're doing.

ND: Like, whose truck was that [*laughter*]?

RBS: No privacy! Whose truck was that? You know. Or somebody has out-of-state-plate cars at their house. We're being watched. To be seen is also to be self-aware. So, that's what I hope my work is also doing:

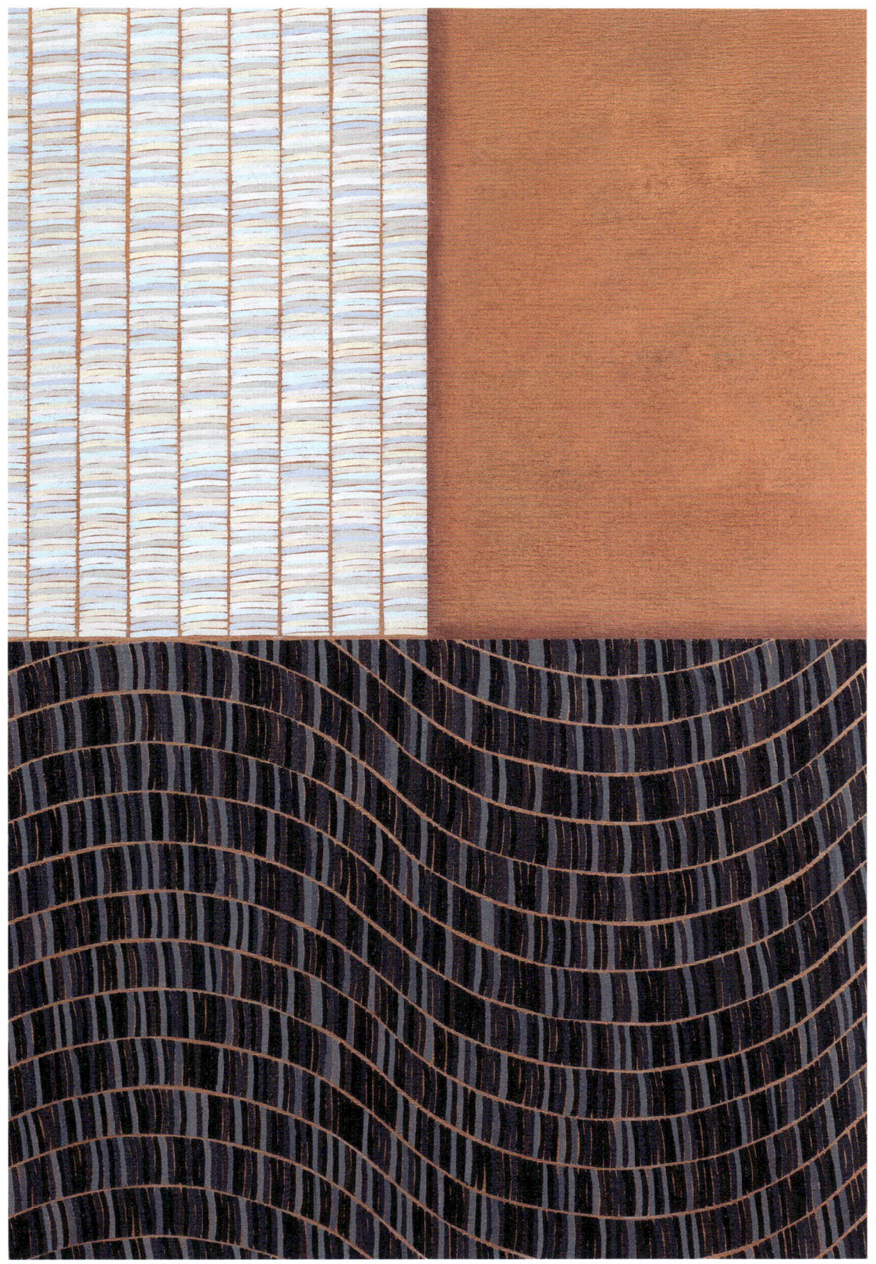

Detail of *She Gives (Quiet Strength IV)*, 2018

it creates those eyes and seeing and helps us notice that we're being seen and then see ourselves in different ways. We witness each other. We hold space where we come to know, and not come to know, in an emotional, spiritual, psychological way—an empathic way.

DWH: I was thinking about *Strata* and what you were talking about, Rose, around the conversation about maturity and what it means to be an elder. *Strata* is a really beautiful, direct illustration of maturity. It is, in its being, longevity. It's an example of growth over extremely long-paced periods of time. It's accumulated experience, accumulated being, the gathering of material, the gathering of life. It's an earthly reference to the wisdom of an elder. That's really beautiful in that it takes us back to how you opened the conversation around prayer and around acknowledging the land we're walking on that nurtures, feeds us, and gives us life.

But as far as maturity, this work is such a beautiful illustration of that. It makes me think of my own body of work, the *Quiet Strength* paintings, which reference the practices of beadwork and quillwork, which are hundreds of thousands of lines made over and over and over again. It feels very similar in that reference. And in that body of work, through repeated motion, I'm also speaking to quiet, paced endurance, an accumulation and an outpouring of love and care and nurturing. The title *Quiet Strength* is a direct reference to Indigenous women and the way that we at times often quietly persevere and deliver, fight through, like you said, carry the baby for longer than our bodies maybe feel like they can or are able to. But we do that. We do it, and to me it also relates to both the work and the nurturing of community. The artwork is a reflection of that caring for community, caring for our children, and caring for ourselves.

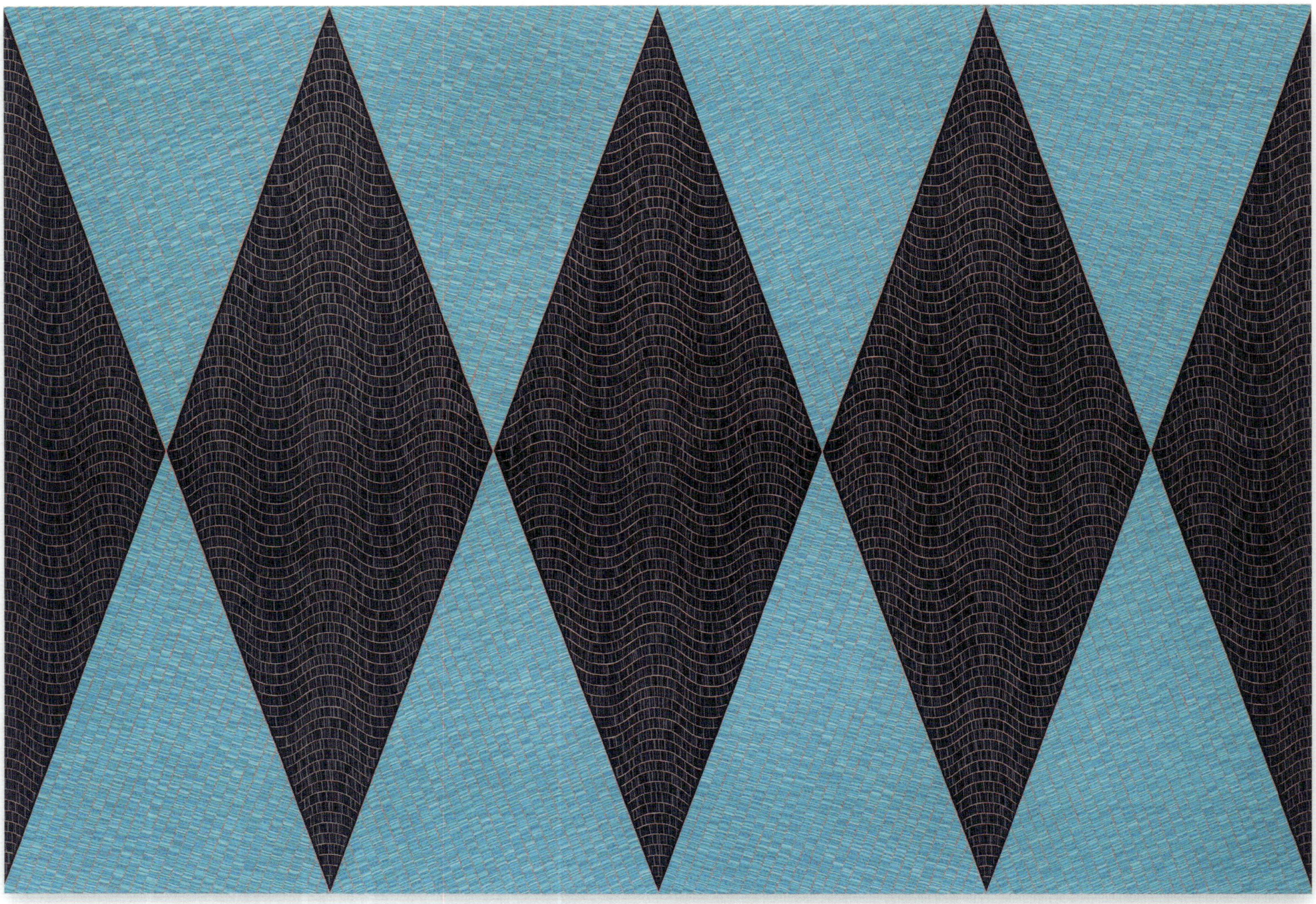

She Gives (Quiet Strength VII),
2020. Dyani White Hawk. Acrylic
on canvas; 213.4 x 304.8 cm.
© Dyani White Hawk. Photo
courtesy of the artist

Detail of She Gives (Quiet
Strength VII), 2020

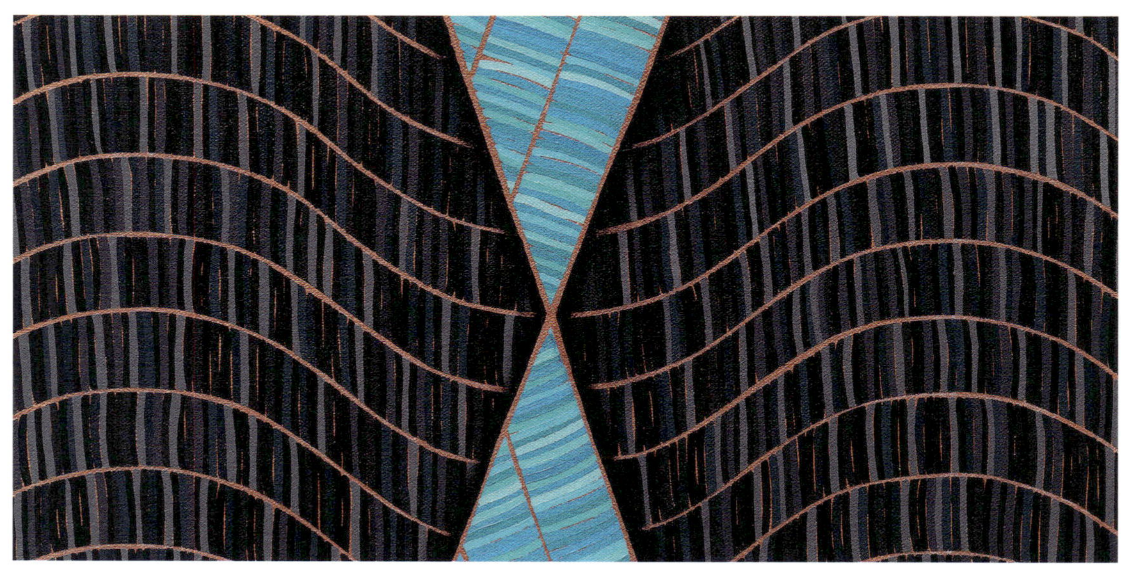

ND: I especially like comparing *Quiet Strength* to *Strata* because they're both knowledge systems. Not book knowledge but knowledge that is a momentum, which means that it has come to us from someplace, and then it's our responsibility to now put it toward others.

To end at your title, Rose, and where you started us off: *Strata*, as a way of knowing the body and being a body in the world. The Earth knows when to break. It knows when to change. We've always been taught that breaking is a negative, it's a weakness. So, what we do is we try to hold, we try to hold and hold and hold until it tips us over, until we can't hold anymore, and then we end up hitting our knees. Whereas there's something about *Strata* that says, "Hey, there's a kind of pressure here, but it doesn't have to fell me or stop me." That's how life happens. New layer. New being. I think there's something really beautiful and generous in the ways you are creating these bodies.

This conversation was held over Zoom on March 1, 2024. The transcript has been edited for publication.

1. White Hawk is referring to a group of three sculptures by Simpson on view at the Denver Art Museum: *Warrior* (2012), *Explorer* (2013), and *Nurturer* (2013).

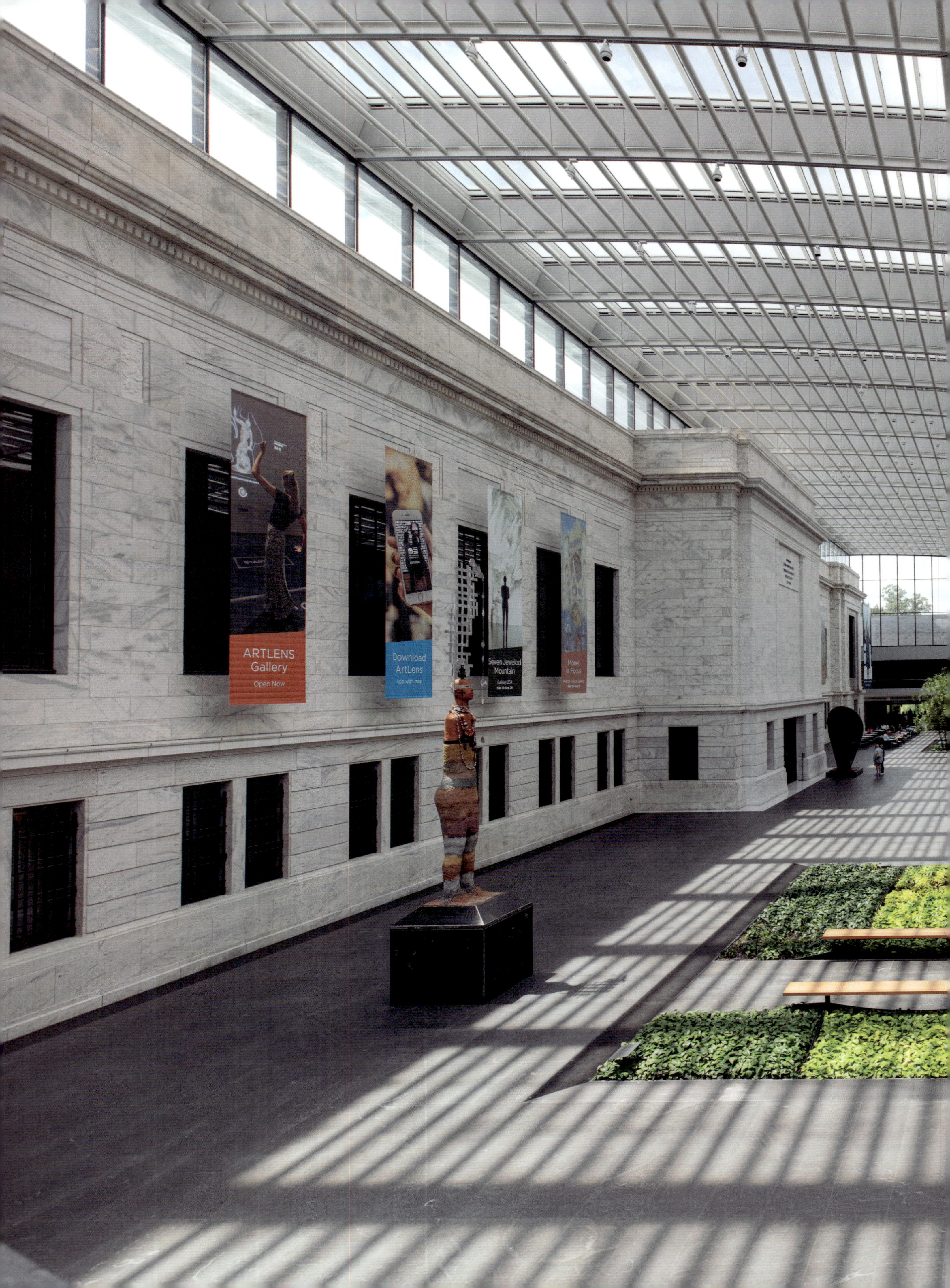
ARTLENS
Gallery
Open Now
Download
ArtLens
App with map
Seven Jeweled
Mountain
Gallery 234
Monet
in Focus

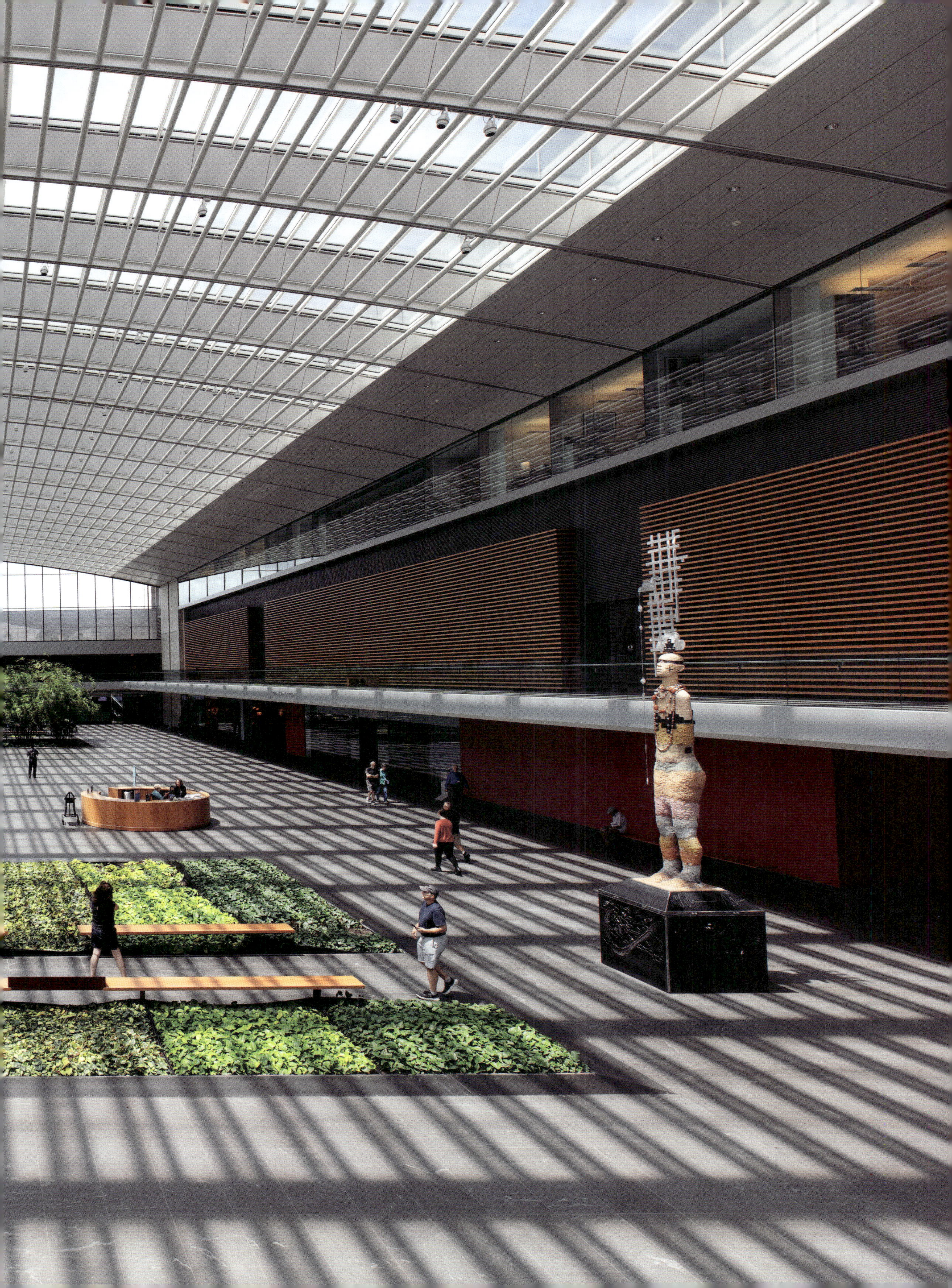

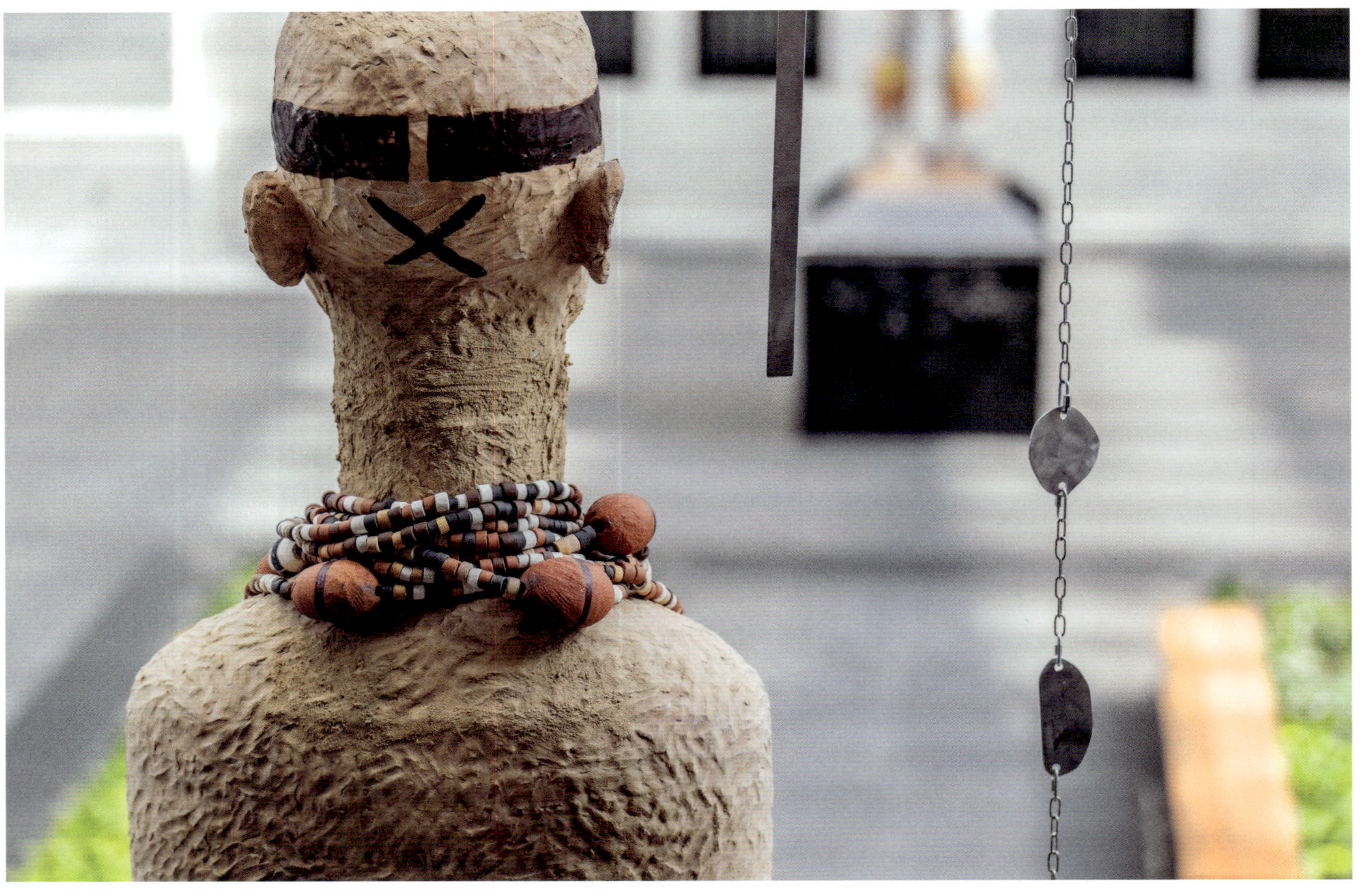

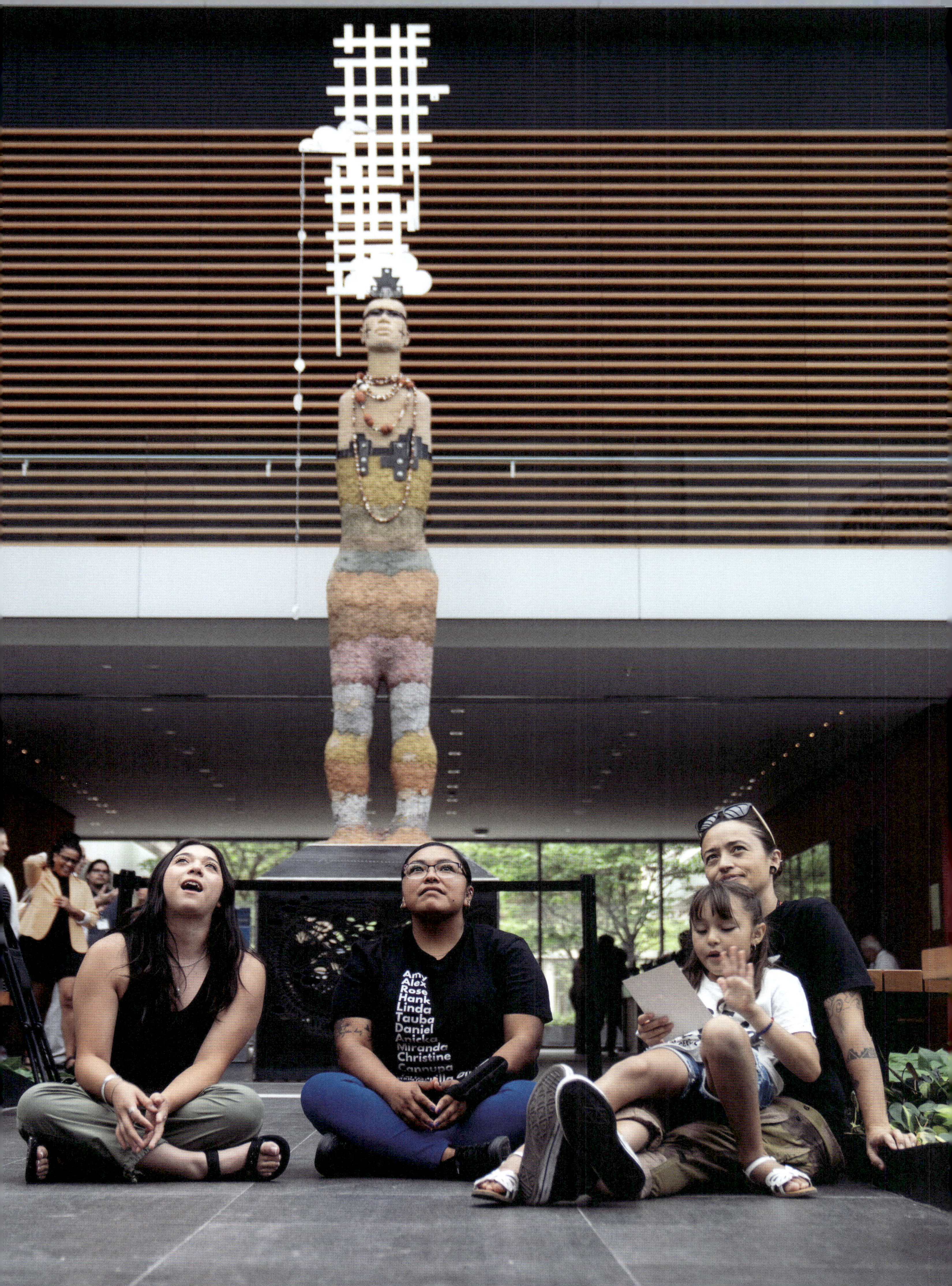

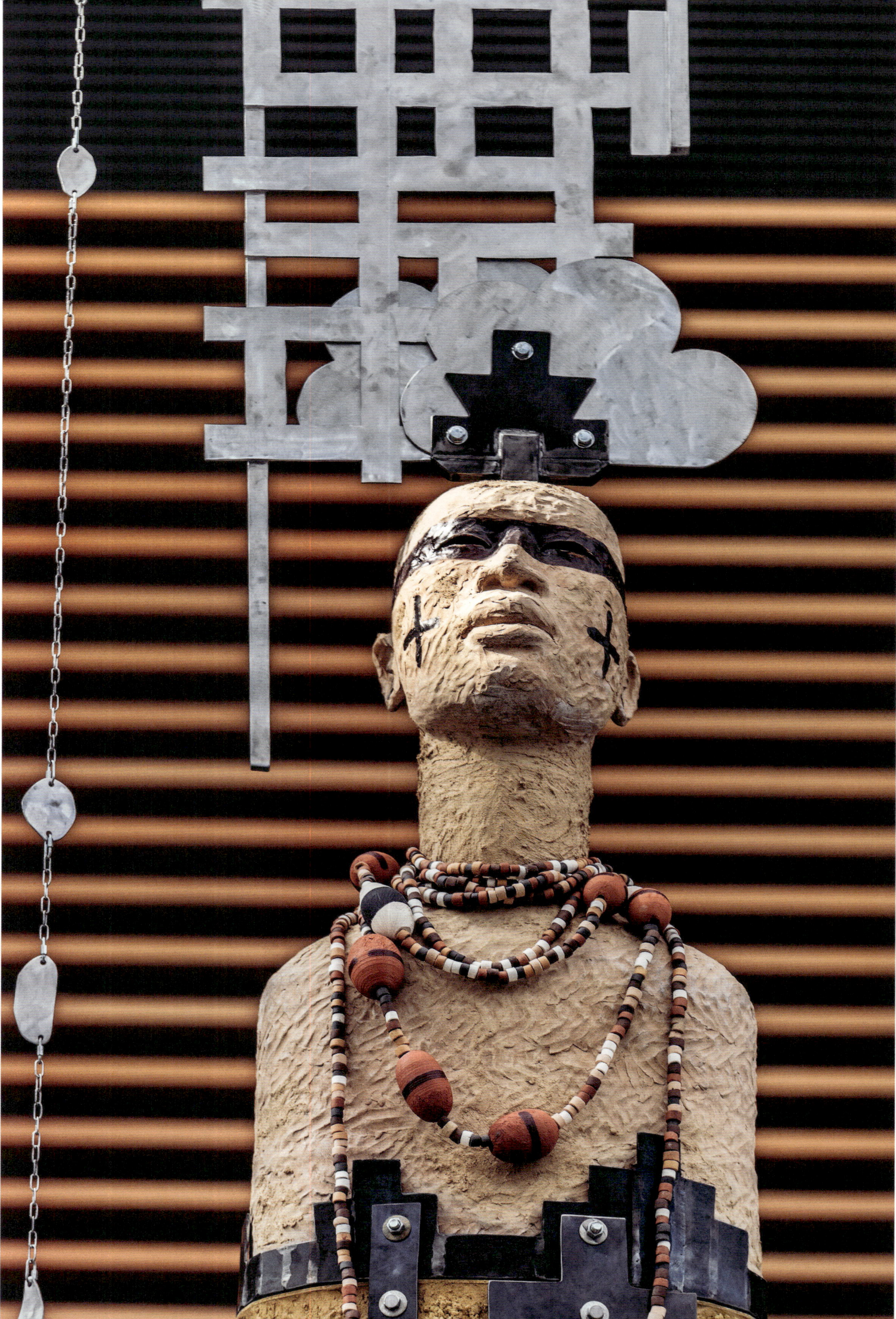

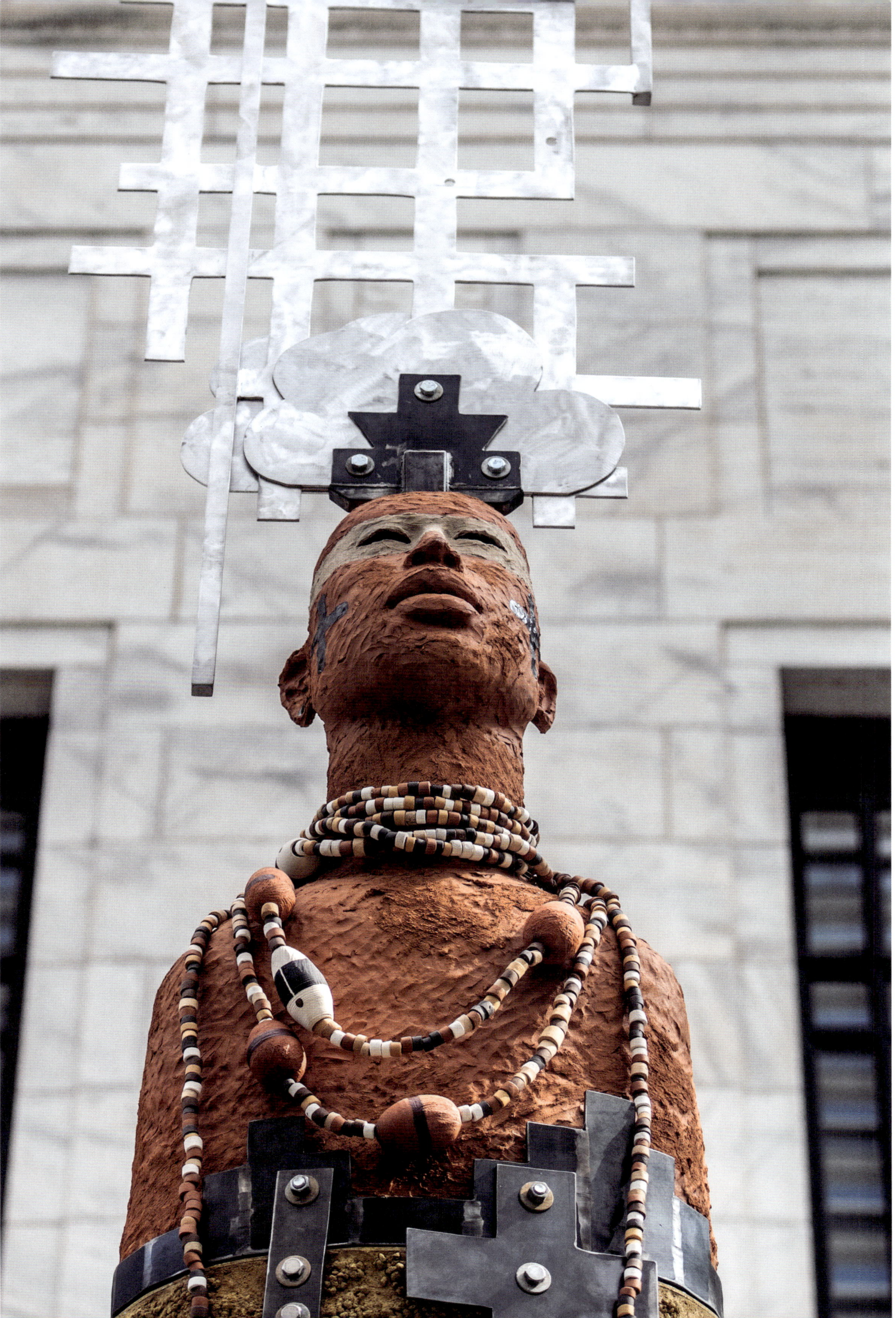

Selected Bibliography

Anaya, Rudolfo. "An American Chicano in King Arthur's Court." In *Old Southwest / New Southwest: Essays on a Region and Its Literature*, edited by Judy Nolte Temple, 113–18. Tucson, AZ: Tucson Public Library, 1987.

Dunbar-Ortiz, Roxanne. *An Indigenous People's History of the United States*. Boston: Beacon Press, 2014.

Finkel, Jori. "Rose B. Simpson Thinks in Clay." *New York Times*, June 16, 2022. https://www.nytimes.com /2022/06/16/arts/design/rose-b-simpson-clay -sculpture.html.

Marsh, Ariana. "Indigenous Sculptor Rose B. Simpson Makes Otherworldly Beings to Reconfigure Her Neural Pathways." *Harper's Bazaar* (March 30, 2023). https://www.harpersbazaar.com/culture/art-books -music/a43454340/indigenous-sculptor-rose-b -simpson-makes-otherworldly-beings-to-reconfigure -her-neural-pathways/.

Mithlo, Nancy Marie. "'A Real Feminine Journey': Locating Indigenous Feminisms in the Arts." *Meridians: Feminism, Race, Transnationalism* 9, no. 2 (March 2009): 1–30.

Nah Poeh Meng. Exhibition text. Poeh Cultural Center, Santa Fe. Ongoing exhibition.

Nilsen, Richard. "Talent for Pottery Runs in the Family." *Arizona Republic*, January 25, 2009, E4.

Powell, Jami C., ed. *Form & Relation: Contemporary Native Ceramics*. Hanover, NH: Hood Museum of Art, 2020.

Scott, Chad. "Rose, Rina, Roxanne and Rose B. Simpson: Four Generations of Santa Clara Ceramics at Norton Museum of Art." *Forbes* (March 21, 2024). https://www.forbes.com/sites/chaddscott/2024 /03/21/rose-rina-roxanne-and-rose-b-simpson-four -generations-of-santa-clara-ceramics-at-norton -museum-of-art/?sh=57479a95f2ad.

Silver, Laura, ed. *Hearts of Our People: Native Women Artists*. Minneapolis: Minneapolis Institute of Art in association with the University of Washington Press, 2019.

Simpson, Rose B. "In the Studio: Rose B. Simpson." Joan Mitchell Foundation, July 8, 2022. https://www.joanmitchellfoundation.org/journal /in-the-studio-rose-b-simpson.

———. "*Maria*, '85 El Camino." In *Maria & Modernism*, edited by Diana F. Pardue et al., 182–87. Phoenix, AZ: Heard Museum, 2024.

———. "My Mother, the Builder." *New Mexico Magazine* (June 17, 2020). https://www.newmexico magazine.org/blog/post/my-mother-the-builder -rose-simpson-roxanne-swentzell/.

———. "Selected Performance and Installation." https://www.rosebsimpson.com/performance #:~:text=In%20the%20spring%20of%202013 ,found%20objects%2C%20and%20ceramic %20components.

———. "Sourced: Inspiration, Innovation, and Material." National Council on Education for the Ceramic Arts, September 25, 2023. YouTube. https:// youtu.be/9i8unoddSv4?si=5xGkMe7yBycYGyCk.

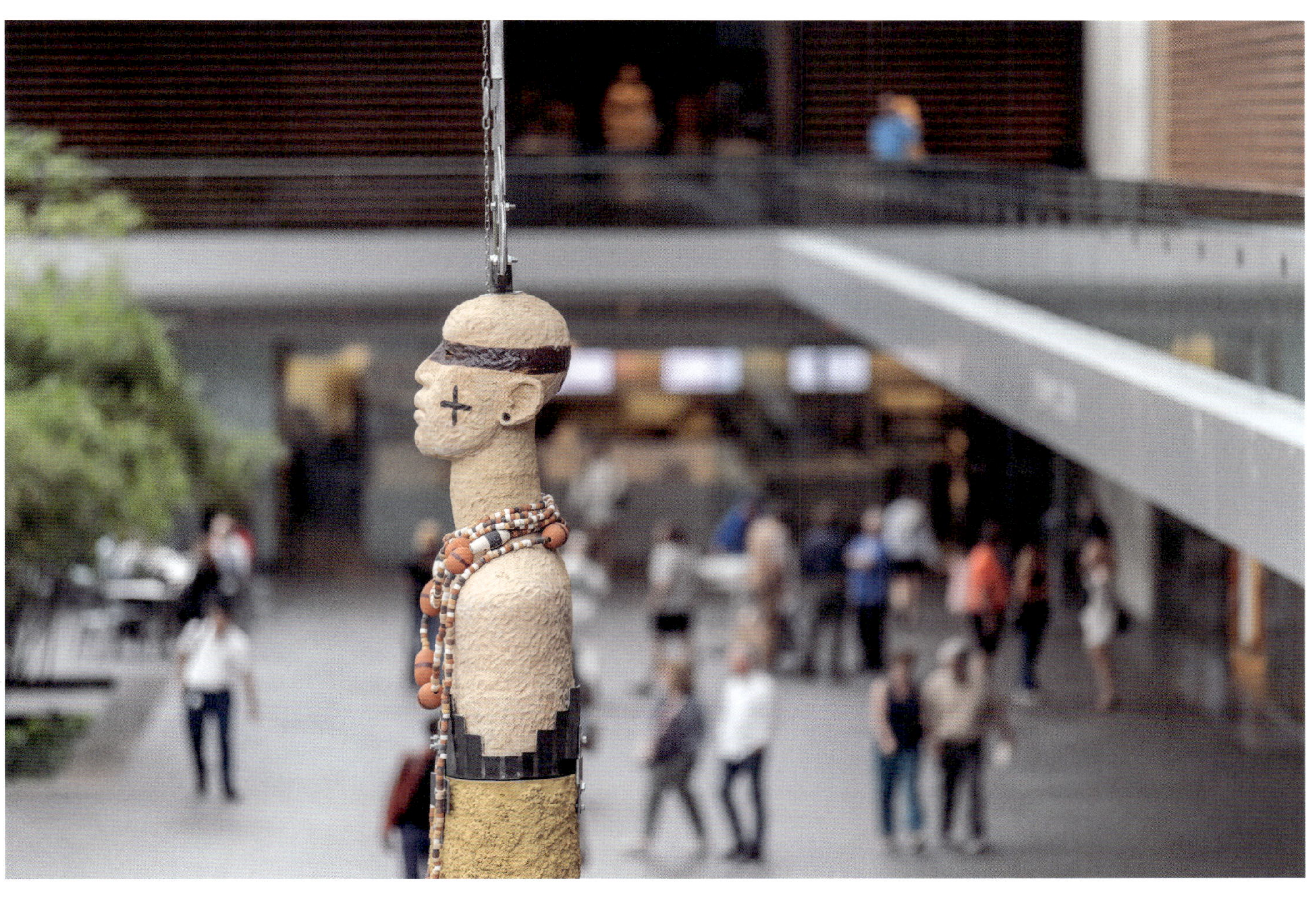

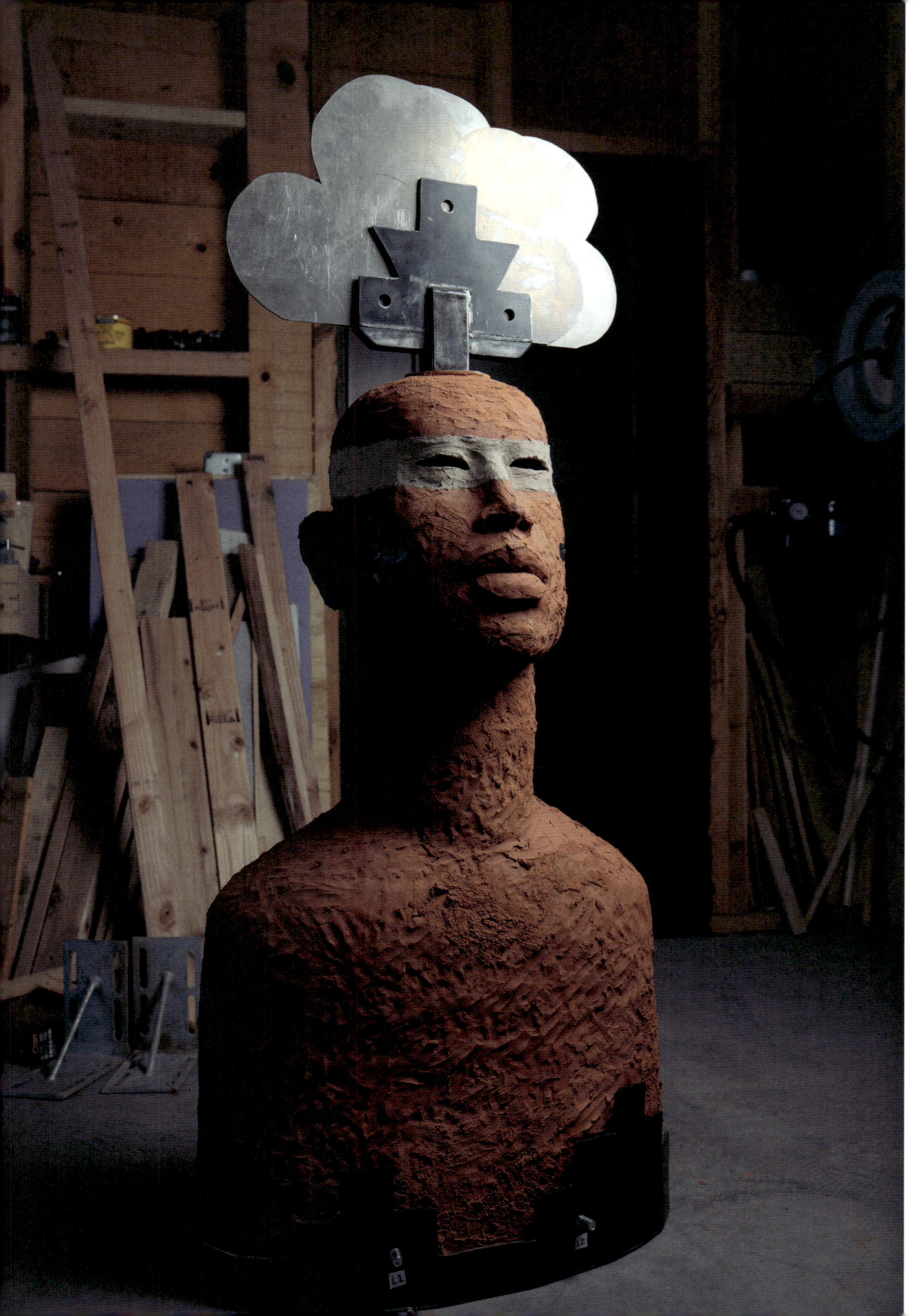

Author and Contributor Bios

AUTHOR

Nadiah Rivera Fellah is curator of contemporary art at the Cleveland Museum of Art.

CONTRIBUTORS

Natalie Diaz (Mojave / Akimel O'odham) is a poet and 2018 MacArthur Foundation Fellow and 2021 Pulitzer Prize awardee. She is the director of the Center for Imagination in the Borderlands and the Maxine and Jonathan Marshall Chair in Modern and Contemporary Poetry at Arizona State University.

Anya Montiel (Tohono O'odham descent) is a curator at the Smithsonian National Museum of the American Indian in Washington, DC.

Karen Patterson is the executive director of the Ruth Foundation for the Arts.

Kate Russell is a photographer based in New Mexico.

Rose B. Simpson (Santa Clara Pueblo) is a mixed-media artist who lives and works in Santa Clara Pueblo, New Mexico.

Dyani White Hawk (Sičáŋǧu Lakota) is a multidisciplinary artist and 2023 MacArthur Foundation Fellow who lives and works in Minneapolis.

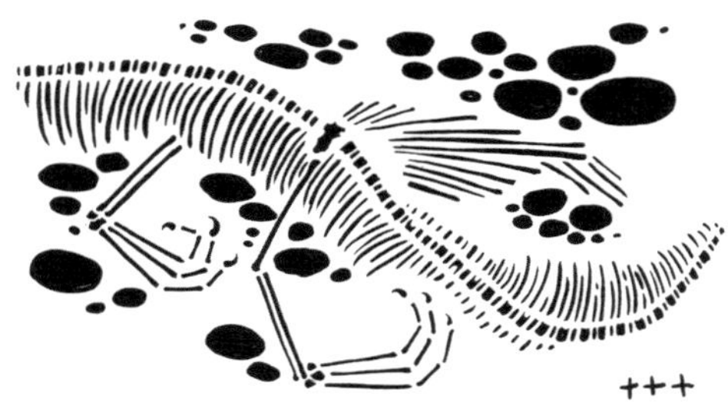

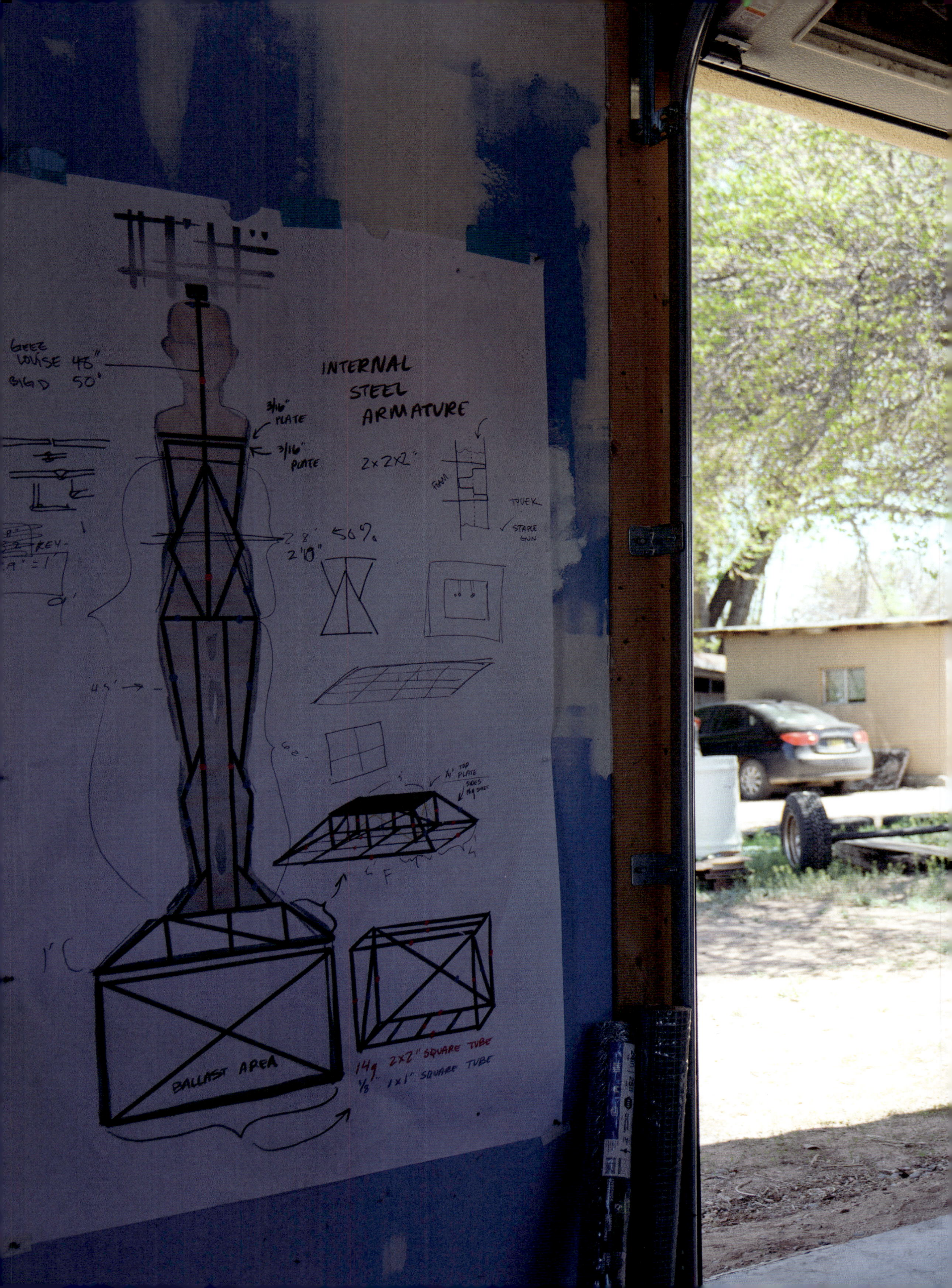
GEEZ
LOUISE 48"
BIG D 50"
INTERNAL
STEEL
ARMATURE
3/16"
PLATE
3/16"
PLATE
2x2x2"
FOAM
TYVEK
STAPLE GUN
2.8' 50%
2'9"
1/4" TOP PLATE SIDES 14g SHEET
BALLAST AREA
14g 2x2" SQUARE TUBE
1/8" 1x1" SQUARE TUBE

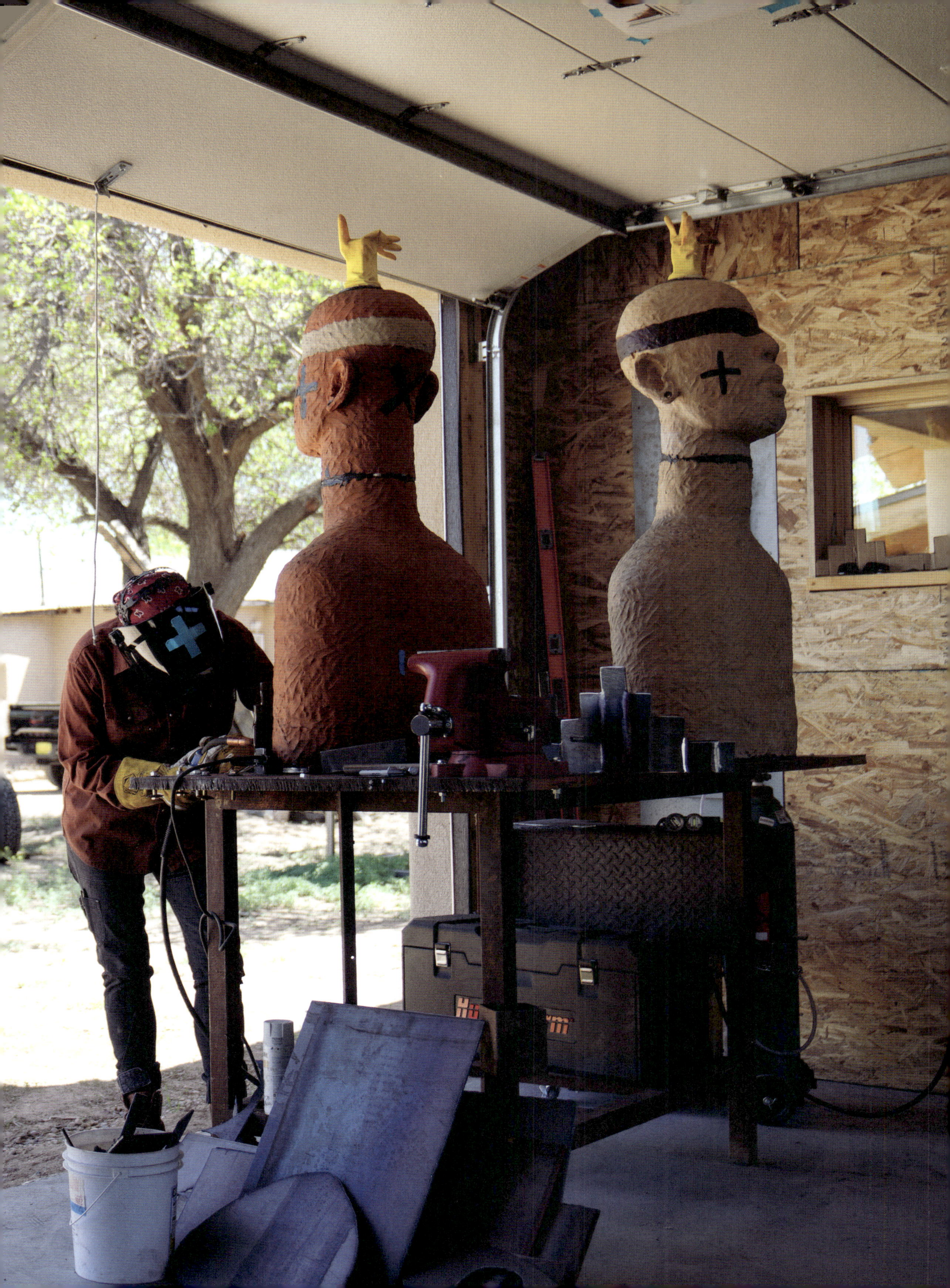

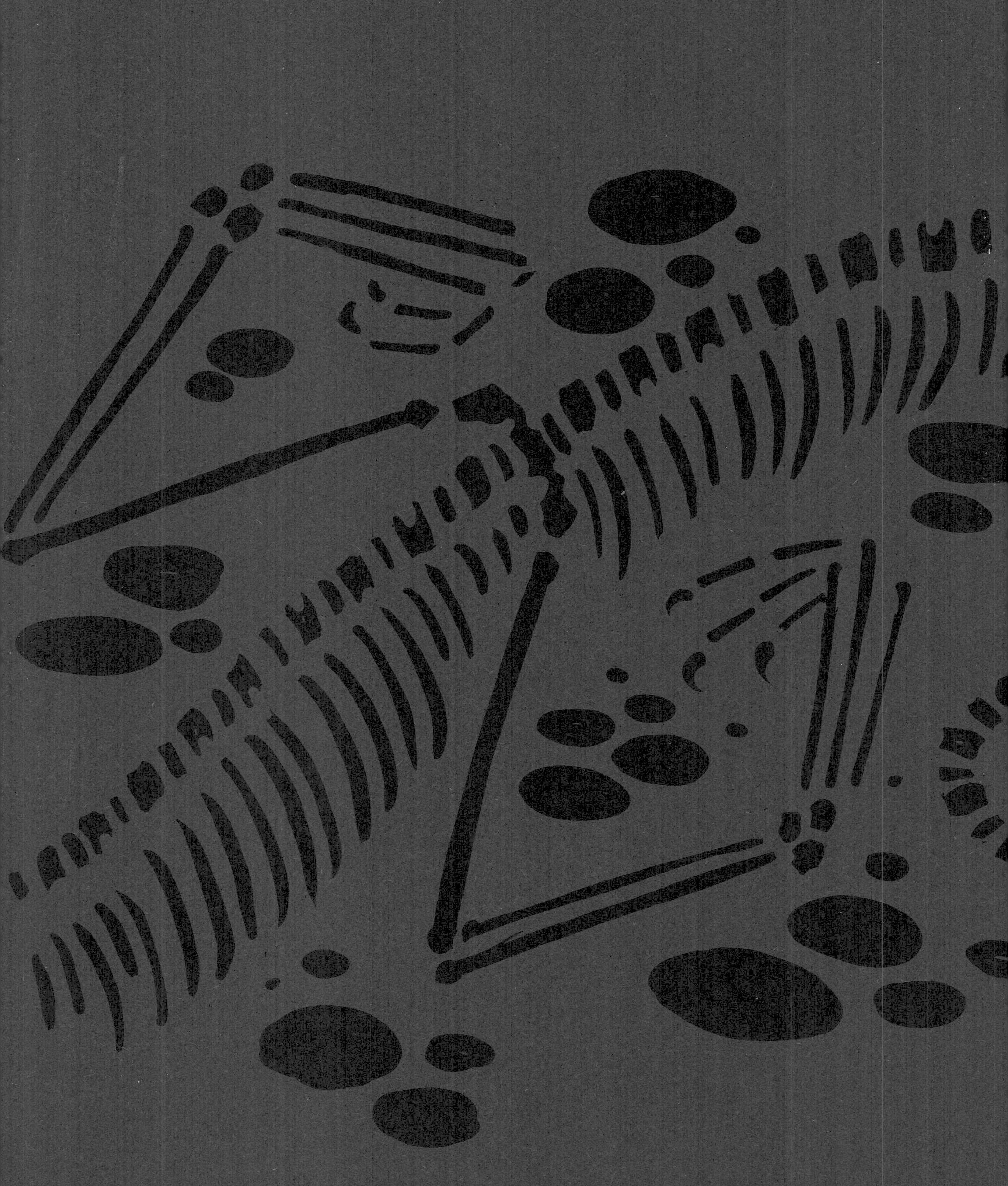